THE KENTUCKY EDUCATION REFORM

THE KENTUCKY EDUCATION REFORM

LESSONS FOR AMERICA

Betty E. Steffy, Ed.D.

College of Education
University of Kentucky
Lexington, Kentucky

TECHNOMIC
PUBLISHING CO., INC.

LANCASTER · BASEL

The Kentucky Education Reform

a **TECHNOMIC**® publication

Published in the Western Hemisphere by
Technomic Publishing Company, Inc.
851 New Holland Avenue, Box 3535
Lancaster, Pennsylvania 17604 U.S.A.

Distributed in the Rest of the World by
Technomic Publishing AG
Missionsstrasse 44
CH-4055 Basel, Switzerland

Printed in the United States of America
10 9 8 7 6 5 4 3 2 1

Main entry under title:
    The Kentucky Education Reform: Lessons for America

A Technomic Publishing Company book
Bibliography:
Includes index p. 301

Library of Congress Catalog Card No. 92-62814
ISBN No. 0-87762-987-0

To Fen

*To the men and women who worked in the Kentucky Department of
Education from April 11, 1990, to June 30, 1991*

and

To the children of Kentucky

CONTENTS

Chapter 4: Empowering Local Schools   75

Chapter 5: Seeking Financial Equity: Kentucky's
Search for the Grail   93

Chapter 6: Primary School   115

Chapter 7: Creating a Level Playing Field   143

THE two most radical packages of educational reform in the United States have occurred in Chicago and Kentucky. The only external and fairly comprehensive evaluation of the Chicago reform effort, completed by North Central Regional Educational Laboratory in April of 1992, indicated that Chicago's educational reform would most likely fail given its current trajectory.

Kentucky's reform, initiated by a lawsuit over school finance, was the most radical comprehensive mandate ever assembled in America. It still has a chance to work.

Betty Steffy's book about the educational reform in the Bluegrass State is based on personal experience. She came to Kentucky before the reform bill was created. She was there when the judges' decisions were rendered, as deputy superintendent of instruction for the Kentucky Department of Education. She organized the major internal thrust to implement the reform legislation before the new commissioner and his staff came on board, the new Office of Accountability was formed, or the State Department of Education was abolished, and along with it her job.

As deputy superintendent for instruction under Dr. John Brock, the last elected state superintendent with full powers, she was an outsider from New Jersey and New York, where she functioned as superintendent of schools in Moorestown and was assistant superintendent of Lynbrook on Long Island. When she arrived, her first responsibility was to win the confidence of Kentuckians: in the Department, in the legislature, and in the field.

Betty Steffy traveled Kentucky, from the Mississippi River to the Appalachian foothills. She covered thousands of miles speaking and listening to Kentucky educators. She spent time in the back country with rural and small district superintendents. They sized her up and decided she knew what she was about. Some still send her vegetables from their gardens, or hams they cure themselves, a rare gesture of friendship by local educators who are naturally suspicious of outsiders and those from the state's capital.

Betty won her spurs in the legislature too. She is a known and trusted educator among many legislators. She can walk the halls in Frankfort and personally speak to many of the key reformers who shaped Kentucky's educational future. She was the only high-level education department administrator to be asked to present her ideas to the Curriculum Subcommittee of the Task Force on School Reform during the critical gestation phase of the reform. Some of her ideas found their way into the final piece of legislation, among them the elimination of norm-referenced testing and the establishment of statewide curriculum goals for all schools.

After the Kentucky reform law passed, now known as KERA (Kentucky Education Reform Act), it was Betty who stepped forward, reached out and organized the thrust to inform local educators, give direction to critical task forces, and inspire staff who would all lose their jobs many months later. Her efforts won editorial praise from one of the state's leading newspapers.

Today from her position at the University of Kentucky, Betty Steffy continues to monitor KERA, to teach classes about it over the compressed video system which beams out from Lexington to the far corners of the commonwealth, and to write about educational reform. She was in a unique position to help shape, lead, reflect on, and evaluate KERA as it unfurled its extensive changes for public schools in Kentucky. She brings this background to this book. She is perhaps one of three or four people in critical high-level public positions in Kentucky reform that could offer readers the insights, background, and data that they will find within these covers. And she remains a friend and passionate observer of KERA, the most radical educational reform ever attempted in the U.S. She provides the combination insider-outsider perspective that will make this book more than a simple exposition of reform rhetoric. She speaks to KERA's effects, and is able to offer a practical perspective on the likelihood of long-term gains or losses. So this is a rare book by a rare author/change agent/educator/professor. She's been there. She knows what she is talking about. She's still involved.

Fenwick W. English
Professor of Educational Administration
University of Kentucky, Lexington

THERE is an old saying, "A task well begun, is half done!"

On April 11, 1990, Governor Wallace Wilkinson signed into law the Kentucky Education Reform Act (KERA). This legislation has been referred to as the most comprehensive, innovative reform legislation ever passed by any state in recent history.

During the fifteen months which followed, the Kentucky Department of Education created the strategies to implement many of the programmatic initiatives embodied in this landmark legislation. While this book is primarily about that time, those programs, and the men and women in the Kentucky Department of Education who saw that vision for what "could be," the book also attempts to describe how the men and women who currently work in the Kentucky Department of Education have taken up the cause and continued the work. Those who toiled diligently during the first few months of implementation recognized the "miracle" that had taken place, a "miracle" that most professional educators in the state believe will never come again. KERA not only created a holistic framework for restructuring the public schools of this state, but it was initially funded with enough resources to enable successful implementation of the new programmatic initiatives.

I worked in the Kentucky Department of Education during the time when the Kentucky Supreme Court decision was rendered, when the reform legislation was being formulated and written, and for a year after the statute became law. As part of the administrative team that designed the first year of implementation efforts, I had a unique opportunity to be directly involved with the public aspects of the implementation as well as the behind-the-scenes activities. From this vantage point I had a unique opportunity to observe, understand, and sometimes shape the design of the programs. This book is written from that perspective. Some may say I was too personally involved to be objective in my description of what happened. Perhaps this is so, but I prefer to believe that my direct involvement has provided me with first-hand experiences that are critical to the accounts recorded in this book. The reader will be the judge.

Even though the statute called for a complete reorganization of the Kentucky Department of Education and termination of all Department employees effective June 30, 1991, the monumental task of designing the implementation strategies began with vigor and enthusiasm. This book is about that time and those strategies. It is about the planning that enabled 130 of Kentucky's 176 school districts to implement a half-day preschool program within six months after the bill was signed into law. It is about the statewide KERA awareness sessions that enabled all Kentucky educators to begin to understand the bill. It is about the creation of the SEEK (Support Education Equity Kentucky) funding formula. Department staff provided each district in the state with preliminary budget projections within six weeks after the bill was signed by the governor. It is about the financial and programmatic policy development process that enabled all facets of the legislation to be addressed. And it is about how the program is currently being implemented, two years after it was enacted.

It is about a task "well begun"! The purpose of this book is to provide a formal record of how the Act was initially implemented under the direction of a state education agency. Problems, issues, successes, and failures will be described. In some cases, the process was exemplary, and could serve as a model for other states. In others, problems were encountered and significant issues had to be addressed. By describing the Kentucky experience, I hope this book will assist other states in designing even better programs to serve the educational needs of the children of this nation.

Betty E. Steffy

CHAPTER 1

State-Legislated Education Reform

History, it has been said, is a river flowing through time. If that is so, then today we are changing its course. On this day, more than any other, I am proud to be a Kentuckian, and I am proud to be your governor.

—Governor Wallace Wilkinson
at the signing of the Kentucky Education
Reform Act (KERA)
April 11, 1990

IS it possible for a state legislature to pass a bill that could alter the course of public education in Kentucky and possibly the United States of America? The state of Kentucky passed such a bill in the spring of 1990. Most agree that in the two years since the bill was passed, the state has only begun to build the infrastructure to support the fundamental restructuring required in this state. No one would have predicted that a state like Kentucky would attempt such a feat, since Kentucky has ranked in the bottom third on indicators of K−12 public education success for years.

Prior to the Kentucky Education Reform Act (KERA), state dropout rates were high. Teacher pay was low. Money supporting the education of each student in the commonwealth was far below the national average. Districts with higher levels of property wealth generated more money to support education than districts with low assessed property value. Unemployment was high. Adult literacy was low.

In the years preceding the passage of the bill, there was an increasing awareness among business leaders, legislators, educators, and the general citizenry that the future of the state was related to the quality of the educational system. For the state to improve economically, attract new business, and generally improve the quality of life of its citizens, education in this state had to improve.

The Kentucky Supreme Court opinion (*Rose v. Council for Better Education*, 1989) declaring the state's education system unconstitutional, was the catalyst that led to the passage of House Bill 940, the

1

Kentucky Education Reform Act (KERA). The emotion surrounding the passage of the bill was captured in the comments of Greg Stumbo, House Majority Leader, minutes before the bill was passed by the House.

> Ladies and gentlemen of the House, after much debate and deliberation, you now have before you what I hope will become the bill that will truly change Kentucky's educational opportunities for children in rural Kentucky and those all over this state. I dream . . . that someday . . . children will sit in these seats, and they will have been afforded opportunities that they might not have had. And I truly mean that! And I think you know what I'm talking about . . . when you look at the parts of this state where I come from . . . and the fact that kids, all too often, start out behind, and all they do is just get further behind. I think that what we have the chance to do today is to see that that never happens again. That no child in Kentucky will ever have to look back and say that he or she didn't receive that full educational opportunity that he or she was entitled to by the constitution of this state.

EVENTS LEADING TO THE PASSAGE OF THE KERA

The Kentucky constitution was enacted in 1891. This document provides for "an efficient system of common schools throughout the state." Initially, this system was supported by a funding mechanism based on student population, but over the years, modifications were made to this system. These modifications included provisions for funding schools on a basis other than student population and a provision for a Minimum Foundation and Power Equalization program to better equalize the amount of money supporting the education of each student in the state. For a variety of reasons, these programs fell short of providing equity in the amount of money supporting the education of each student in the state, regardless of the property wealth of the district.

In 1985, sixty-six school districts, seven boards of education and twenty-two public school students banded together to form the Council for Better Education. Acting as attorney for the Council, former Governor Bert Combs filed a class action equity suit in Franklin Circuit Court. Judge Ray Corns issued a judgement in October, 1988, stating that the funding system for schools was "discriminatory" and "inefficient." On appeal, the Kentucky Supreme Court found the entire educational system unconstitutional. The Court said:

> This decision applies to the entire sweep of the system—all its parts and parcels. This decision applies to all the statutes creating, implementing and financing the system and to all regulations, etc., pertaining thereto.

This decision covers the creation of local school districts, school boards, and the Kentucky Department of Education to the Minimum Foundation Program and Power Equalization Program. It covers school construction and maintenance, teacher certification—the whole gamut of the common school system in Kentucky. . . . Since we have, by this decision, declared the system of common schools in Kentucky to be unconstitutional, Section 183 places an absolute duty on the General Assembly to re-create, re-establish a new system of common schools in the Commonwealth. . . .

. . . We view this decision as an opportunity for the General Assembly to launch the Commonwealth into a new era of educational opportunity which will ensure a strong economic, cultural and political future. (*Rose*, pp. 215–216)

The General Assembly was charged to re-create this new system by the end of the next session of the General Assembly which was set to convene in January of 1990.

In response to the Supreme Court decision, the leadership of the General Assembly formed the Task Force on Education Reform. Membership on this Task Force was limited to members of the House, the Senate, and representatives from the governor's office. The elected state superintendent of public instruction was not asked to serve on the committee. No representative from the state's education associations was asked to serve. No State Department of Education employee, teacher, or administrator was invited to be a member of the Task Force.

After formation, the Task Force divided into three subcommittees: curriculum, finance, and governance. Each subcommittee hired a consultant to assist the committee. On March 7, 1990, the Task Force adopted its final report. Within hours after the adoption, House Bill 940 was introduced. The bill was signed into law on April 11, 1990. Before he signed the bill, Governor Wallace Wilkinson made these comments.

Think with me for a moment what this day means. Someday you are going to be able to tell your children that you witnessed one of the most historic days in Kentucky's history. You are going to be able to tell them that you were there when the governor signed into law a new school system. A school system that made Kentucky great. Today, we begin building that new system. It is a system where geography is a subject to be taught, not a factor which determines the quality of a child's education. A system where our teaching professionals are allowed to make their own decisions instead of following instructions from a remote voice in Frankfort. A system where each student can learn at his or her own pace and to his or her own potential. A new management culture in our schools. New ideas and new ways of doing things and with them a new feeling of competitiveness and achievement.

> These are the gifts of education reform, gifts that were made possible by
> a new and more equitable method of financing schools and enough money
> to get the job done right. Funding for disadvantaged schools. Funding for
> the resources and materials we need. Funding for new and improved
> school facilities. Funding for books and computers. Funding for pay
> raises and bonuses.
>
> History, it has been said, is a river flowing through time. If that is so, then
> today we are changing its course. On this day, more than any other, I am
> proud to be a Kentuckian, and I am proud to be your governor.

Since the day the governor spoke those words, approximately one
billion new state and local dollars have been expended to support
education reform in Kentucky. A new governor has been elected and a
new commissioner of education has been chosen. Local schools have
been empowered to make instructional decisions and over 400 school
councils have been formed. The State Department of Education and the
State Board of Elementary and Secondary Education have been reorganized. New state standards for curriculum have been established and
a new authentic student performance assessment system has been implemented. To coordinate the educational and human services within a
community, centers have been established in 250 school communities.
The Office of Educational Accountability, a "watchdog" for the General
Assembly, was established and began to investigate local district wrongdoing. These investigations led to the removal of school board members
from office and superintendent resignations. Vacancies in the offices of
local school district superintendents have been filled in over 30 percent
of the districts in the state. Average teacher salaries in the state have
increased 17 percent. Approximately 18,000 disadvantaged three- and
four-year-old children are participating in preschool programs and districts are beginning to replace grades Kindergarten through third, with
a new, success-oriented primary program. KERA has had an impact on
higher education because of a joint resolution, passed by the House and
the Senate, requiring state colleges and universities to develop comprehensive plans to support the implementation of the reform. Business
leaders, community groups and professional organizations have joined
forces to sustain public support for the reform. Educators all over the
state are working harder than ever before to ensure the success of this
initiative.

When the bill was first passed, the fear was that there would be a
tremendous, statewide backlash from the citizens of the commonwealth
because of the major tax increase that accompanied the legislation. That

backlash never came. During the 1992 meeting of the General Assembly, there were no substantial changes in the Act. In fact, there was an attempt to maintain financial support for the reform even though the state experienced a shortfall in projected revenue due to the recession. Although funding for some of the reform programs was less than had been predicted, in essence, the reform continued with strong financial commitment. This was due primarily to the tenacious persistence of the leadership of the General Assembly. This leadership understands the relationship between educational improvement and economic development for this state, and intends to maintain support for the reform for as long as it takes to be effective. Most educators in Kentucky understand that this opportunity to significantly change the educational system in Kentucky will not come again within their professional lifetimes. Because of the comprehensive nature of the reform, because it includes most of the innovative programmatic initiatives currently being discussed nationally, and because it was legislated by a state general assembly, it has the potential for impacting the future of public education in this country. With increasing interest in public school privatization and vouchers, the ability of the state of Kentucky to succeed with this endeavor has great significance.

This book is meant to provide a public record of how a state agency guided the implementation of this landmark legislation, to describe how programs were developed and initiated, and to assist others as they attempt to implement reform initiatives in other parts of this country.

COMPONENTS OF THE REFORM

Characteristics of an Efficient Educational System

The Kentucky Supreme Court defined the essential and minimal characteristics of an efficient educational system. They are summarized as follows:

(1) Its establishment, maintenance, and funding are the sole responsibility of the General Assembly.

(2) It is free to all.

(3) It is available to all Kentucky children.

(4) It is substantially uniform throughout the state.

(5) It provides equal educational opportunities to all Kentucky children.

(6) It is monitored by the General Assembly to assure that there is no waste, no duplication, no mismanagement, and no political influence.

(7) Schools are operated under the promise that an adequate education is a constitutional right.

(8) Sufficient funding provides each child an adequate education.

(9) An "adequate education" is defined as one that develops the following seven capacities:
- communication skills necessary to function in a complex and changing civilization
- knowledge to make economic, social, and political choices
- understanding of government processes as they affect the community, state, and nation
- sufficient self-knowledge and knowledge of one's mental and physical wellness
- sufficient grounding in the arts to enable each student to appreciate his or her cultural and historical heritage
- sufficient preparation to choose and pursue one's life's work
- skills enabling students to compete favorably with students in other states

Basic Principles and Structural Issues

The work of the curriculum subcommittee led to the development of the heart of the programmatic initiatives in KERA. David Hornbeck, the consultant to that subcommittee, is credited with crafting the design for most of these initiatives. When the committee began its deliberations, they were guided by thirteen principles. Three of the most significant are discussed here.

The first guiding principle was, "All children can learn at relatively high levels!" This is not a very profound statement. Almost every school district philosophy statement in the country has terminology similar to this. However, in actuality, many educators accept this statement for the children of families with middle class values, who are native Americans, who provide support to the school and an enriching home environment. They have less confidence in the principle for children from broken homes, living in poverty, who are non-English speaking, who have been identified as needing special services, and who have parents who were school dropouts. In reality, this translates into more than 25 – 30 percent of the children in schools today.

The second principle states that what is currently known about learning is sufficient to enable all children to be successful in schools. We are not in need of a new educational theory. We are not in need of a new textbook series. Perhaps not all teachers and administrators have the skills necessary to teach and administer schools where all children can be successful, but the knowledge and materials are available to do the job.

The third principle states that what children learn should be approximately the same across the state. This means that it should not be necessary to live within the "most affluent" school district in the state in order to ensure that a child receives an education that meets state standards. Whether the child lives in a hollow or a colonial mansion; whether or not the child is labeled as "special"; whether or not the child is from a single parent home; whether or not the child comes to school hungry; or whether or not the child's parents speak English; that child has the right to an education that will enable him/her to achieve at relatively high levels. Creating this type of school system is the challenge of KERA.

In working to produce such a system, the Act provided for five major structural changes in the way public education in the state of Kentucky would be organized. The first structural change was to move from an "inputs" system to an "outcomes" system. This meant that the General Assembly through statute, and the State Department of Education through regulations, would cease looking at requirements such as the number of books in the library, and the amount of time for instruction in a content area to determine the effectiveness of a school system. Rather, the state would look at what students know and are able to do as the measure of the district's effectiveness. Further, the unit for measuring the degree of student success would become the school, instead of the district. Districts would remain as accountable units; however, the individual school would become the primary, state-designated unit of measure.

The second structural issue is the development of a system of school sanctions and rewards. Under the provisions of KERA, it would no longer be acceptable to simply maintain demonstrated student achievement at a certain level within a school. Now, the school must continue to improve over time. Schools unable to improve the number of students achieving high state standards would receive sanctions. Schools able to significantly improve the number of successful students would be rewarded. The rewards would be increased money for the school, while the sanctions could mean the loss of a job for a tenured educator.

The third structural change involved moving from a state assessment system based on norm-referenced test district results, to a school-based, performance assessment system aligned with new state curriculum standards. In the recent past, the state had relied on the California Test of Basic Skills as the formal measure of successful district and student success. The state required the administration of this test at each grade level. Districts were required, by statute, to publish the results of these tests, along with other district data, to the general public each year in October. While the state department did not rank the districts on the basis of the test results, the major newspapers in the state did. The publication of this ranking was one of the reasons for the formation of the Council for Better Schools and the filing of the initial equity lawsuit. The districts argued that since the property values were low, they could not possibly generate the amount of money per pupil that the more property affluent districts could. Further, they argued that this discrepancy in the amount of money available per pupil was the reason for the discrepancy in the achievement of students. They contended that with the same amount of money as the more academically achieving districts, they could produce the same results. The gauntlet was thrown, and the legislature responded.

Over the next few years, it is the intent of the legislature to provide for state and local equity among districts. Now, it is up to local districts to produce student academic achievement. The districts that filed the suit argued that money was the problem. The state Supreme Court, in declaring the entire educational system unconstitutional, argued that the problem was more than money. Now, districts are faced with proving that the money can help produce the results. These results will be based on student achievement on authentic performance tasks, instead of norm-referenced tests. The challenge is significant for all of Kentucky and all of the nation. With equitable funding, can districts produce comparable high levels of student achievement? Time will tell!

The fourth structural change deals with the locus of school district decision making, which is a governance issue. KERA mandates that all 1,350+ schools in the state be empowered, through the formation of school councils, to make instructionally related decisions at the school level. Teachers have long said that they are not involved in the decision-making process. They contend that decisions are far too often made in the state capital or at the district level. Frequently, they have indicated that they know best what is appropriate, in terms of decision making, to enable all students to learn at relatively high levels. KERA gives teachers the power to make decisions at the school level through the formation of school councils. KERA provides school councils with sweeping powers regarding the selection of instructional materials, the utilization of instructional time, the development of school discipline codes, extracurricular activities, and fundraising activities. Yet, after two years, the number of school councils is surprisingly small. Teachers have voted to form school councils in less than a third of the schools in the state. However, there is still time. All schools in the state are not mandated to have councils until 1996. What is most important is that KERA provides the opportunity for a structural change in teacher empowerment.

The fifth structural change dealt with provisions for professional development. Legislators realized that the comprehensive changes embodied in KERA would require all educators to upgrade their skills. Consequently, the law mandated that teacher inservice focus on the following topics during the 1990−92 biennium for the four state-required teacher inservice days: overview of the law, school-based decision making, primary school, performance assessment, research-based instructional practices, and motivating students with diverse cultural backgrounds. In addition, all principals were required to receive professional development. Superintendents were required to demonstrate a high level of competence in such areas as leadership, performance assessment, curriculum, law, and school-based decision making by passing an assessment procedure that is being developed. To support this professional assessment, a special line item was provided in the state budget. Recognizing that implementation of the programmatic initiatives in KERA would require massive professional development, districts were given $1.00 per student the first year, $5.00 the second year, and $15.00 the third and fourth years of the implementation to plan professional development activities.

These basic principles and structural changes, which provide the foundation for KERA, must be dealt with as an integrated whole. For example, school-based councils, in and of themselves, will not achieve the results intended by the integration of all of these components. The decision-making authority of the councils is directly related to the new state standards. The standards are linked to the new authentic assessment system. Professional development was designed to provide educators with the skills they need to implement the state standards. Creating a success-oriented learning environment and building strong parent-school partnerships is designed to enable more students to achieve the state standards. Each component of the restructuring initiative is directly related to other components, forming a school restructuring web.

Five Important Programmatic Initiatives

Although the educational system was crafted to measure student success based on performance, the bill did provide for the development of five important programmatic initiatives. It appeared as though the curriculum subcommittee sat down with a group of educators and discussed why all students were not being successful in schools.

One barrier to learning that teachers always mention is the perceived lack of parental support for education. Middle- and upper-class parents are viewed as understanding the importance of supporting the instruction children receive in school with a home environment where books are valued, children are read to frequently, the amount of TV watched and the type of TV programs viewed are monitored, good nutritional habits are practiced, and proper medical attention is provided. Because children from lower economic circumstances may not have such a learning environment, KERA provided for the formation of Family Resource Centers to serve elementary schools where 20 percent of the students attending the school could qualify for free lunch and the formation of Youth Services Centers for secondary schools which met the same criteria. Ideally, these centers would link the social service community with the educational community so that pregnant teenagers could receive appropriate medical attention; parenting classes would be made available to the community; and before-school and after-school day care, as well as summer and vacation day care could be provided. The vision was that these centers would enable parents to view school as a helpful place to go for information and assistance. It was hoped that by the time a young child reached school age, the parents would lose their negative feelings about school and would interact with the school environment in the same supportive way as parents with typical middle-class values.

The next problem that was named by our group of educators was the fact that all children do not come to the schoolhouse door with the same social and readiness skills. The Preschool program was designed to provide children who would qualify for free lunch with a preschool experience that would enable them to gain these important social and readiness skills. The program mandated significant parental involvement and was designed to function collaboratively with the Head Start program. While it is a voluntary program, state department officials have predicted that between Head Start and the state Preschool program, the state is serving over 75 percent of the children in the state who would qualify. Between the family help and support offered by the Family Resource Centers, and the readiness skills offered by the Preschool program, children from economically deprived backgrounds should be better prepared to enter the formal schooling process at age five.

The next problem facing our group of educators was the fact that all children do not learn in the same way and at the same rate. All too often, our factory model, graded school environment does not provide adequately for these differences. Consequently, KERA provided for the implementation of a success-oriented primary school to replace grades kindergarten through three. This program is designed to provide "the gift of time" necessary for all children to achieve at relatively high levels. This program was supplemented with funding to pay for additional instructional time for approximately one-third of the student population in Kentucky schools. This supplemental program was called Extended School Services as money was made available to extend the school day, offer Saturday classes, extend the school year, or offer summer school. Districts have great discretion as to how these funds can be used. The intent was to enable teachers to identify student needs and to provide for those needs so that by the time the child reached the age appropriate for entering fourth grade, the child would demonstrate high levels of academic proficiency.

Finally, our group indicated that the schools in which they worked lacked the appropriate technology to support the type of individualized instruction envisioned by KERA. To assist districts in acquiring this needed technology, the legislature provided for the development of a strategic technology plan to be implemented over a five-year period. When completed, this plan will link all districts and classrooms in the state and provide a computer for every five students.

Perhaps this approach sounds too simplistic, but the programmatic initiatives have been created. They have been incorporated in the statute, and implementation plans are currently being carried out. The legislature is tenacious in its position that if these programs are successfully implemented, the educational system in Kentucky will truly be restructured and all children in this state will benefit.

How Learning Will Be Different

When the system is fully in place, a process that will take approximately six years, the learning environment in Kentucky schools will change. The new learning environment will be characterized by the following descriptors:

(*1*) A major focus on learning outcomes

(*2*) High expectations for nearly all students

(*3*) An emphasis on what is most important to learn

(*4*) An emphasis on performance assessment

(*5*) A learning environment emphasizing a variety of learning experiences

(*6*) An emphasis on active learning using multiple senses

(*7*) An emphasis on holistic learning

(*8*) More emphasis on cooperative and group learning

(*9*) Greater emphasis on quality learning experiences

(*10*) Greater emphasis on using real-life experiences as content for learning

A noble dream! Many legislators, employees of the Legislative Research Commission (LRC) and expert consultants, who testified while the Task Force was deliberating, never believed that their work would result in the passage of the bill. The governor had run on a platform of no new taxes. The relationship between the governor and the leaders of the General Assembly was "strained" to say the least. Without the support of the governor, there was little hope for gaining the funding necessary to support the reform. Yet, in the end, the governor's support was there. The budget bill to support the implementation was passed with HB 940. There were rumors of legislative arm-twisting, some evidence of "pork barreling," and many conversations behind closed doors, in order to gain the votes necessary to pass the bill; but pass it did.

SCHOOL GOVERNANCE

Clearly, there has been a significant shift in the locus of control for public education in Kentucky. Prior to the Supreme Court decision, there was a general feeling that local school districts had the power and authority to create whatever type of school system they wanted. If the district was doing a good job, the credit went to the district board, staff, and administration. If the district was producing poor results, the blame went to the district board, staff, and administration. With KERA, the locus of accountability has shifted to state government. The executive, judicial, and legislative branches have responsibility for an accountable state education system, while local districts have become a vehicle to achieve that accountability.

Local School Boards

At the same time, the autonomy of a local school district and its elected board of education has changed. More power has been shifted to the state and to local school councils. Local school district boundaries were not changed with the enactment of KERA, although there were a variety of proposals that would have modified the current system. In addition, the number of board members elected remained unchanged. In Kentucky, all 176 districts operate with five elected board members. The 123 county districts have five board members, each representing a particular division of the district. The fifty-three independent districts elect their board members at large.

One of the most significant changes in board operations was removing the board's hiring function. Under KERA, the only person the local board may hire is the superintendent of schools. When there is a vacancy for superintendent, the district will form a local steering committee made up of two teachers, one board member, one parent, and one principal. The steering committee will review applicants and make recommendations to the board, although the board is not bound by the recommendation of the committee.

Another caveat in KERA regarding local school board authority is the local school board's ability to terminate the superintendent's contract. The local board retains the right to terminate the contract, but may do so only with the approval of the commissioner of education. Before KERA was enacted, it was not unusual for a newly seated board to remove the superintendent from office and seat a new superintendent. With five-member boards, a 2-3 board might become a 3-2 board with the election of one new board member. With the board election, the district may have a new superintendent.

To fully comprehend the unique political arena in which many districts in Kentucky operate, it is important to understand that for a significant number of counties in this state, the local school district is the largest employer in the county. Because of the geography of the state, having a "good job" can mean working for the schools or some other agency of local or state government. Since school board members made hiring decisions, there was a perception that sometimes these decisions were politically motivated. There was also a perception that sometimes relatives of school board members were given preference in securing positions. Because of this perception, KERA includes language which makes a person ineligible for election to a local school board if he/she has a relative employed in the district. A relative is defined as a father, mother, brother, sister, husband, wife, son, daughter, aunt, uncle, son-in-law, or daughter-in-law.

Other provisions of KERA regarding school boards include a provision for limiting contributions to local board candidates' races to $100 from an individual and $200 from a political action committee (PAC). Board members are explicitly prohibited from influencing the hiring of school employees, and candidates for local school boards are prohibited from soliciting or accepting any money or services from any employee of the school district. The extent of abuses of board power is unsubstantiated. Certainly, the state has many hard working, dedicated school board members. These provisions of KERA are mentioned because they were recommendations made through the work of the subcommittee on governance to the Task Force on School Reform and became part of the legislation. Whether these violations of board power were real or perceived, under KERA, they will ostensibly cease.

Local Superintendent

KERA vests responsibility for all personnel actions in the district with the superintendent, including hiring, transfer, dismissal, suspension, promotion, and demotion. The superintendent simply informs the local board of his/her actions. This change was made because of the perception that local school board members used their power to influence the hiring of school personnel. With some exceptions, the superintendent, like board members, is prohibited from hiring relatives.

Readers from districts where there have been long-standing policies at the local district level prohibiting nepotism or cronyism, may be surprised that in the 1990s, it was necessary for a state legislature to include such provisions in school reform legislation. The Kentucky legislature did consider it important and necessary to include them. Only time will tell whether the provisions of KERA are sufficient to eliminate the real or perceived misuse of board and superintendent power.

State Superintendent of Public Instruction

Another important provision of KERA is related to the position of the elected state superintendent of public instruction and to the State Department of Education. Since the state superintendent of public instruction was a constitutional officer, it was not possible to eliminate the position without an amendment to the state constitution. In the past, Kentucky voters had not supported the elimination of this constitutional position. However, KERA reduced the duties of the position to the point where the state superintendent was simply a figurehead. The salary for the position was reduced to $3,000 a year effective January, 1992. This enabled the superintendent of public instruction, seated prior to the passage of KERA, to maintain a position as figurehead and his current salary until his term of office was over. KERA provided for an appointed commissioner of education. The first commissioner was selected by a committee made up of representatives of the governor's office and the legislature. A national search was conducted and Dr. Thomas Boysen was selected as the first commissioner of education for Kentucky. Dr. Boysen took office January 1, 1991, six months after KERA took effect. The seated superintendent of public instruction, Dr. John Brock, attempted to facilitate the transition to the best of his ability.

The legislature's action to eliminate the position was tied to the perception that the state superintendent used the position to reward political favors. There was a general feeling among the legislature that many of the employees of the Kentucky Department of Education were not the "brightest and best." This perception led to the provision calling for the elimination of all positions in the Kentucky Department of Education, effective June 30, 1991. The new commissioner of education was given the authority to completely reorganize the Department. By fall of 1991, most of the reorganization of the Department was complete. However, the process has continued. At the present time, almost all of the administrators occupying the top four levels of the organization are new to the state of Kentucky, the Department, and/or the position.

Politics in Kentucky School Districts

The purpose of this book is not to focus on politics in Kentucky school districts. The purpose here is to prepare a record of how this state attempted to restructure the instructional delivery system within schools to meet the needs of all children under the mandate of state legislated reform. However, it is doubtful that the programmatic initiatives and the funding would have materialized if the business leaders, parents, and citizens of this state did not believe that through the reform, whatever remnants of political patronage and politics that remained operational within this state would be removed.

While there was no statewide citizen revolt because of the tax increase enacted to support KERA, there has been evidence of citizen backlash in isolated districts. One case bears discussion because it highlights the desire of at least one school district to maintain and preserve old ways of doing things. The ramifications of the actions that took place in this district have been felt at the highest levels of the leadership in the General Assembly. These actions call into question whether the present local school district model, currently in place in Kentucky, supports or impedes reform. While the reader is asked to remember that this is simply one district in a state made up of 176 districts, it remains a troublesome example. In the future, the General Assembly may have to revisit the governance issue if other examples are seen. An editorial that appeared in the May 31, 1992, issue of the *Lexington Herald Leader*, describes the present situation.

> It was predictable that a judge somewhere in Kentucky would rule a big part of the state's school reform law unconstitutional. The law is complex, and much of state constitutional law is a mystery even to those who know most about it.
>
> It was predictable, too, that such a ruling would center on the parts of the law that are aimed at rooting out corruption and patronage in local schools. These political abuses are a way of life in some school districts, and can't be expected to die easily.
>
> But predictable as it may have been, what has happened in Harlan County in recent days is little short of an outrage. There, the old and new politics of schools clashed with lamentable results.
>
> On the Friday before Election Day, Harlan Circuit Judge Ron Johnson announced that he planned to reinstate three Harlan County school board members who had been removed from office by the state board of education. But Johnson didn't issue a written order.

The effect was that the state couldn't appeal the decision. And that gave the three ousted school board members a free hand to campaign against state Rep. Roger Noe, the Harlan Democrat who was an architect of the reform law and one of the House's most thoughtful members.

Last Tuesday, Noe lost the Democratic primary to Rick Fox, who had campaigned against the school reform act. Last Friday, Johnson finally got around to issuing his ruling reinstating the three ousted board members — at least for now.

The case is clearly headed to the state Supreme Court, which set the whole school reform process in motion with a landmark 1989 decision. There's every reason to expect that the high court will back the law and the state school board, and that reform will eventually come to Harlan County's schools.

Reform is inevitable, in Harlan County and elsewhere in Kentucky. Kentuckians clearly will no longer tolerate the kind of political abuses that plague many school districts. That knowledge doesn't help the state's children now. But it may make it a bit easier to swallow what happened in Harlan last week.

Roger Noe was chairman of the Joint Education Subcommittee of the General Assembly. He has served in the state legislature for sixteen years. He was a member of the Task Force on Education Reform. It is somewhat ironic that he should lose this position as a consequence of the implementation of one of the accountability provisions of KERA.

One accountability provision in KERA is the establishment of the Office of Educational Accountability (OEA). The office is an independent arm of the Legislative Research Commission (LRC) with the primary responsibility of monitoring the implementation of the Kentucky Education Reform Act. OEA reports to the leadership of the General Assembly, which included Roger Noe. The duties of the Office of Educational Accountability include reviewing the state's school finance system; verifying the accuracy of school district and state performance; and investigating unresolved allegations of wrongdoing at the state, regional, or district level. In fulfilling this last responsibility, the office conducted an investigation that led to the removal of three Harlan County school board members from office by the State Board of Elementary and Secondary Education. The entire board and the local superintendent were under investigation at the time. One board member resigned because of health reasons, one board member was newly elected and remained in office, the superintendent resigned before the State Board hearing, and three board members were removed from office. The community protested the State Board action and implied that politics was involved. Some feel this action contributed to Roger Noe's loss in the May, 1992, primary. Even though the district had received over 25 percent of new state money because of KERA, many local citizens blamed KERA for the removal from office of the local board members.

These events are not representative of the vast majority of school districts in this state. Of the 176 school districts in Kentucky, most are working exceedingly hard to implement the new initiatives in KERA. However, there are a small number of districts where the OEA is investigating similar wrongdoing. These tend to be districts where unemployment rates are high, where the school system is the largest employer in the county, where positions on the board of education are seen as powerful, political seats, and where there has been a long tradition of autocratic practices within local government and school administration. Even though there are dedicated educators and concerned citizens working and living within these areas, it appears that the internal county pressures are such that it is almost impossible for the system to correct itself internally. It is within these districts that the State Board of Elementary and Secondary Education, representing the executive branch of state government; the Office of Educational Accountability, representing the legislative branch of state government; and the Supreme Court, representing the judicial branch of state government, are working in concert to enable these districts to rid themselves of past practices which seem to have interfered with the ability of the districts to improve the system. Much of the statutory language related to governance in KERA is directed to the abuses of this small number of Kentucky school districts.

Harlan County is clearly an exception, but there are other Harlan Counties in Kentucky and their existence can no longer be tolerated. Roger Noe may have been a casualty in the implementation of KERA. There will likely be others. The individuals in these districts who want to maintain the power structure the way it has always been will not give up that power easily. The lawsuits, both within the state judicial system and the federal court system, will continue for many years.

In the end, if the vision of KERA is fulfilled, the children of this state will prevail. It may take additional, stronger statutory language, but the joint commitment by business leaders, educators, and the people of Kentucky is to stay the course.

This book is not about the Harlan Counties of the state. This book is about the programmatic initiatives currently underway, which hold the potential for changing the way teachers teach and children learn. It is a book about pioneers in education reform. It is about districts and educators who began to pilot the primary school concept within the first year of the legislation. It is about how Kentucky educators created a new system of state standards for what children should know and be able to do when they graduate from high school. It is about beginning the largest state-supported collaborative network between the social service community and the education community to coordinate services for families and youth. It is about replacing standardized student assessment with a state authentic assessment system linked to sanctions and reward. It is about combining the forces of the federal Head Start program with the state Preschool program to provide young children with a better preparation for formal schooling.

Behind the description of the programs are the educators of Kentucky. Even though they were not invited to formally participate in the development of the Act, it is these same educators who are laying the foundation for its success. Many are working harder than they ever have before. There are persistent rumors of burnout and early retirements, yet the momentum continues to grow. As some make their contribution and step aside, others are there to take their place. The synergy that comes from the collective work of the group is beginning to emerge, and with it, a strong resolve to do whatever it takes to change a river's course.

REFERENCES

Council for Better Education v. Wilkinson. No.85-CI-1759. Franklin Circuit Court, Div. I. Judgements dated May 31, 1988, and October 14, 1988.

Editorial, *Lexington Herald Leader*, May 31, 1992.

Kentucky Department of Education. 1990. *Kentucky School Laws.* Frankfort, Kentucky: Banks-Baldwin Law Publishing.

Miller, Mary Helen, Kevin Noland, and John Schaaf. 1990. *A Guide to the Kentucky Education Reform Act of 1990.* Frankfort, Kentucky: Legislative Research Commission.

Rose v. Council for Better Education, Inc., No. 88-SC-804-TG, Kentucky, September 28, 1989.

Stumbo, Gregory (Speaker). Kentucky General Assembly, Frankfort, Kentucky, 1990.

Wilkinson, Wallace (Speaker). Signing of House Bill 940, Frankfort, Kentucky, April, 1990.

CHAPTER 2

What Students Will Know and Be Able to Do: Kentucky's New Curriculum

WRITTEN in 1891, the Kentucky state constitution, Section 183, states:

> Education is perhaps the most important function of state and local governments. . . . It is required in the performance of our most basic public responsibilities . . . It is the very foundation of good citizenship. Today, it is a principal instrument in awakening the child to cultural values, in preparing him for later professional training, and in helping him to adjust normally to his environment. In these days, it is doubtful that any child may reasonably be expected to succeed in life if he is denied the opportunity of an education. Such an opportunity, where the state has undertaken to provide it, is a right which must be made available to all on equal terms.

This statement is as true today as it was over a hundred years ago, and the skills and knowledge that make up that education continue to evolve. What makes up an "adequate" education is different today than it was at the turn of the century.

The Kentucky Supreme Court, in an opinion rendered in June, 1989, defined an "adequate" education as one that develops the following seven capacities.

(*1*) Communication skills necessary to function in a complex and changing civilization

(*2*) Knowledge to make economic, social, and political choices

(*3*) Understanding of governmental processes as they affect the community, state, and nation

(*4*) Sufficient self-knowledge and knowledge of one's mental and physical wellness

(*5*) Sufficient grounding in the arts to enable each student to appreciate his or her cultural and historical heritage

(*6*) Sufficient preparation to choose and pursue one's lifework intelligently

(7) Skills enabling students to compete favorably with students in other states

In two short years, these words have been operationalized into a new state curriculum and an authentic, performance assessment system.

HISTORICAL PERSPECTIVE

Over the past few decades in Kentucky, much of the curriculum embodied in the skills and information taught in school was driven by the Kentucky Essential Skills Test (KEST), the California Test of Basic Skills (CTBS), the state textbook adoption process, and the Kentucky Program of Studies. The Program of Studies is a state-produced document that briefly describes the content of courses taught at each grade. It also lists the certification required to teach each course. In the past, if a school district wanted to offer a course that was not listed in the Program of Studies, the district would have to receive approval from the State Board of Elementary and Secondary Education. In addition, until the passage of KERA, state statutes defined specific time requirements for content areas. The State Department monitored compliance with course content, certification, and time requirements through an elaborate accreditation process. Districts failing to comply were required to develop school improvement plans to eliminate "accreditation deficiencies." Deficient districts then received interim accreditation visits from state officials to monitor progress toward removing the deficiencies. Districts that were unable to meet the goals stated in their school improvement plans faced State Department intervention, and possible sanctions.

KERA eliminated the district accreditation process, removed the subject time requirements, and fundamentally changed the definition of curriculum. These changes began in February, 1989, when Governor Wallace Wilkinson (1989) issued an executive order that created the Council on School Performance Standards.

> Whereas, it is the function of the public schools to guide, nurture and teach the children and youth of the Commonwealth in the acquisition of the body of knowledge and skills that it has determined they should know and be able to do at various stages in their education, and

> Whereas, the essence of what the Commonwealth desires children to be able to know and do is embodied in the curriculum of the public schools; and

Whereas, the public needs to know the degree of success each child experiences in acquiring all the designated body of knowledge and skills as he or she progresses through the educational process, and

Whereas, there needs to be established a credible process, common to all public schools, for documenting the educational progress of every child in the Commonwealth, and

Whereas, the public desires to know the educational progress of children on an individual school basis:

Now, therefore, pursuant to the authority vested in me by KRS 12.029, I, Wallace G. Wilkinson, Governor of The Commonwealth of Kentucky, do hereby create a Council on School Performance Standards which shall advise the Governor, the General Assembly, the Superintendent of Public Instruction and the State Board for Elementary and Secondary Education regarding the following:

1. The extent to which the Kentucky Program of Studies will satisfy the present and future educational needs of the Commonwealth's children and youth, and what may be required to strengthen it;

2. Standards for student performance at various stages in a child's educational program which can provide a basis for fairly and accurately assessing the educational progress of every child in the public schools;

3. Appropriate methods of assessing learning, suitable for statewide use, which schools can use to document the extent to which children are acquiring all the knowledge and skills expected of them at specific points in their educational program, given their relative ability to do so;

4. The extent to which the curriculum of the public schools can be appropriately adapted to the differences in learning styles of children, taking into consideration the inherent ability of children to attain the expected knowledge and skills.

. . . To achieve these goals, the Council may hold public hearings, create standing or ad hoc committees, employ consultants, and commission the writing of issue papers. The Council shall report its initial findings and recommendations to the Governor, Superintendent of Public Instruction, State Board for Elementary and Secondary Education, and the General Assembly on or before August 1, 1989.

The Council was composed of twelve members, appointed by the governor. They represented higher education, business leaders, teachers, administrators, State Board members, the superintendent of public instruction, and the secretary of education. They began their work by holding focus group interviews with business leaders, graduates, parents, employers, and educators around the state. Each group was asked what a high school graduate of the year 2000 should know and be able to do.

Using information collected from the interviews, the University of Kentucky Survey Research Center prepared a twenty-two minute telephone survey. The survey was administered to 838 Kentucky residents of voting age. The survey population included 201 opinion leaders and 637 members of the general population (report of the Council on School Performance Standards, 1989). The survey showed that the overall rating of education in Kentucky was not very good. While 3.8 percent of those surveyed rated Kentucky education as "excellent," 17.9 percent rated it "poor," 43.4 percent rated it "fair," and 34.9 percent rated it "good." Survey respondents were also asked to rate the importance of specific instructional skills or knowledge such as the ability to perform basic reading, writing, speaking, and math skills; the ability to learn how to think and solve problems; proficiency in the use of computers and technology; and the importance of work, employment, and earning a living.

In addition to work on the survey, five subcommittees were formed. Three of the subcommittees began to describe what children should know and be able to do at the elementary, middle school, and high school levels. Another subcommittee described what children should know and be able to do after completing vocational school, and the final subcommittee prepared a report regarding assessment.

As the Council was preparing its interim report, during the summer of 1989, the Supreme Court decision declaring Kentucky's educational system unconstitutional was rendered. Even so, the interim report was delivered to the State Board of Elementary and Secondary Education in August of 1989, as required in the governor's executive order. By that time, the General Assembly had formed the Task Force on Education Reform. In September, 1989, the Council presented its report, entitled *Preparing Kentucky Youth for the Next Century: What Students Should Know and Be Able to Do and How Learning Should Be Assessed*, to the curriculum subcommittee of the Task Force. The six broad learning goals identified in this report became part of House Bill 940 and were later enacted as a statute. The statute reads as follows:

158.6451 Council on School Performance Standards; development of goals for Commonwealth's schools; model curriculum framework

(1) Upon July 13, 1990, the Council on School Performance Standards established by Executive Order 89-151 shall be reconvened by the chairman to frame the following six (6) goals for the schools of the Common-

wealth in measurable terms which define the outcomes expected of students:

(a) Schools shall expect a high level of achievement of all students.

(b) Schools shall develop their students' ability to:

1. Use basic communication and mathematics skills for purposes and situations they will encounter throughout their lives;

2. Apply core concepts and principles from mathematics, the sciences, the arts, the humanities, social studies, and practical living studies to situations they will encounter throughout their lives;

3. Become a self-sufficient individual;

4. Become responsible members of a family, work group, or community, including demonstrating effectiveness in community service;

5. Think and solve problems in school situations and in a variety of situations they will encounter in life; and

6. Connect and integrate experiences and new knowledge from all subject matter fields with what they have previously learned and build on past learning experiences to acquire new information through various media resources. . . .

The Council shall make periodic progress reports and a final report by December 1, 1991. . . . (KDE, 1990, p. 232)

In the preparation of the interim report, approximately seventy-five people worked consistently on the project. That number grew to nearly 200 as the work of defining the new state curriculum progressed.

The Council was reconvened on June 4, 1990. The executive director, Dr. Roger Pankratz, was reemployed; and the Council approved a work plan schedule developed by Dr. Pankratz that outlined the work of the Council for the next eighteen months. The work plan called for the formation of eleven task forces: Primary/Elementary, Middle School, High School, Language Arts, Arts and Humanities, Science and Technology, Mathematics, Social Studies, Practical Living, Vocational Studies, and Computers and Other Applied Technology. A nomination, interview, and approval procedure was established for the selection of task force chairpersons. Once selected by the executive director, each chairman had to be approved by the Council. These individuals were recognized as leaders in their fields, had skills in resolving group conflict, were highly respected by their peers, had the time available to devote to this project, and possessed excellent writing skills. The charge to these task forces was to define the "big ideas" associated within their areas and to define the performance assessment measures appropriate for grades four, eight, and twelve. These "big ideas" became the seventy-five valued outcomes that are the basis of Kentucky's new, integrated curriculum. The eighteen months between the reformation of the Council and the December, 1991, State Board approval of the valued outcomes were filled with heated debate, frustration, hard work, long hours, exhilaration, growth, and dedication. This came from scores of Kentucky educators who understood the importance of the task and what it meant for the future of Kentucky's children.

The executive director of the Council and his small staff were given office space in the Department of Education. While this was not a Department initiative, staff at the Department attempted to assist the Council and worked cooperatively with the executive director. The work of the Council progressed in the midst of a Department reorganization that replaced the vast majority of the top administrative staff in the Department (see Chapter 9). The executive director maintained a positive working relationship with the old Department administration that was in place during the first year of KERA implementation; then quickly established a positive working relationship with the new administration during the transition to the newly restructured Department. This continuity was essential since the design and development of the new performance assessment system was under the direction of the Department and work on the assessment design was progressing simultaneously with work on the curriculum.

A formal process to apply for membership on a task force was established and over 450 educators applied. Each task force was to be made up of the chairman, one Department of Education representative, and eleven members. In choosing the members, attention was given to breadth of expertise, both in Kentucky and nationally; geographic location; ethnicity; and present role. Each committee included teachers, administrators, higher education faculty, and state department representatives. Teachers were more heavily represented on each committee than any other group. Among the teachers selected, care was taken to include teachers with elementary, middle, and secondary experience in addition to experience with special needs children such as gifted children or learning disabled children.

Some task forces worked together more harmoniously than others. Often, this was related to the divergence in content areas represented on the task force. For example, the Arts and Humanities task force included art, music, drama, and literature content expertise. Agreeing on the "big ideas'' to be addressed in these fields and relating them to the six goals in the statute was a difficult undertaking. The state curriculum was not organized around individual content areas such as science, math, and social studies. Rather, the six basic learning goals: Basic Communication and Math Skills; Core Concepts (in science, math, social studies, arts and humanities, and practical living); Self-Sufficiency; Responsible Group Membership; Thinking and Problem Solving; and Integration of Knowledge became the organizer for the curriculum.

The content areas were envisioned to be the means for achieving the fundamental goals established in the law, not to be ends in and of themselves. They would serve as the vehicle to achieve the valued outcomes. With the passage of time, the implementation of the primary school (see Chapter 5), and the expansion of the critical attributes of the primary school to the middle school and high school, the architects of the new state curriculum envisioned a day when children would experience a truly integrated curriculum from the time they entered primary school until they graduated from high school. The implications for certification, Carnegie units, textbook publishers, and graduation requirements were understood. Only time will tell if Kentucky has designed a state curriculum that can break the mold of the segmented factory model that is common in our schools today. To date, the valued outcomes have been incorporated into the design of the state's new performance system and we have taken the initial, small steps in that direction.

A valued outcome has been defined as the ability to demonstrate consistent, quality performances on authentic tasks related to a skill area, core concept, personal attribute, or thinking process (*Technical Report*, 1991, p. 5). Because valued outcomes focus on "big ideas," they do not include all of the enabling skills and knowledge required to demonstrate achievement of the outcome. The seventy-five valued outcomes are listed below as they relate to each of the six learning goals.

Goal One: Basic Communication and Math Skills

Valued Outcomes:

- (*1*) Students use research tools to locate sources of information and ideas relevant to a specific need or problem.
- (*2*) Students construct meaning from a variety of print materials for a variety of purposes through reading.

(*3*) Students construct meaning from messages communicated in a variety of ways for a variety of purposes through observing.

(*4*) Students construct meaning from messages communicated in a variety of ways for a variety of purposes through listening.

(*5*) Students communicate ideas by quantifying with whole, rational, real, and/or complex numbers.

(*6*) Students manipulate information and communicate ideas with a variety of computational algorithms.

(*7*) Students organize information and communicate ideas by visualizing space configurations and movements.

(*8*) Students gather information and communicate ideas by measuring.

(*9*) Students organize information and communicate ideas by algebraic and geometric reasoning such as relations, patterns, variables, unknown quantities, deductive and inductive processes.

(*10*) Students organize information through development and use of classification rules and classification systems.

(*11*) Students communicate ideas and information to a variety of audiences for a variety of purposes in a variety of modes through speaking.

(*12*) Students construct meaning and/or communicate ideas and emotions through the visual arts.

(*13*) Students construct meaning and/or communicate ideas and emotions through music.

(*14*) Students construct meaning and/or communicate ideas and emotions through movement.

(*15*) Students use computers and other electronic technology to gather, organize, manipulate, and express information and ideas.

Goal Two: Core Concepts

Valued Outcomes — Science

(*1*) Students use appropriate and relevant scientific skills to solve specific problems in real-life situations.

(*2*) Students identify, compare, and construct patterns and use patterns to understand and interpret past and present events and predict future events.

(3) Students identify and describe systems, subsystems, and components and their interactions by completing tasks and/or creating products.

(4) Students use models and scales to explain or predict the organization, function, and behavior of objects, materials, and living things in their environment.

(5) Students understand the tendency of nature to move toward a steady state in closed systems.

(6) Students complete tasks and/or develop products that identify, describe, and direct evolutionary change that has occurred or is occurring around them.

Valued Outcomes — Math

(1) Students demonstrate understanding of *number* concepts.

(2) Students demonstrate understanding of concepts related to *mathematical* procedures.

(3) Students demonstrate understanding of concepts related to *space* and *dimensionality*.

(4) Students demonstrate understanding of *measurement* concepts.

(5) Students demonstrate understanding of *change* concepts on patterns and functions.

(6) Students demonstrate understanding of concepts related to *mathematical structure*.

(7) Students demonstrate understanding of *data* concepts related to both *certain* and *uncertain* events.

Valued Outcomes — Social Studies

(1) Students recognize issues of justice, equality, responsibility, choice, and freedom; and apply these democratic principles to real-life situations.

(2) Students recognize varying forms of government and address issues of importance to citizens in a democracy, including authority, power, civic action, and rights and responsibilities.

(3) Students recognize varying social groupings and institutions and address issues of importance to members of these groupings, including beliefs, customs, norms, roles, equity, order, and change.

(4) Students interact effectively and work cooperatively with the diverse ethnic and cultural groups of our nation and world.

(5) Students make economic decisions regarding production and consumption of goods and services related to real-life situations.

(6) Students recognize the geographic interaction between people and their surroundings in order to make decisions and take actions that reflect responsibility for the environment.

(7) Students recognize continuity and change in historical events, conditions, trends, and issues in order to make decisions for a better future.

(8) Students observe, analyze, and interpret human behaviors to acquire a better understanding of self, others, and human relationships.

Valued Outcomes – Arts and Humanities

(1) Students create products and make presentations that convey concepts and feelings.

(2) Students analyze their own and others' artistic products and performances.

(3) Students appreciate creativity and the values of the arts and the humanities.

(4) Through their productions and performances or interpretations, students show an understanding of the influence of time, place, personality, and society on the arts and humanities.

(5) Students recognize differences and commonalities in the human experience through their productions, performances, or interpretations.

(6) Students complete tasks, make presentations, and create models that demonstrate awareness of the diversity of forms, structures, and concepts across languages and how they may interrelate.

(7) Students understand and communicate in a second language.

Valued Outcomes – Practical Living

(1) Students demonstrate positive individual and family life skills.

(2) Students demonstrate effective decision making and evaluative consumer skills.

(3) Students demonstrate skills and self-responsibility in understanding, achieving, and maintaining physical wellness.

(4) Students demonstrate positive strategies for achieving and maintaining mental and emotional wellness.

(5) Students demonstrate the ability to assess and access health systems, services, and resources available in their community that maintain and promote healthy living for its clients.

(6) Students perform psychomotor skills effectively and efficiently in a variety of settings.

(7) Students demonstrate knowledge, skills, and values that have lifetime implications for involvement in physical activity.

Valued Outcomes — Vocational Studies

(1) Students demonstrate strategies for selecting career path options.

(2) Students produce and/or make presentations that communicate school-to-work/post-secondary transition skills.

(3) Students demonstrate the ability to complete a post-secondary opportunities search.

Goal Three: Self-Sufficiency

Valued Outcomes

(1) Students demonstrate positive growth in self-concept through appropriate tasks or projects.

(2) Students demonstrate the ability to maintain a healthy lifestyle.

(3) Students demonstrate the ability to be adaptable and flexible through appropriate tasks or projects.

(4) Students demonstrate the ability to be resourceful and creative.

(5) Students demonstrate self-control and self-discipline.

(6) Students demonstrate the ability to make decisions based on ethical values.

(7) Students demonstrate the ability to learn on their own.

Goal Four: Responsible Group Membership

Valued Outcomes

(1) Students effectively use interpersonal skills.

(2) Students use productive team member skills.

(3) Students individually demonstrate consistent, responsive, and caring behavior.

(4) Students demonstrate the ability to accept the rights and responsibilities for self and others.

(5) Students demonstrate an understanding of, appreciation for, and sensitivity to a multicultural and world view.

(6) Students demonstrate an open mind to alternative perspectives.

Goal Five: Thinking and Problem Solving

Valued Outcomes

(1) Students use critical thinking skills in a variety of situations that will be encountered in life.

(2) Students use creative thinking skills to develop or invent novel, constructive ideas or products.

(3) Students create and modify their understanding of a concept through organizing information.

(4) Students use a decision-making process to make informed decisions among options.

(5) Students use problem-solving processes to develop solutions to relatively complex problems.

Goal Six: Integration of Knowledge

Valued Outcomes

(1) Students address situations (e.g., topics, problems, decisions, products) from multiple perspectives and produce presentations or products that demonstrate a broad understanding. Examples of perspectives include economic, social, cultural, political, historic, physical, technical, aesthetic, environmental, and personal.

(2) Students will use what they already know to acquire knowledge, develop new skills, or interpret new experiences.

(3) Students expand their understanding of existing knowledge (e.g., topics, problems, situations, product) by making connections with new and unfamiliar knowledge, skills, and experiences.

While the valued outcomes define what is most important for students to learn, they do not dictate how teachers are to teach the skills necessary to acquire the valued outcomes; nor do they dictate the sequence for teaching those skills or the instructional strategies teachers should use.

All of these decisions are to be made at the district, school, and classroom level. Whatever process teachers use to achieve these valued outcomes, these instructional strategies should enable all students to demonstrate on the state's new authentic assessment system, that they have acquired these skills (see Chapter 3). Since the state performance assessment is aligned to the valued outcomes, it is assumed that there will be congruence among the written, taught, and tested curriculum at the district, school, and classroom level. The state's sanctions and rewards system will assess each school's ability to achieve the valued outcomes at grades four, eight, and twelve.

PROCESS

The work plan developed by the executive director of the Council on School Performance Standards was followed with only minor modification from April, 1990, to December, 1991. These activities are summarized below to provide the reader with an understanding of how the work progressed.

(*1*) April – May – June, 1990
 - In June a Council meeting was held to reemploy staff and adopt the work plan schedule.
 - Applications for task force membership were mailed to 178 school districts and major professional education organizations in the state.
 - Applications for task force membership were received and processed.

(*2*) July – August – September, 1990
 - Recruitment and selection of task force members was conducted. In excess of 450 applications were received and processed. All applications were read by two to five reviewers. Recommendations were made by task force leaders. Final approval was given by a special Council committee.
 - A selection process to identify task force leaders was conducted involving (1) nominations/interviews, and (2) approval by council.
 - A Council meeting was held to approve task force leaders and a process was established to complete task force member selection.

- Council staff participated in the second round of Kentucky Department of Education statewide regional meetings.
- The Director conducted orientation/training for task force leaders in Louisville.
- An orientation and training meeting for eleven task forces was conducted in Frankfort.
- Council staff provided materials and information to 125 task force members as a follow-up to the orientation session.
- Council staff corresponded with 325 applicants for task force membership who were not selected inviting them to become advisory members.
- The executive director provided information to school personnel and civic groups.

(3) October – November – December, 1990
- Council staff mailed packets to more than 200 advisory members to task forces.
- The director presented the work of the Council at the Regional Teacher Education Conference sponsored by AACTE, with a focus on Kentucky School Reform.
- The executive director met with all eleven task force leaders individually to go over task force progress and to address concerns.
- The executive director and three task force leaders participated in a Performance Assessment Conference conducted by OERI and made a formal presentation to key U.S. Department officials.
- The executive director and four task force leaders presented the work of the Council at the Lexington conference held for National Laboratories and Research and Development Centers.
- A two-day work session was held for eight task forces in Louisville.
- The executive director met with the assessment consultants employed by the State Board for Elementary and Secondary Education.
- A Council meeting was held to review the work of the task forces and approve the 1991 work plan schedule.
- A task force leaders' retreat was held to plan the next four months' agenda and detailed work plan schedule.

- The first scheduled meeting of Business and Community Leaders' Advisory Council to review the work of task forces was held.
- Council staff mailed out the second round of packets to advisory members requesting input for valued outcomes and ideas for assessment tasks.
- Council staff provided information about the work of the Council to school personnel and civic groups through formal presentations and speaking engagements.

(4) January – June, 1991
- The Council processed feedback on valued outcomes and assessment tasks.
- The executive director conducted a task force leaders' meeting to plan for February work session.
- The executive director implemented a two-day work session for eleven task forces, processed information, and determined which learning outcomes were most important.
- The executive director conducted a two-day meeting for task force leaders to process task force work session results.
- The Council developed a draft document that framed the six school goals in measurable terms for grades four, eight, and twelve.
- The Council on School Performance Standards met to approve the draft document for release to the public.
- The executive director conducted public hearings and processed comments on the draft document.
- The executive director planned and conducted work sessions for all task force members to review the public comments on the draft document and revise the document to address concerns.
- Task force leaders continued to work on revising the draft documents based on the results of the meeting with task force members.

(5) July – December, 1991
- Council continued to make revisions.
- The draft technical report was presented to the Council for approval.
- Staff was trained to conduct public awareness sessions.
- A videotape was produced to use in public awareness sessions.

- Council approved the final plan in the form of a technical report.
- The technical report was presented to the State Board for Elementary and Secondary Education.
- State Board approved the plan.

COUNCIL TECHNICAL REPORT

The technical report became the basis for statewide inservice on the valued outcomes during 1992. The document not only listed the seventy-five valued outcomes, it also provided background information about KERA, how the valued outcomes would be linked to performance assessment, and how instruction in Kentucky would change. The report was sent to each school district in the state. Massive, statewide inservice took place to acquaint educators, parents, and community leaders with the valued outcomes. Some districts began to form study groups to design a process to align the present district curriculum with the valued outcomes.

While few disagreed with the importance of the valued outcomes, many educators had difficulty in understanding exactly what they meant in terms of student behavior. Many educators decided to wait until the State Department issued the required curriculum framework before beginning the task of aligning the local district curriculum with the valued outcomes.

CURRICULUM FRAMEWORK

158.6451 (4) By July 1, 1993, the State Board for Elementary and Secondary Education shall disseminate to local school districts and schools a model curriculum framework that is directly tied to the goals, outcomes, and assessment strategies developed pursuant to this section. . . . The framework shall provide direction to local districts and schools as they develop their curriculum. The framework shall identify teaching and assessment strategies, instructional material resources, ideas on how to incorporate the resources of the community, a directory of model teaching sites, and alternative ways of using school time. (KDE, 1990, p. 232)

In early June, 1992, the Division of Curriculum Development of the Kentucky Department of Education held its first public meeting to introduce the draft copy of the framework. The main document addressed goals 1, 3—6, and the math and vocational education components of goal 2. The rest of goal 2, including science, social studies, arts and humanities, and practical living studies was scheduled to be distributed in September, 1992.

This draft framework was developed over a nine-month period under the leadership of the newly hired division director. The Division not only had a new director, but had also been reorganized as part of the restructuring of the Department. In this restructuring, new staff members were moved to the Division from other units within the Department, some members of the old Division kept their jobs or left the Department, and the Division had been operating with an acting director through the most difficult parts of the Department reorganization (see Chapter 9). In addition, morale within the Division was low. Under the leadership of the new director, the group began to assume an identity, gain confidence and expertise, and rise to the challenge of developing a document referred to in the legislation as a curriculum framework. Even in draft form, without all of the required components, the document is a valuable resource for school districts.

The purpose of the curriculum framework is to provide local districts and schools with assistance as they align local curriculum with the state goals and valued outcomes. While districts are not required to use any part of the framework, educators across the state have found it to be a valuable resource.

In the fall of 1991, building on the mission of the Kentucky Department of Education, the Division of Curriculum Development created a series of beliefs to guide their work in creating the framework. The dialogue that led to the development of these beliefs helped the Division coalesce, and to become focused, committed, and dedicated to the task before them. These beliefs (*Kentucky's Preliminary Curriculum Framework*, 1992, p. 11) were used as guiding thoughts in the development of the curriculum framework.

We believe all children can learn at high levels, and they

.....possess a curiosity and desire to learn.
.....respond positively to success and enthusiasm.
.....develop and learn at different rates.
.....demonstrate learning in different ways.
.....learn by being actively involved, by taking risks, and by making connections.

Successful schools are for students, and they

.....expect a high level of achievement.
.....provide the time and instruction to achieve student success.

.....provide connections with home and community experiences.

.....insure a safe, positive environment.

.....create opportunities to explore and grow.

Effective instruction facilitates learning, and it

.....addresses identified outcomes.

.....assures success and risk taking.

.....employs a variety of effective techniques to address learning diversity.

.....aligns curriculum, instruction, and assessment.

.....connects curricular offerings to the life experiences of students.

.....encourages self-directional and life-long learning.

The work of the Division was assisted by several committees made up of educators from across the state. The committees included Integrated Curriculum Committee, Primary Committee, Language Arts Committee, Mathematics Committee, Vocational Education Committee, and an Advisory Committee.

The major part of the framework is devoted to the identification of "demonstrators" for each of the valued outcomes. Demonstrators are defined in the framework as expansions of the valued outcomes that further define what students should be able to do (p. 111). "They will indicate how students are progressing toward the outcome" (p. 111).

Figure 2.1 is an example of two pages from the draft framework. At the top of the page, the curriculum goal is listed. In this case the valued outcome relates to goal 1. Then the valued outcome is stated. This valued outcome deals with the student's ability to communicate ideas and information through writing. Demonstrators are listed for elementary, middle school, and high school. Elementary school is defined as primary through fifth grade. (Note: primary school replaces grades kindergarten through third.) The demonstrators are not linked directly to a grade level, but they do become progressively more comprehensive as you read *up* the column. Theoretically, students who can successfully complete all of the demonstrators listed in a column would be able to perform well on the state's assessment system at grades four, eight, and twelve. Included with the demonstrators is a column entitled Possible Integrated Learning Links. The items listed in this column are "suggestions for connections across other content areas" (p. 111).

The next section, called "Instructional Strategies," is a listing of possible strategies a teacher could employ in designing instruction to achieve this valued outcome. The section entitled "Ideas for Incorporating Community Resources" is another listing of suggestions; this time,

```
┌─────────────────────────────────────────────────────────────────────┐
│         GOAL 1: BASIC COMMUNICATION AND MATH SKILLS                    │
└─────────────────────────────────────────────────────────────────────┘
```

```
┌─────────────────────────────────────────────────────────────────────┐
│  VALUED OUTCOME:  Students communicate ideas and information to a      │
│  variety of audiences for a variety of purposes in a variety of       │
│  modes through writing.                                                │
└─────────────────────────────────────────────────────────────────────┘
```

DEMONSTRATORS	ELEMENTARY	MIDDLE SCHOOL	HIGH SCHOOL
POSSIBLE-INTEGRATED LEARNING LINKS	Publish (make public) writing.	- Publish (make public) writing.	- Publish (make public) writing.
	- Refine writing through revising and editing.	- Edit the writing.	- Analyze and revise draft to improve organization, focus, and language.
Video/Film Scripts	- Respond to a piece of writing (self and peer) using established criteria.	- Revise the draft.for clarity of expression.	
Journals		- Respond to a piece of writing (self and peer) using established criteria.	- Create and use criteria to evaluate own and others writing.
Advertisements	- Create initial draft to give shape to ideas/information.		
Notation		- Create initial draft to give shape to ideas/information.	- Write in a variety of modes and purposes for a variety of audiences.
Public Service Announcements	- Write in a variety of modes and purposes for a variety of audiences.	- Write in a variety of modes and purposes for a variety	
Speeches			- Choose writing to express personal interests and ideas both in and out of school.
Limericks	- Choose writing to express personal interests and ideas both in and out of school.	- Choose writing to express personal interests and ideas both in and out of school.	
	- Communicate ideas in an organized manner (e.g., mapping, clustering, webbing).	- Communicate ideas in an organized manner (e.g., mapping, clustering, webbing).	- Communicate ideas in an organized manner (e.g., mapping, clustering, webbing).
	- Express thoughts/ideas through verbal and/or symbolic representation (e.g., pictures, scribbles, words).		

The demonstrators represent interdependent stages of an entire process. Students must be instructed in all stages of the process at each age level.

```
┌─────────────────────────────────────────────────────────────────────┐
│                    INSTRUCTIONAL STRATEGIES                            │
└─────────────────────────────────────────────────────────────────────┘
```

Clustering-Graphic Organizers	Handbook	Dramatizing
Journals/Response Logs	Advance Organizers	Peer Response
Brainstorming	Metacognition	Reflecting
Independent Reading	Graphic Organizers	Writing Process
Conferencing	Higher Order Thinking	Whole Language
		Writing to Learn

```
┌─────────────────────────────────────────────────────────────────────┐
│           IDEAS FOR INCORPORATING COMMUNITY RESOURCES                  │
└─────────────────────────────────────────────────────────────────────┘
```

- Read/write letters to/for individuals with disabilities.
- Interview individuals in the community (e.g., students, business men and women, senior citizens, or representatives of a variety of culture) about childhood memories; organize data; and publish results.
- Produce a brochure for a local non-profit agency.
- Invite local celebrity to talk to class about lifetime experiences.
- Write a biography of the celebrity.
- Interview a variety of ethnic groups in the community and write a cultural history of the area.

Figure 2.1. Kentucky Draft Framework. Source: Kentucky Department of Education, 1992.

```
CORE CONCEPT:  WRITING
```

ELEMENTARY ACTIVITIES

- Write new lyrics for familiar songs.
- Create a class joke book.
- Create greeting cards using a variety of expressive media.
- Graph the results of a science investigation.
- Construct a graphic organizer (e.g. Venn Diagram, story map,
    cluster, web) to record writing ideas.
- Share writing in an author's chair.
- Use telecommunications to establish a project partnership with a school
    in another geographic location.
- Explore the use of writing in real life by interviewing people from
    different occupations. Chart the types of writing used.

MIDDLE SCHOOL ACTIVITIES

- Write an information guide for next year's class of students.
- Identify a partent-teen conflict. Exchange dialogue in written form to
    resolve the conflict. Reverse roles and repeat.
- Explain how to solve a mathematics problem using words, but no
    numbers.
- Write a fairy tale from a different point of view and share with a
    younger audience.
- Select an animal or object and describe its view of the world.
- Write to a pen pal from another country and compare lifestyles.
- Research a planet. Create a life form from that planet. Interview
    the "creature" about life on the planet and write a news article on
    the visitor.
- Identify and study a school or community problem. Design a plan of
    action with multiple solutions. Present the plan to the appropriate
    audience.

HIGH SCHOOL ACTIVITIES

- Write the results of an experiment you have conducted.
- Write a dramatization of a historical event.
- Write a story, short poem, or play and submit it to a literary
    magazine.
- Create an informative brochure describing yourself.
- Keep a portfolio of your writing. Reflect on your strengths and
    weaknesses and on progress over time.
- Exchange letters with a pen pal from another region or country.
- Create a layman's guide explaining how to maintain your automobile.
- Write a song (e.g., rap, opera, rock, country) about one of your
    teachers.

Figure 2.1 (continued). Kentucky Draft Framework. Source: Kentucky Department of Education, 1992.

40

suggestions to help the school form stronger connections with the community and provide students with real-life applications of skills. The last section in the draft document is a listing of suggested instructional activities at the elementary, middle, and high school levels that could lead to the development of the demonstrators and the valued outcomes.

INSTRUCTIONAL PAST-PRACTICE IN KENTUCKY

The status of the written curriculum in most Kentucky school districts is not much different from the status of the written curriculum in many school districts in the country. The curriculum has been largely textbook driven, dealing more with ''covering'' the material than assuring student mastery of ''big ideas.'' Elementary teachers focused on basic skills taught to the ''average'' student. By fourth grade, approximately 20 percent of the students in the class had been retained.

Many of the elementary schools in Kentucky are K – 8, self-contained schools although the middle school concept is expanding in acceptance as older buildings are being replaced and new middle schools are being built. In other cases, it is not uncommon for a district to close older elementary schools, turn the high school into a middle school and build a new high school. The high schools are generally traditional in organization, with six fifty-five minute periods of instruction.

In addition, the high school curriculum is content-focused. Teacher tests generally assess whether students can demonstrate knowledge of the content covered in the course. The number of students enrolled in the state's high schools declines from grades nine through twelve because of the student dropout rate. Even though the state has worked hard to reduce the number of dropouts, it is not uncommon for a district to lose 25 percent of the student population from the ninth grade to graduation.

Of course, Kentucky high schools, like most high schools in the nation, can point to the academic achievement of some graduating seniors as evidence that the schools are producing highly competent graduates. And they are! The problem is that they are not producing enough of them.

Current curriculum guides often include a listing of discrete, content-related skills with little linkage to the ''big ideas'' reflected in the valued outcomes. It is not uncommon for a State Department curriculum consultant to ask for a copy of a district's curriculum guide and be handed a state skills list that was developed several years ago when the state used a criterion-referenced skills test to gauge the effectiveness of school districts.

School districts are accustomed to following the dictates of the State Department, whether the issue is the number of minutes of instruction for mathematics or the number of required books in the library. Districts relied on the State Department to dictate what tests would be used to assess student achievement, score the tests, and send districts the results.

Meanwhile, local boards of education focused their activities on items related to budget development, new construction, hiring staff, approving contracts, and setting policy. Until quite recently, it was not common for a school district to have a strategic plan or to evaluate the effectiveness of the instructional program in any systematic, comprehensive way other than through the results of the state achievement tests.

Moving from a state-dictated instructional system to one where the local district and the schools within the district are expected to design and implement an instructional program that will lead to the valued outcomes will be a difficult transition for many schools and districts in the state.

CURRICULUM FRAMEWORK OFFERS GUIDANCE

To assist schools/districts in this transition, the draft of the curriculum framework contains a large section entitled "Transforming the Learning Environment." In this section of the framework, the Department has identified several current authors/programs that the Department thinks will aid districts in changing the learning environment from one characterized by "learners as passive isolated consumers of facts in a large classroom group to learners as active processors and producers of information, learning in large and small groups, project teams, and independently" (p. 15). The topics covered in this section include outcome-based instruction, alternative ways of learning, integrated curriculum, and curriculum/assessment connections.

Outcome-based instruction is commonly linked to the work of Bill Spady. It is characterized by the Department as a

> process, not a program; a commitment to success for all students closely linked to a standard of performance, rather than a schedule of perfor-

mance; an attitude which focuses educational needs on the needs of the learner, not the conveniences or needs of the educational system; and has performance outcomes aligned to instruction and methods of assessment. (p.17)

Clearly the themes of outcome-based instruction are compatible with the vision and intent of KERA.

The work of Howard Gardner, detailed in his book, *Frames of Mind: The Theory of Multiple Intelligences*, is presented as a model for alternative ways of learning. The theory identifies seven domains of intelligence: linguistic — the capacity for language; logical/mathematical — the capacity for classification and abstract reasoning; musical — the capacity to discern pitch, rhythm, timing; spatial — the capacity to visualize from different perspectives; bodily kinesthetic — the capacity to use the body to accomplish complex activities; interpersonal — the capacity for comprehending aspects of character in other people; and intrapersonal — the capacity to assess personal strengths and motivations (p. 21). Teachers are encouraged to learn more about this and other models in order to provide students with instructional activities that are linked to the various "intelligences." Information about the Foxfire approach is also included in this section. During the next year the Department intends to add material to the framework regarding this approach.

The work of Heidi Jacobs (1991) and Robin Fogarty (1991) are examples of how to integrate curriculum. The Department of Education takes the position that integrated instruction supports student-centered classrooms, teaching teams, heterogeneous learning environments, use of a variety of instructional materials, performance assessment, arranging school schedules around teaching, alternative graduation requirements, community-based learning, and alternative demonstrations of learning.

PROSPECTS FOR SUCCESS

The vast majority of the valued outcomes are content free. That is to say, demonstrating a valued outcome is not directly linked to a specific body of knowledge such as the Civil War or the writings of Shakespeare. In the future, it is envisioned that content will be used as a vehicle to demonstrate the acquisition of the valued outcomes, not as an end itself. This envisioned transformation is depicted in Figure 2.2 where the content areas are not seen as the ultimate ends for instruction, but as the

<u>The Vision Realized:</u>

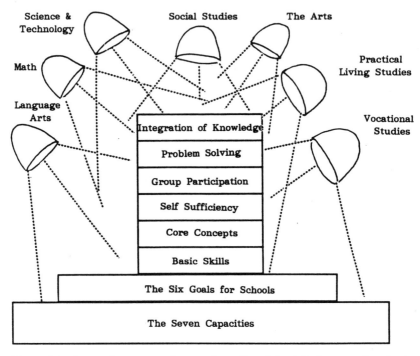

Figure 2.2. Content Integration. Source: Council on School Performance Standards, 1991.

means for achieving the seven capacities and the six curriculum goals. A transformation such as this will require a major shift in the organization and instructional priorities of most secondary schools.

At the present time, most secondary teachers in the state have been unaffected by the reform. Generally, they use the same textbooks they used before, give the same type of tests, and grade students using the same point system. Few secondary teachers in the state have a thorough understanding of KERA, the valued outcomes, or the new state performance assessment system. The process of moving from the traditional, teacher-directed, content-focused learning environment to a student success-oriented environment, based on the integration of knowledge and the application of that knowledge to achieving the valued outcomes, is a quantum leap that will take time, patience, extensive professional development, and a dramatic change in the attitude of many secondary educators. Full integration of instruction with students learning at high levels and demonstrating competence through authentic performance may not happen within the professional lifetime of many secondary educators. The initiative may cause some to retire or seek employment in other fields. So be it!

This initiative is more than a Kentucky initiative. It is a national initiative. It will not go away with the next meeting of the Kentucky General Assembly. It is the foundation for the transformation of Kentucky schools and it will happen!

REFERENCES

Council on School Performance Standards. 1989. *Preparing Kentucky's Youth for the Next Century: What Students Should Know and Be Able to Do and How Learning Should be Assessed.* Frankfort, Kentucky: Kentucky Department of Education.

Council on School Performance Standards. 1991. *Kentucky's Learning Goals and Valued Outcomes: Technical Report.* Frankfort, Kentucky: Kentucky Department of Education.

Fogarty, Robin. 1991. "Ten Ways to Integrate Curriculum," *Educational Leadership* (October):61−65.

Gardner, H. 1984. *Frames of Mind: The Theory of Multiple Intelligences.* New York: Basic Books.

Jacobs, Heidi Hayes. 1991. "Planning for Curriculum Integration," *Educational Leadership* (October):27−28.

Kentucky Department of Education. 1990. *Kentucky School Laws.* Frankfort, Kentucky: Banks-Baldwin Law Publishing.

Kentucky Department of Education. 1991. *The Kentucky Education Reform Act: 1990 Implementation Report.* Frankfort, Kentucky.

Kentucky Department of Education. 1992. Draft of *Kentucky Preliminary Curriculum Framework*, Frankfort, Kentucky.

Rose v. Council for Better Education, Inc. Kentucky, No. 88-SC-804-TG, September 28, l989.

Spady, William. Founder of The Network for Outcome-Based Schools.

Wilkinson, Wallace, Governor. Executive Order 89-151, February, 1989.

CHAPTER 3

Assessing Student Performance: High-Stakes Testing

> Without quality assessment, it is impossible to identify accurately the learning needs of individual students and student groups, to review the appropriateness of curriculum goals and content, or to evaluate the quality of teaching. In effective learning environments, assessment and instruction are inexorably linked. (KDE, 1991b, p. 2)

THE state of Kentucky will assess the achievement of students, the effectiveness of teachers and administrators, and the success of KERA by reviewing data from the state's new authentic assessment system, which will evolve over a five-year period of time. It replaces the previous state accountability system, which was linked to norm-referenced testing as well as student attendance and dropout rates. Since the evolving authentic assessment system will be used as the basis for granting state sanctions or rewards at the school-site level, it has been labeled "high-stakes" testing.

Some view this component of KERA as the most effective way to generate change at the classroom level. Teachers are encouraged to "teach to the test." In the minds of many State Department officials, the ideal classroom of the future will be one where it will be impossible to tell the difference between instruction and assessment.

Because of this new focus, standardized testing has undergone great scrutiny in recent years. It has been described as a testing system gone amok (Shepard, 1989). Test scores are sometimes used to fire superintendents, admonish teachers, and increase the value of homes in a community. Test scores have also played an increasingly important role in educational decisions over the past few years. With time, the flaws in these tests have become increasingly evident. "There is growing, if far from universal, impatience with student assessment that addresses chiefly facts and basic skills, leaving thoughtfulness, imagination, and pursuit untapped" (Wolf, Bixby, Glenn, and Gardner, 1990). "In contrast to testing in most other countries, testing in the U.S. is primarily controlled by commercial publishers and non-school agencies that produce norm-referenced, multiple-choice instruments designed to rank students cheaply and efficiently'' (Darling-Hammond, 1991). Even though students in the United States are among the most tested in the world (Wolf, LeMahieu, and Eresh, 1992), this country currently lacks an effective accountability and assessment system. States like Vermont, New York, Maryland, California, and others are currently expanding the use of authentic assessment measures in an effort to improve the quality of teaching and learning (O'Neil, 1992).

The goals of this new form of assessment include practices which ''capitalize on the actual work of the classroom, enhance teacher and student involvement in evaluation, and meet some of the accountability concerns of the district'' (Chittenden, 1991, p. 22). In moving toward this, Lauren Resnick (1989, pp. 66−67) suggests three principles to serve as guidelines for expanded use of the authentic assessment as a measure of school accountability. First, ''You get what you assess.'' Therefore, tests must be carefully fashioned to assess what is really valued by the community, the teachers, and the students. If we want students to be good writers, then we should make them write. If we want them to be good debaters, then they must practice the art and craft of the debate. Secondly, ''You do not get what you do not assess.'' Those activities that are not assessed tend to disappear from classrooms over time. If we expect students to be able to use mathematical concepts to solve complex problems, then we must assess their ability to do that. Finally, the most critical principle is to ''build assessments toward what you want educators to teach.'' If you want teachers to change what they are doing in classrooms, then you must change the mechanism of assessment. For example, KERA's authentic assessment includes actual writing, which involves short answers and essays. This way, teachers will be encouraged to teach more writing skills and include more opportunities for students to write in the classroom.

In this new arena of authentic assessment, we are asking students to learn how to drive the ''academic car.'' In order to demonstrate that you have the skill and knowledge necessary to be licensed to drive a vehicle in any state, you must pass two parts of an assessment: a criterion-referenced, paper and pencil test; and a performance event of driving the car. For most people, the paper and pencil part of the test is the less difficult. The real test comes when the driver is behind the wheel of the car and actually demonstrates through his/her performance that he/she has mastered the skills necessary to be a licensed driver. For too long, our schools have been content to rely on pencil and paper demonstrations of academic achievement. Now, we are asking students to drive the academic car through performance events and portfolio assessment.

In their publication, *Beyond Standardized Testing*, Archbald and Newmann (1988, p. 2) pointed out that traditional forms of assessment can "depress student learning, teacher commitment, and public support." Grant Wiggins (1991) has identified nine characteristics of authentic assessment which tend to invigorate teaching, learning, and public support.

Authentic assessment:

1. involves tasks which we value, and at which we want students to excel . . . tasks worth learning and "teaching to"

2. simulates the challenges facing adults or workers in a field of study

3. is constructed of "ill-structured" challenges that require knowledge in use, effective use of a repertoire of knowledge, and good judgment in solving the problem(s)

4. focuses on the students' ability to produce a quality product and/or performance; effectiveness and craftsmanship become more appropriately central than "right answers" as criteria

5. involves de-mystified tasks and standards; allows for thorough preparation and self-assessment by the student

6. relies on trained assessor judgment, in reference to clear and appropriate criteria (as opposed to those most easily observed or scored)

7. is typically composed of interactions between assessor and assessee. Focuses on the students' ability to justify answers and respond to follow-up or probing questions

8. involves patterns of response and behavior, consistency of performance, habits of mind

9. is multi-modal, calling upon different means of displaying mastery in an integrative "performance"

In constructing the authentic assessment system embedded in KERA, Kentucky is attempting to create such an encouraging environment. During the spring of 1992, authentic assessment tasks were administered to grades four, eight, and twelve.

WHAT THE STATUTE SAYS ABOUT ASSESSMENT

158.6453 Assessment of achievement of goals; development of statewide assessment program; publication of annual performance report by districts

(1) The State Board of Elementary and Secondary Education shall be responsible for creating and implementing a statewide, primarily performance-based assessment program to ensure school accountability for student achievement of the goals set forth in KRS 158.645. The program shall be implemented as early as the 1993−94 school year but no later than the 1995−96 school year. The board shall also be responsible for administering an interim testing program to assess student skills in reading, mathematics, writing, science, and social studies in grades four (4), eight (8), and twelve (12). The tests shall be designed to provide the state with national comparisons and shall be the same as, or similar to those used by the National Assessment of Educational Progress. The interim testing program shall begin during the 1991−92 school year and shall be administered to a sample of students representative of each school and the state as a whole. The test scores shall be used, along with other factors described in KRS 158.6451, to establish a baseline for determining school success during the 1993−94 school year. (KDE, 1990, p. 233)

The statute also provided for the employment of three or more authorities in the field of performance assessment to assist the Board in the design of bid specifications for the interim and full-scale performance assessment. The Board employed five consultants. During the time when bid specification development work was underway, the Council on School Performance Standards was developing the valued outcomes, the state was actively engaged in selecting the first commissioner of education, and membership on the State Board of Elementary and Secondary Education was being restructured in compliance with KERA.

ASSESSMENT CONTRACT AWARDED

In May, 1991, Advanced Systems in Measurement and Evaluation, Inc., and Far West Laboratory for Educational Research and Development submitted the successful proposal for the development of the Kentucky authentic assessment system. The five-year contract was awarded in the fall of 1991, after the new commissioner was hired and the new State Board was seated, but before the work of the Council on School Performance Standards was complete. The proposal was developed without knowledge of the exact format of the valued outcomes. Since the interim assessment process had to be administered in the spring of 1992 because of statutory mandate, this program was developed primarily in response to the request for proposal and was not directly linked to the valued outcomes.

The first year of the interim assessment has been linked to twenty-nine of the seventy-five valued outcomes; one in reading, one in writing, thirteen in mathematics, six in science, and eight in social studies (*Ed News*, January-February, 1992, p. 13). Direct linkage to all of the valued outcomes will take place over the next four years.

TRANSITION TEST

The interim assessment system that was administered during the spring of 1992 at grades four, eight, and twelve, was made up of three separate parts: writing portfolio, performance event, and transition test. Of the three, the transition test was considered to be the most conventional. The statute called for this to be a test similar to the NAPE. It included multiple choice items in addition to open-ended questions and writing prompts. Specifically, the test consisted of fifty to fifty-five multiple choice items, four open-ended questions that required about a half-page response, and one response question. Students were given two class periods to complete the response question. Different forms of the test were administered in each classroom. In addition, a technique called matrix sampling was used. Using this technique, different forms of the test use a set of common questions and some different questions. This allowed for a wide variety of test questions to be asked in each school without increasing the time required for the test. Student results on the tests will reflect answers to only the common questions. School scores will reflect both the common test items and the matrix test items. Testing took eleven class periods to administer, two for each of the five content areas tested and one for response to a student questionnaire. All students completed this assessment and it was scored by Advanced Systems. The only way a student could be excused from participating in this assessment was for the individual student's portfolio to state that undergoing the assessment would result in harm to the student.

While assessing student achievement in social studies, mathematics, science, and reading, this achievement was not based on specific skill acquisition, as it is for most state criterion-referenced tests. There were no skill lists distributed to teachers to use as a basis for instruction. While teachers had access to the valued outcomes, these are stated in general terms and a number of skills could be included in any one of them.

For example, one of the valued outcomes in science is, "students identify and describe systems, subsystems, and components and their interactions by completing tasks and/or creating products.'' The statement is supposed to reflect the integration of knowledge and the ability to apply that knowledge as a high school graduate. Educators were not provided with any additional information that would assist them in understanding the meaning of this valued outcome at the fourth- or eighth-grade level, and therefore may have interpreted the outcomes differently. This assistance will be forthcoming from the State Department when the curriculum framework is developed and distributed.

Thus, the 1991−92 school year assessment was designed to establish a "baseline" score for each school building in the state and establish a target "threshold" score for the 1993−94 assessment. Teachers were not expected to have aligned the classroom curriculum with the valued outcomes during this initial year of establishing baseline scores. Alignment refers to the relationship among the written, taught, and tested curriculum (English, 1992). However, there is an expectation that teachers will align instruction with the state assessment system. Currently, information about the discrete skills assessed on each performance event, transition test item, and portfolio assessment is not clear.

PERFORMANCE EVENT

Performance events assessed student achievement in science, social studies, and mathematics. These events took approximately one class period and were administered by school staff and an outside facilitator. Many of the performance events began with a group problem-solving activity and then required students to complete an individual activity in writing. All students at the fourth-grade level participated in the performance event assessment. At grade eight, up to six classes participated in the performance event assessment. At twelfth grade, a random sampling of ninety students was assessed. The performance event assessment was used to determine a school score only. No individual student assessment data was generated from this assessment.

Feedback from the students regarding the performance event assessment was quite positive. Statements such as, ''This is fun!'' and ''Can't we do this more often?'' were commonly reported. Still, while students appeared to enjoy the activities, teachers are still struggling with identifying exactly what skills were assessed. With the exception of assembling the needed materials, there was little teacher instructional preparation for this activity. As information about the scoring rubrics for these events is made public, teachers will gain a better understanding of how to disaggregate the skills embodied in the valued outcomes and incorporate them into daily instruction.

PORTFOLIO ASSESSMENT

The assessment measure that generated the most attention during this initial interim assessment year was the writing portfolio. Prior to this year, the state assessment system did not include holistic writing assessment. The valued outcome assessed by the portfolio is that ''students communicate ideas and information to a variety of audiences for a variety of purposes in a variety of modes through writing.'' Writing assessment is just the beginning. Over the next few years, the portfolio will be expanded to include a variety of materials and assess a variety of valued outcomes. During the 1992−93 school year mathematics portfolios will be added. In the years to come, the portfolio will evolve into an integrated content portfolio reflecting a wide variety of student work.

Orientation to the portfolio began in the fall of 1991. Advanced Systems set up an elaborate, statewide system to orient teachers to the process and guide them in beginning to develop individual student portfolios. Notably, the legislature had provided several million dollars to enhance student writing in the state, over the past several years. Many districts across the state had developed competitive grants and received funds to support the development of integrated language arts instruction. Through this process, the state was moving toward adding a writing requirement to the state's assessment program. The movement toward portfolio assessment was a natural evolution in this process. In fact, the state's present system of regionally placed writing consultants was funded through the Writing Project, not as a new KERA initiative. Because of the professional development that had taken place in the past, there was a general understanding across the state about holistic scoring and the writing process. Advanced Systems was able to capitalize on the established network and formalize the program much more quickly because of the work that had been done in the past.

An elaborate training and communication system was established by Advanced Systems. Led by a state coordinator, regional coordinators were hired and trained to facilitate the process. Within each region, cluster leaders were identified. A cluster leader was a district teacher with responsibility for training and developing a communication system with approximately fifteen to twenty teachers. Cluster leaders were volunteers from districts. Formally, they received no additional pay for the work they performed, although many districts attempted to reimburse them or reduce their teaching duties to reward them for the work they were doing. Regional coordinators were employed by the state. Cluster leaders were utilized to conduct local cluster meetings in the fall of 1991, to explain the portfolio process and distribute materials, to train teachers in the scoring of portfolios, and to score their own students' portfolios.

After portfolio scores were established for all students in grades four, eight, and twelve, the scores were sent to Advanced Systems. To ensure consistency in scoring, a procedure was established to collect a sample of five portfolios from each teacher and have them scored again. If inconsistencies were noted, all the portfolios for that teacher were rescored.

In order to assemble a writing portfolio, teachers were encouraged to increase the amount of student writing done in all classes and to develop writing folders for each child at grades four, eight and twelve. Writing folders at the elementary level were kept by the self-contained, classroom teacher. Writing folders for eighth- and twelfth-grade students were generally kept by the English or Language Arts teacher. All of these teachers were encouraged to instruct students in the writing process and to expand the use of this process in classroom instruction.

Portfolios were assessed holistically on six criteria: idea development, organization, support, sentences, wording, and mechanics, using a five-point scale. Idea development refers to the degree to which the writer establishes and maintains a purpose and communicates with the audience. Organization focuses on the degree to which the writer demonstrates unity and coherence. Support alludes to the degree to which the writer includes details that develop the main point(s). Sentences touch upon the degree to which the writer includes sentences that are varied in structure and length, constructed effectively, and complete and correct. Wording refers to the degree to which the writer exhibits correct and effective vocabulary. Mechanics refers to the degree to which the writer demonstrates technically correct spelling, punctuation, capitalization and usage. Figure 3.1 depicts the Kentucky Writing Assessment Holistic Scoring Guide and the Analytic Annotation Guide.

1	2	3	4	5
• Little or no awareness of audience and/or purpose • Little or no organization; thought patterns difficult, if not impossible, to follow • Few or no details • Errors in sentence construction interfere with communication • Incorrect and/or ineffective wording • Errors in surface features interfere with communication	• Poor awareness of audience and purpose • Random and/or weak organization • Limited and/or inappropriate details • Incorrect and/or ineffective sentence structure • Inappropriate wording • Errors in surface features are disproportionate to length and complexity	• Some attempt to establish and maintain purpose and to communicate with the audience • Some lapses in unity and coherence • Unelaborated or repetitious details • Simplistic sentence structure • Simplistic language • Some errors in surface features that do not interfere with communication	• Focused on a purpose; some evidence of voice • Predictable organization • Elaborated and appropriate details • Predictable pattern in sentence structure • Acceptable, appropriate language • Few errors in surface features relative to length or complexity	• Establishes and maintains clear focus; evidence of distinctive voice • Careful but subtle organization • Rich, interesting, and/or pertinent details • Effective variety in sentence structure and length • Effective and/or rich language • Control of surface features

Analytic Annotation Guide

		COMMENDATIONS	NEEDS
IDEA DEVELOPMENT	The degree to which the writer • establishes and maintains a purpose • communicates with the audience	IX voice IY original and/or insightful	IJ greater sense of purpose IK greater investment by author
ORGANIZATION	The degree to which the writer demonstrates • unity • coherence	OX evidence of planning OY order/sequence easily followed	OJ more evidence of planning OK clearer focus/stronger unity
SUPPORT	The degree to which the writer includes details that develop the main point(s)	SUP-X appropriate details SUP-Y rich, interesting details	SUP-J more appropriate details SUP-K more elaboration of details
SENTENCES	The degree to which the writer includes sentences that are • varied in structure and length • constructed effectively • complete and correct	SX variety in structure and length SY complete and correct sentences	SJ greater variety in structure and length SK more complete and correct sentences
WORDING	The degree to which the writer exhibits correct and effective • vocabulary • word choice	WX successful use of vivid, rich language WY effective and varied vocabulary	WJ closer attention to appropriate word choice WK more varied vocabulary
MECHANICS	The degree to which the writer demonstrates technically correct • spelling • capitalization • punctuation • usage	MX spelling enhances readability MY capitalization, punctuation, and usage aid clarity	MJ appropriate spelling to aid reader MK greater control of punctuation, capitalization, and usage

Figure 3.1. Kentucky Writing Assessment: Holistic Scoring Guide. Source: Kentucky Department of Education, 1991.

At the fourth-grade level, the portfolio contained the items listed below.

(*1*) Table of contents

(*2*) Best piece

(*3*) Letter to the reviewer written by the student explaining why she/he selected the best piece and how the piece was developed

(*4*) One short story, poem, or play

(*5*) One personal narrative

(*6*) One piece, the purpose of which supports/defends a position or solves a problem

(*7*) One prose piece from a content area other than English/Language Arts

At the eighth-grade level the contents of the portfolio contained the following.

(*1*) Table of contents

(*2*) Best piece, chosen by student

(*3*) Letter to reviewer written by the student explaining why she/he selected the best piece and how the piece was developed

(*4*) A personal narrative

(*5*) An information and/or persuasive piece on a cultural event, public exhibit, sports event, media presentation, or a piece of writing, current issue, math problem, or scientific phenomenon

(*6*) Two prose pieces, the purpose of which will be to predict an outcome, defend a position, evaluate a situation, or solve a problem. Any of the pieces may come from subject areas other than English or Language Arts, but a minimum of one piece *must* come from another subject area.

The portfolio for grade twelve contained the following.

(*1*) Table of contents

(*2*) Best piece, chosen in collaboration with the teacher

(*3*) Letter to reviewer written by the student explaining why she/he selected the best piece and how the piece was developed

(*4*) One short story, poem, play, or personal narrative

(*5*) Two prose pieces from content areas other than English or Language Arts, the purpose of which will be to predict an outcome, defend a position, evaluate a situation, or solve a problem.

(6) A personal response to a cultural event, public exhibit, sports event, media presentation, or to a book, current issue, math problem, or scientific phenomenon

Impact of this newly designed authentic system was felt most severely by teachers for fourth and eighth grades and by the English teachers at the high school. As the year progressed, more teachers at other grades began to realize that this new assessment system would impact them as well, even though their grade or subject was not directly affected this year. For example, learning to write effectively is a process that takes place over a number of years and in almost all classes. It is not an event that happens only at fourth grade. The sequential skills necessary for a student to be able to demonstrate writing abilities begin to be taught in the first year of primary school.

CONTINUOUS ASSESSMENT

In addition to mandating the development of a state authentic assessment system, KERA required districts to develop their own continuous assessment program to evaluate how students were progressing toward the state-assessed benchmark. The concept of a district continuous assessment plan developed at the local district level is foreign to most Kentucky districts. The practice in Kentucky over the past several years has been for the state to assess student achievement annually at each grade level, using a standardized instrument. Districts are not accustomed to being responsible for the development of student assessment mechanisms beyond the classroom, and certainly not used to developing authentic assessment measures based on the new valued outcomes.

To assist districts with the development of their continuous assessment systems, Advanced Systems has developed continuous assessment materials and made them available to districts on a voluntary basis. These materials are referred to as ''scrimmage tests'' since districts use them to prepare teachers and students for the ''real'' assessment. These tests mirror the context and tasks found on the accountability tests. While helpful to districts, they are not meant to substitute for the entire continuous assessment program at the district level. Figure 3.2 delineates the relationship among the valued outcomes, state accountability assessment, continuous assessment and local school curricula.

Both the accountability assessment and the continuous assessment systems are linked directly to the six goals and the valued outcomes. This does not mean that a school would be prevented from going beyond the valued outcomes. Schools are free to add their own unique curriculum to the instructional program and evaluate student achievement of that curriculum in any way they see fit. The two columns under continuous assessment refer to the annual scrimmage tests available on a voluntary basis from advanced systems and the periodic, interval assessments that

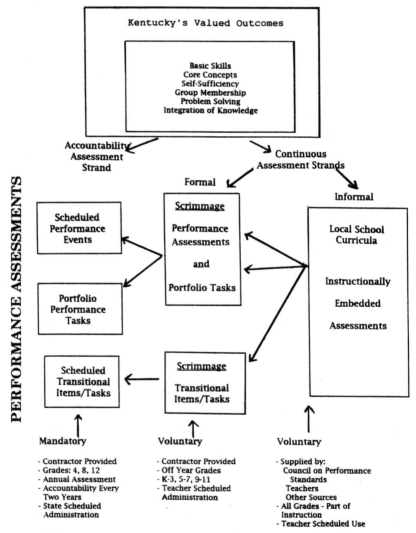

Figure 3.2. Relationship of Valued Outcomes and Performance Assessment Tasks to Accountability, Assessment, Continuous Assessment, and Curriculum Development. Source: Kentucky Department of Education, 1991b.

teachers design to routinely assess student progress. The column under local school curricula is blank because decisions regarding this area are at the discretion of the district and the school.

As a result, most districts have continued to use the CTBS test as another component of the district's continuous assessment testing program. Districts explain this decision by indicating that Chapter I requires a norm-referenced test as part of the student referral process. In reality, many educators are reluctant to give up an assessment system that they perceive to be efficient and cost effective, in favor of developing an expensive, experimental one. Presently, a national task force is looking at a variety of recommendations to change Chapter I requirements when it is reauthorized. A movement to authentic assessment measures is one of the recommendations under consideration.

Parents in many districts have been vocal with their skepticism regarding the newly evolving authentic assessment measures. They want data that enables them to compare the achievement of their children with other children, and with children in other schools and districts. As the authentic assessment system evolves, parental awareness sessions need to be developed at the school and district level to explain the new system and to gain parental support for it. During the fall of 1992, student, school, and district scores will be released. Everyone receiving this information, including the students, needs to understand what it means and how the information will be used.

ACADEMIC STANDARDS ACCOUNTABILITY

In the interim, we have an academic standards accountability system that is viewed as experimental. Even though performance assessment is being talked and written about extensively across the country, many teachers, administrators, and parents are still non-believers.

However, KERA has mandated the system and Advanced Systems has a $25 million contract to develop the process over the next four years. Figure 3.3 depicts how the three components of transition test items, performance events, and portfolios will evolve over that period of time. As you can see, during this initial, interim testing year, the transition test contributes the largest part of a school's baseline, academic score. The portfolio and performance event assessment are important, but they do not weigh as heavily in determining the school score. In the spring of 1993, and again in the spring of 1994, alternate forms of the three

60

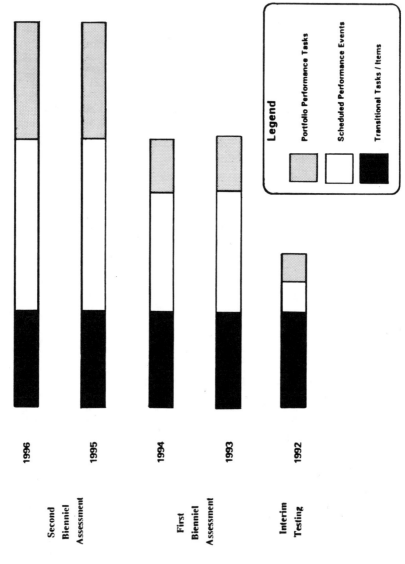

Legend

Portfolio Performance Tasks

Scheduled Performance Events

Transitional Tasks / Items

1996

Second
Bienniel
Assessment

1995

1994

First
Bienniel
Assessment

1993

Interim
Testing

1992

Figure 3.3. Relative Emphasis of Task Types over Time. Source: Kentucky Department of Education, 1991b.

assessments given this year will be repeated in grades four, eight, and twelve. At the same time, the portfolio assessment and the performance event assessment will be expanded. By the spring of 1996, it is predicted that the three types of assessment will have approximately equal weight in determining a school score.

During 1992, there was limited assessment of three of the six learning goals: basic skills, core concepts, and problem solving. This assessment addressed five content areas: reading, writing, math, social studies, and science. As shown in Figure 3.4, during 1993 and 1994, there will be a wider assessment of the content areas including reading, writing, math, social studies, science, arts, humanities, practical living, and vocational. By 1995 and 1996, the assessment will be broad and will include all of the content areas listed above plus the three additional learning goals of self-sufficiency, group membership, and integrated knowledge. The current and developing systems are complex, yet integrated.

The seven capacities named in the Supreme Court decision and the six learning goals identified by the Council on School Performance Standards have been further operationalized by the seventy-five valued outcomes (see Chapter 2). The valued outcomes have become the foundation for the development of the state's academic assessment system. The components of this system include a transition test with multiple forms, portfolio assessment, and performance events. All three strands of the accountability assessment system are evolving and will not be finalized until 1996. The state authentic assessment system is just one component of the state accountability system. The state accountability system includes both academic and non-academic standards. The authentic assessment system is designed to measure the academic standards.

NON-ACADEMIC STANDARDS

The non-academic standards that make up the second part of the state's accountability system include school attendance rates, school retention rates, and school dropout rates. Attendance and dropout rates were part of the previous state accountability system, but these were district rates, instead of school rates. In addition to attendance and retention and dropout data at the school level, the non-academic indicators will include a measure of successful transition to the workplace, military, and/or post-secondary education. Schools are also required to remove physical and mental barriers to learning.

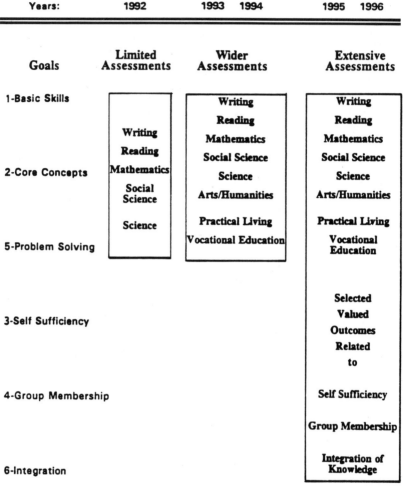

Figure 3.4. Performance Assessments of Kentucky's Valued Outcomes Increasing over Time. Source: Kentucky Department of Education, 1991b.

Work leading to the designation of procedures for defining these non-academic standards was begun by a subcommittee of the Council on School Performance Standards. In September, 1991, the Council produced a draft of how these standards would be defined.

Attendance

In elementary schools, the Average Daily Attendance will be 96% for the year.

In middle schools and junior high schools, the Average Daily Attendance will be 95% for the year.

In secondary schools, the Average Daily Attendance will be 94% for the year.

Dropout Rate
In a middle school, no more than 1% of the students will drop out.

In a junior high school, no more than 2% of the students will drop out.

In a secondary school, no more than 5% of the students will drop out.

The dropout rate is defined as the annual percentages of students leaving school prior to graduation in grades 7–12 and include withdrawals in attendance accounting codes W 6, W 10, W 11, and W 14.

Retention Rate
In any school, no more than 4% of the total number of students will be retained.

Physical and Mental Barriers to Learning
The local school district and each school within the district shall have policies and procedures to assist in the identification and reduction of physical and mental health barriers to learning. The policies and procedures shall provide for:

(1) systemic efforts to define and identify physical and mental health barriers to learning which may impede successful attainment of the goals and capacities in the Kentucky Education Reform Act;

(2) systemic screening of students to identify physical and mental health barriers impacting the learning of individual students;

(3) referral of students for medical, educational, social, mental health, and family support services including prevention; evaluation and intervention to in-school and district programs, public and non-public agencies;

(4) coordination with existing community, regional and state resources for provision of services to students, and

(5) the development of a written plan to assist in reducing physical and mental health barriers to learning which includes:

(a) a systematic needs assessment process to provide current data for long-term and annual planning, including data on the service needs of the district and school student population;

(b) strategies and activities to implement to reduce physical and mental health barriers to learning; and,

(c) evaluating the implementation of the plan and effectiveness of the activities and strategies for reducing the identified physical and mental health barriers to learning.

Transition
Eighty percent of the graduates of a school district will make a successful transition to either work, military service, or post-secondary education.

The task force also suggested that students in the commonwealth should be given an identification number to assist in the accurate tracking of students from district to district.

The precise formula, the weights attached to each part of the formula, and the formula for developing a school's "threshold" score had not been finalized by late spring, 1992. However, the development and administration of this formula is mandated by KERA (KDE, 1990, p. 233):

158.6455 Determination of and rewards to successful schools

It is the intent of the General Assembly that schools succeed with all students and receive the appropriate consequences in proportion to that success.

(1) The State Board for Elementary and Secondary Education shall promulgate administrative regulations to establish a system of determining successful schools and dispensing appropriate rewards. The system shall be based on the following:

(a) A school shall be the unit of measure to determine success;

(b) School success shall be determined by measuring a school's improvement over a two (2) year period;

(c) A school shall be rewarded for an increased proportion of successful students, including those students who are at risk of school failure;

(d) A threshold level for school improvement shall be established by the board to determine the amount of success needed for a school to receive a reward. The threshold definition shall establish the percentage of increase required in a school's percentage of successful students as compared to a school's present proportion of successful students, with consideration given to the fact that a school closest to having one hundred percent (100%) successful students will have a lower percentage increase required;

(e) Rewards shall be given to the school on behalf of full-time, part-time, and itinerate instructional staff of a school who generate the reward when the school achieves at least one percent (1%) gain over its threshold as defined in paragraph (d) of this subsection. Substitute teachers shall not be used in calculating the reward;

(f) Rewards shall be calculated by applying the percentage set by the General Assembly in the biennial budget to the current annual salary of each certified staff person employed in the school on the last working day of the year of the reward. The reward for part-time and itinerant staff shall be calculated for the proportion of time spent in the school. In determining the percentage to be applied to a school for calculation of the rewards for the school's staff, consideration shall be given to the fact that schools already having a high percentage of successful students shall have a lower requirement for a percentage increase in its number of successful students. The staff person's identity in connection to his share of the reward shall be maintained when his share of the reward is deposited to the school's account;

(g) The certified staff members shall by majority rule collectively decide on the ways the reward funds shall be spent. Each individual staff person shall use the amount he earned in accordance with the decisions made by the total staff. Rewards shall not be added to a staff person's base salary and shall not be defined as compensation for retirement purposes. . . .

Figure 3.5 depicts the relationship between the academic and non-academic components of the accountability index and how this index relates to the rewards and sanctions component of the statute. The General Assembly provided $33 million for the rewards component of KERA during the 1990−92 biennium. These monies are being held in an escrow account. An additional $1 million was added to the escrow account in the budget bill for the 1992−94 biennium. Initially, teachers were quite skeptical about the rewards since money was not appropriated a few years ago when the General Assembly had promised teachers a $300 bonus if they had a good performance evaluation. When it came time to pay the bonus, the money was not appropriated. Teachers have never forgotten.

During the recent General Assembly session, it was clear that not all KERA initiatives—including earned rewards—were going to be funded to the extent originally planned because of the state recession. Superintendents from some of the state's more "affluent" districts suggested that the state should dip into the escrow accounts to fund all initiatives. The General Assembly rejected this suggestion.

There is still a lot of distrust among educators as to whether rewards will actually be given. By fall of 1992, districts will receive student, school, and district data from the first year of interim authentic assessment, and will receive their baseline and threshold scores. At this time, there is anticipation of renewed interest in both rewards and sanctions.

Many issues, including those listed here, have arisen around the rewards and sanctions component of KERA. There are over fifty schools in the state that do not have one of the grades that are tested. The question of whether these schools will participate in the sanctions and rewards component has to be determined. If they do participate, how that participation will be determined must be addressed. In addition, schools with high percentages of yearly, student migration are concerned about being held accountable for students who have attended the school for a short time. Schools with very high academic achievement are concerned

66

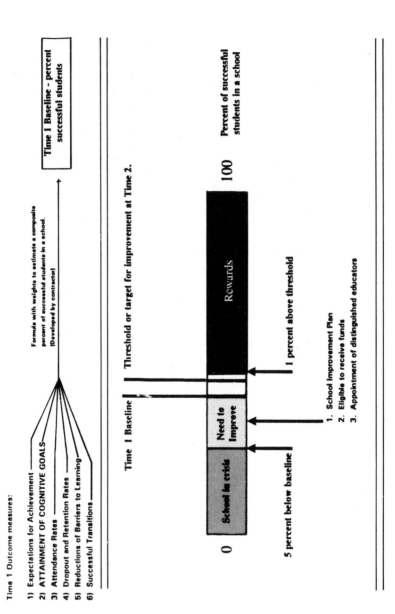

Figure 3.5. Determining Rewards and Sanctions. Source: Kentucky Department of Education, 1991b.

about the tendency toward regression to the mean, and some educators are concerned about the sampling techniques used at eighth and twelfth grade to determine who participates in the performance event. Statisticians are concerned about the reliability of determining the 1 percent increase beyond threshold to qualify for rewards, especially in small schools. Some educators are concerned about requiring all students, including those identified as special education students, to participate in the assessment. Unless the student's IEP states that it will be detrimental, the student must participate in the assessment. The list of concerns continues. State policy makers will attempt to resolve these issues over the next few months.

Table 3.1 describes what will happen at a school depending on the results of the 1993 and 1994 state assessment results. Even though the state assessment program is evolving over the next four years, the sanctions and reward component will begin in 1994. The rewards distributed to staff at a school improving more than 1 percent above the threshold, will increase incrementally based on the actual percentage of increase. For instance, a school improving 5 percent above the threshold score would receive more of a reward than a school improving 2 percent above the threshold. Schools that show no gain will be required to develop a school improvement plan. These schools will be eligible for school improvement funds. If the school scores decline, but the decline is less than 5 percent, then the school must develop a school improvement plan and the school will be assigned a Kentucky Distinguished Educator.

KENTUCKY DISTINGUISHED EDUCATORS

Kentucky Distinguished Educators are certified educators who have been selected by the State Department to serve as "education ambassadors" within the state. During the summer of 1992, five Kentucky Distinguished Educators were selected and given a sabbatical from their district. The Kentucky Distinguished Educators selected the first year planned to assist the department in designing a training program for future distinguished educators. The State Department has estimated that they may need approximately seventy-five Kentucky Distinguished Educators to assist schools who fall below their threshold in 1994.

KERA empowers these individuals with significant responsibilities when they are placed in schools with deficient scores.

Table 3.1. The Reward Matrix.

	Condition	Result
1993 – 94	Improvement > 1%	Rewards are distributed to school staff (not counting substitute teachers).
1993 – 94	No gain 1st Biennial Review	Develop school improvement plan. Eligible to receive school improvement funds.
1993 – 94	No gain 1st Biennial Review, Decline < 5%	Develop a school improvement plan. Eligible to receive school improvement funds. One or more Kentucky Distinguished Educators will be assigned to the school to provide assistance.
1993 – 94	Decline > 5%, 1st Biennial Review	School is declared a "School in Crisis." Full/part-time certified staff placed on probation. Parents notified of right to and procedures for transferring students to a successful school. One or more Kentucky Distinguished Educators assigned to the school to evaluate certified staff every six months and make recommendations to the superintendent of district regarding retention, transfer, and dismissal until the school is no longer in crisis. Dismissal recommendations are binding.
	Decline > 5% for the district	Actions same as immediately above. If the recommendation by the Kentucky Distinguished Educator(s) is to dismiss the superintendent, the local board shall do so. If two consecutive biennial reviews are declining, the district shall be declared an educational development district and the local board members and superintendent removed.

The State Board for Elementary and Secondary Education shall adopt an appeals procedure to provide school/district relief from special circumstances beyond their control.

158.782 "Kentucky Distinguished Educator"; purposes; program criteria; monetary awards; compensation; assignments

(1) The State Board of Elementary and Secondary Education shall promulgate administrative regulations to set forth the criteria for the Kentucky Distinguished Educators Program which shall be implemented by July 1, 1991. The designation of "Kentucky Distinguished Educators" shall be given to the state's most outstanding and highly skilled certified educators who deserve recognition and are willing to fulfill the following purposes of the program:

(a) Serving as teaching ambassadors to spread the message that teaching is an important and fulfilling profession;

(b) Assisting the Department of Education with research projects and staff development efforts;

(c) Accepting assignments in schools whose percentage of successful students declined as described in KRS 158.6455. The assignments shall require the educator to:

1. Work in a school full-time for a designated period of time to assist the school staff with implementing its school improvement plan. The educator shall have the authority to make decisions previously made by the school staff;

2. Help to increase the effectiveness of the staff, parents, the civic and business community, and government and private agencies in improving the school's performance; and

3. Evaluate and make recommendations on the retention, dismissal, or transfer of certified staff in a "school in crisis."

4. Complete an intensive training program, provided by the Department of Education and approved by the State Board for Elementary and Secondary Education, prior to being assigned to assist a school's staff with implementing its school improvement plan. The training program shall include, but shall not be limited to instruction in the methods of personal evaluation, school organization, school curriculum, and assessment. (KDE, 1990, pp. 237–238)

Even though the statute indicated that the distinguished educator program was to begin in 1991, due to the reorganization of the Department of Education, the program did not get underway until the spring of 1992.

Early plans from the Department of Education called for a program that would train approximately eighty Distinguished Educators over a two-year period of time. The eight state universities in Kentucky were engaged to assist in the training. The program was designed so that each university would create a training program for approximately ten distinguished educators. Since the eight state universities are geographically spread across the state, the Department felt candidates would come from the geographic areas served by the universities.

The presidents of the universities agreed to participate in the program as part of the university system support for the implementation of KERA. Legislative approval was required to modify the program in this way. Approval was not secured, so the Department decided to reduce the number to five, as originally stated in KERA, and utilize the skills of these distinguished educators to help design the training program. The status of university involvement in the program had not been clarified by the summer of 1992.

SCHOOLS IN CRISIS

If a school's scores decline more than 5 percent, the school is declared a "school in crisis" and all full/part-time staff are placed on probation. Parents are notified that the school has been designated a school in crisis. This time, one or more distinguished educators may be assigned to the school. The distinguished educator(s) evaluates the staff and makes recommendations to the superintendent every six months regarding staff retention, transfer, and dismissal until the school is no longer in crisis. According to the statute, dismissal recommendations are binding.

If the proportion of successful students declines by more than 5 percent in the district, then the distinguished educator's powers to recommend dismissal expand to include the superintendent. If the district has a record of decline in the number of successful students for two biennial reviews, then the district is declared an education development district and the board members and the superintendent shall be removed under provisions of state statute.

PLANS AND REPORTS REQUIRED FOR DEFICIENT AND DEVELOPMENT DISTRICTS

KERA sets out very specific planning and reporting procedures for districts with these designations.

158.710 Responsibilities and functions of educationally deficient districts and education development districts; plans required; reports required

Each educationally deficient district and education development district shall assume the following responsibilities and functions in implementing the provisions of KRS 158.680 to 158.710:

(1) The district shall develop a plan to improve the education of all students enrolled in preschool and the primary program through grade twelve (12). In developing the plan and prior to approval by the local board of education, the district shall involve local citizens, parents, students, teachers, and administrators. The district, pursuant to KRS 158.685 shall involve *Department of Education consultants in the development of the plan;

(2) Educationally deficient districts and education development districts pursuant to KRS 158.685 shall submit a plan each year, or more frequently if ordered by the State Board for Elementary and Secondary Education, listing new process goals, the interim performance goals, and timelines until the deficiency has been eliminated;

(3) Local school personnel shall ascertain areas of strength and areas needing improvement in the school program as revealed by the test results and other student assessments and with the advice and counsel of the representatives mentioned in subsection (1) of this section, shall develop appropriate programs to address educational areas needing improvement for all students in preschool and the primary program through grade twelve (12);

(4) The district improvement plan developed and submitted to the department shall include the following:

(a) Performance goals or interim performance goals;

(b) Product goals;

(c) A list of individuals, by occupation, or groups involved in developing the plan;

(d) The areas of needed improvement as revealed by the district assessment results;

(e) A list of priorities for program implementation;

(f) The objectives and activities deemed appropriate and necessary for alleviating the observed educational areas of needed improvement;

(g) A calendar of events and timeline, for implementation;

(h) A brief report, each succeeding year, or more frequently if required by the State Board for Elementary and Secondary Education, after submission of the initial plan, of the program status and progress made in areas of needed improvement.

(5) The district improvement plan shall be coordinated with the master staff development plan and the Department of Education shall provide technical assistance in the planning, implementation, and evaluation of this coordination.

(6) Effective June 30, 1996, KRS 158.650 to 158.710 shall become null and void. (KDE, 1990, p. 236)

The statute also stipulates that if an educationally deficient district fails to meet the process goals, interim performance goals, or timelines set in the district improvement plan, this failure shall constitute grounds for removal of the board and superintendent. The state board would then appoint new board members for a term of four years. The new board would hire a new superintendent with the approval of the chief state school officer.

The provisions of the statute are specific and severe. Since they become null and void effective June 30, 1996, it is generally believed that these provisions will be closely reviewed at that time to determine if they have been effective. If they have not been effective in providing a mechanism for districts to improve student achievement, it is expected that the legislature will enact a different model.

There is speculation that future modifications may include a reconfiguration of school boundaries, changing the number and qualifications of local district school boards, and/or other more dramatic innovations. Essentially, the legislature is determined to do whatever seems necessary to ensure that the number of successful students in grades four, eight, and twelve increases.

DISTRICTS FACING ASSESSMENT DILEMMA

Districts are now faced with the dilemma of aligning the local district curriculum with the state assessment to insure that the number of successful students increases enough to enable the district to achieve the threshold scores for each of the schools in the district. They are attempting to do this for the twenty-nine valued outcomes assessed in this first year of state accountability assessment. The problem is compounded by the general nature of the valued outcomes and the fact that the valued outcomes are stated for exiting twelfth graders. A few of the valued outcomes which the state says were assessed during the spring of 1992 are listed below.

(1) Reading
   — Students construct meaning from a variety of print materials for a variety of purposes through reading.
(2) Mathematics
   — Visualizing: Students organize information and communicate ideas by visualizing space configurations and movements.
   — Measuring: Students gather information and communicate ideas by measuring.

(*3*) Science
- Nature and Scientific Activity: Students use appropriate and relevant scientific skills to solve specific problems in real-life situations.
- Evolution: Students complete tasks and/or develop products that identify, describe, and direct evolutionary change that has occurred or is occurring around them.

(*4*) Social Studies
- Structure and Function of Economic Systems: Students make economic decisions regarding production and consumption of goods and services related to real-life situations.
- Historical Perspective: Students recognize continuity and change in historical events, trends, and issues in order to make decisions for a better future.

Consistently, when groups of teachers are given these valued outcomes and asked to write down what a student should be able to do at the fourth-, eighth-, or twelfth-grade level to demonstrate that he/she can apply these ''big ideas,'' there is no consistency in their answers. Consequently, many districts are anxious to obtain the scoring rubrics and the test items used in 1992 to help them in rewriting the district and school curriculum.

The situation is further complicated by the formation of local school councils that have statutory power to select instructional materials, configure the school day, and make curricular decisions regarding the appropriate instruction required to achieve the valued outcomes. Some teachers look at the list of valued outcomes and say, ''We already do that.'' Others don't know what the valued outcomes mean for them. Yet, they all understand that a high-stakes accountability system has begun. In some cases, they feel helpless to control the variables. In other cases there is a frenzy of activity to define what they mean at the local level. Universally, there is concern about the future and how Kentucky's high-stakes testing will affect the future professional careers of teachers and administrators as well as how this high-stakes testing will affect the achievement of the children in this state.

REFERENCES

Archbald, Doug A. and Fred M. Newmann. 1988. *Beyond Standardized Testing: Assessing Authentic Academic Achievement in the Secondary School*. Reston, Virginia: National Association of Secondary School Principals.

Chittenden, Edward. 1991. "Authentic Assessment, Evaluation, and Documentation of Student Performance," in *Expanding Student Assessment*, Vito Perrone, ed., Virginia: Association for Supervision and Curriculum Development, pp. 22 – 31.

Darling-Hammond, Linda. 1991. "The Implications of Testing Policy for Quality and Equality," *Phi Delta Kappan* (November):221 – 224.

English, Fenwick. 1992. *Deciding What to Teach and Test*. California: Corwin Press.

Kentucky Department of Education. 1990. *Kentucky School Laws*. Frankfort, Kentucky: Bank-Baldwin Law Publishing.

Kentucky Department of Education. 1991a. *The Kentucky Education Act: 1990 Implementation Report*. Frankfort, Kentucky.

Kentucky Department of Education. 1991b. *Kentucky Instructional Results Information System*. Frankfort, Kentucky.

Kentucky Department of Education. 1992. *Ed News* (January-February).

Kentucky Department of Education. 1992. *Guidelines for the Generation of Student Work for Portfolios*. Frankfort Kentucky.

O'Neil, John. 1992. "Putting Performance Assessment to the Test," *Educational Leadership* (May):14 – 19.

Perrone, Vito. 1991. *Expanding Student Assessment*. Virginia: Association for Supervision and Curriculum Development.

Resnick, Lauren. 1989. "The Uses of Standardized Tests in American Education," *Proceedings of the 1989 Educational Testing Service Invitational Conference*. Princeton, New Jersey: Educational Testing Service, pp. 63 – 79.

Shepard, Lorrie A. 1989. "Why We Need Better Assessment," *Educational Leadership* (April):4 – 9.

Wiggins, Grant. 1991. "Characteristics of Authentic Assessment," included in materials distributed by the Kentucky Department of Education for professional development training over Kentucky Education Television Star Channel network.

Wolf, Dennie, Janet Bixby, John Glenn III and Howard Gardner. 1990. "To Use Their Minds Well: Investigating New Forms of Student Achievement," to appear in *Review of Research in Education*, Gerald Grant, ed.

Wolf, Dennie Palmer, Paul G. LeMahieu and JoAnne Eresh. 1992. "Good Measure: Assessment as a Tool for Education Reform," *Educational Leadership* (May): 14 – 19.

CHAPTER 4

Empowering Local Schools

THERE are approximately 1,350 public school sites in the state of Kentucky. By June, 1992, over 400 of these schools had formed school-based councils. When House Bill 940 was first introduced, one of the most controversial sections of the bill dealt with school-based decision making (SBDM). The Kentucky Education Reform Act (KERA) mandates that by July 1, 1996, all schools in the state shall operate school councils. The only schools that are exempt from this provision are schools that have met their threshold score (achieved state-mandated scores on cognitive and non-cognitive indicators, see Chapter 3) and choose to apply for an exemption; and schools where the district is made up of only one school.

In creating this section of the bill, legislators were responding to the plea for more direct involvement in school decision making by parents and teachers. Many teachers have contended that they are not involved in making the instructional decisions that impact their ability to enable students to achieve at high levels. They suggest that no one really knows the needs of the students in a particular school better than the staff of that school.

Parent involvement in schools has traditionally been confined to a supportive role, not one that includes parents in the process of instructional decision making. Fundraising, volunteering, and providing a supportive home environment for schooling have been the primary roles for parents. Most parents believe that no one knows a child, and the educational needs of a child, better than the parent. Thus, many parents believe that they have a right to assist the schools in making instructional decisions that impact their children. School-based decision making in Kentucky schools promotes active involvement from parents and teachers in addition to the traditional involvement of administration.

In defining the composition, responsibilities, and areas of accountability for councils, the statute is very specific.

THE STATUTE

160.345 Required adoption of school councils for school-based decision making; composition of council; responsibilities

(1) The term "teacher" for the purpose of this section means any person for whom certification is required as a basis of employment in the public schools of the state with the exception of principals, assistant principals, and head teachers.

(2) By January 1, 1992, each local board of education shall adopt a policy for implementing school-based decision making in the district which shall include, but not be limited to, a description of how the district's policies . . . have been amended to allow the professional staff members of a school to be involved in the decision making process as they work to meet educational goals. . . . The policy shall also address and comply with the following:

(a) Each participating school shall form a school council that shall be composed of two (2) parents, three (3) teachers, and the principal or administrator. The membership of the council may be increased, but it may only be increased proportionately. The parent representatives on the council shall not be relatives of any employee of the school.

(b) The teacher representatives shall be elected for one (1) year terms. The parent members shall be elected by the parent members of the parent teacher organization of the school or, if none exists, the largest organization of parents formed for this purpose. The principal or head teacher shall be the chair of the school council.

(c) The school council shall have the responsibility to set school policy which shall provide an environment to enhance the students' achievement and help the school meet the goals established by KRS 158.645 and 158.6451. The principal or head teacher shall be the primary administrator and the instructional leader of the school, and with the assistance of the total school staff shall administer the policies established by the school council and the local board.

(d) All certified staff at the school may be participants in the school-based decision making. The staff shall divide into committees according to their areas of interest, such as, but not limited to, grouped grade levels, subject areas, and special programs. Each committee shall elect, by a majority of the committee a chair, who shall serve for a term of one (1) year. The committee shall submit its recommendations to the school council for consideration.

(e) The school council and each of its committees shall determine the frequency of the agenda for their meetings. Matters relating to formation of school councils that are not provided for by this section shall be addressed by local board policy.

(f) The meetings of the school council shall be open to the public and all interested persons may attend. However, the exceptions to open meetings provided in KRS 61.810 shall apply. (KDE, 1990, p. 277)

COUNCIL FORMATION

By statute, councils could be formed anytime after July 13, 1990, the day the law took effect. Almost immediately, there were differences in interpretation regarding the language of the statute. The Kentucky School Boards Association, representing local district school board members; the Kentucky Education Association, representing the state's 32,000 teachers; the State Department of Education; and the Prichard Committee, a powerful, state citizens group, were all called upon to interpret the language.

Role of the District School Board

Initially, the Kentucky Education Association and the Kentucky School Boards Association appeared to disagree regarding policy development. The statute mandated that each local school board would develop board policy to guide the implementation of school-based decision making. The board policy had to address the following:

(1) School budget and administration, including discretionary funds; activity and other school funds; funds for maintenance, supplies, and equipment; and accounting and auditing

(2) Assessment of individual student progress, including testing and reporting of student progress to students, parents, the school district, the community, and the state

(3) School improvement plans, including the form and function of strategic planning and its relationship to district planning

(4) Professional development plans

(5) Parent, citizen, and community participation including the relationship of the council with other groups

(6) Cooperation and collaboration within the district, with other districts, and with other public and private schools

(7) Requirements for waiver of district policies

(8) Requirements for record keeping by the school council

(9) A process for appealing a decision made by a school council

To assist local school boards in broadening the governance structure of the school district to include school-based decision making, the Kentucky School Boards Association developed a guide entitled *Reaching New Heights* (Harvey, 1991). In this document, the association clearly took a supportive position to SBDM.

> The addition of school-based decision making to the governance structure of the school district has not eliminated the concept of a school district under the oversight of a board of education. In fact, it has strengthened that concept by decentralizing the process of decision making and inviting diversity of programming within the district, thus enabling a local board to focus on broader and more strategic objectives and policies. Ideally, the relationship between the board of education and the school council would be a harmonious one, each working together and within its sphere to promote student learning, striving toward school and district goals mutually determined and supported by all. (p. 8)

The issues that led to a difference in interpretation between the Kentucky School Boards Association and the Kentucky Education Association were related to the oversight role of the district board in reviewing school plans and policies, and to the development of an appeal process for local council actions.

Role of the Education Coalition

Shortly after John Brock was elected superintendent of public instruction, he organized a group composed of top level executives from ten major statewide organizations and agencies. The Education Coalition was composed of representatives from the following groups: Catholic Conference of Kentucky, Kentucky Association of School Administrators, Kentucky Association of School Superintendents, Kentucky Chamber of Commerce, Kentucky Congress of Parents and Teachers, Kentucky Department of Education, Kentucky Education Association, Kentucky Education Foundation, Kentucky School Boards Association, and the Prichard Committee for Academic Excellence. The Coalition continued to meet after KERA was enacted. They worked collaboratively to develop a position statement regarding school-based decision making.

The position statement of the Coalition, issued in August, 1991, (Harvey, pp. 33 – 39) included the following points:

(*1*) The local school board has authority for all activities with local schools.

(2) School councils and boards should seek ways to work collaboratively to improve student academic achievement.

(3) Local board policies should facilitate school decision making.

(4) District review of school policies should be confined to a review for consistency in the following areas: state and federal laws and regulations, concerns for health and safety, concerns for liability, financial resources available, contractual obligations to personnel and other providers of goods and services, and the authority delegated to the council by the board within the statutes.

(5) School councils will need training and support as they develop their planning skills.

(6) Board parameters for school plans include the following guidelines: be brief, three to six pages; include broad goals, specific objectives, and plans for implementation; provide for program evaluation; relate school plans to district plans, and identify specific areas in which the council will work.

(7) Include an appeal process with the following steps:
   – Appeal to the council for reconsideration.
   – Appeal to the superintendent.
   – Appeal to the school board.

(8) Parents are included on school committees.

(9) The district shall form a district-wide steering committee to coordinate activities and share information.

Training

Several associations, the Department of Education, and many private consultants began to conduct training. The School Boards Association focused on training present board members regarding the role and responsibility of the local school council while the state education association began to inform teachers about the new decision-making authority they would have under the law. In addition, the association used its regional network of field representatives to conduct training.

During the first eight months after the passage of KERA, the State Department provided awareness sessions regarding the bill, provided guidelines to local boards to assist them in developing local district policy, and developed a training program for council members in conjunction with the Gheens Academy, the professional development center for Jefferson County Schools. The awareness sessions provided participants with knowledge of the bill, defined the concept, and described the role of the principal and the superintendent in facilitating the formation of school councils. This training provided council members with skills in areas such as consensus decision making, developing an agenda, team planning, and running effective meetings.

Councils Begin Their Work

The decision to form a school council is made at the school by the teaching staff of that school.

> 160.345 (5) After July 13, 1990, any school in which two-thirds of the faculty vote to implement school-based decision making shall do so. By June 30, 1991, each local school board shall submit to the chief state school officer the name of at least one (1) school which shall implement school-based decision making the following school year. The board shall select a school in which two-thirds of the faculty vote to implement school-based decision making. If no school in the district votes to implement school-based decision making, the local board shall designate one (1) school of its choice. (KDE, 1990, p. 278)

The ink was hardly dry from signing KERA into law when news articles began to appear about school faculties meeting to discuss the possibility of forming councils. The legislature expected that large numbers of schools would vote to form councils in July, 1990. In actuality, a relatively small number of school councils were formed and began to function prior to January, 1991, when local school boards were required to have their policies to guide the functioning of councils enacted anyway.

A few superintendents and principals encouraged teachers to form councils right away. In many cases, these were situations where there was already a great deal of faculty and parent involvement in the decision-making processes of the school or where school administrators believed in the concept of shared decision making and encouraged the staff and parents to get involved. In other cases, the staff saw this as an opportunity to take a more active role in the school, with or without the support of the local board, administration, or the building principal.

In a few instances, the staff was anxious to form a council because the school needed a new principal and the statute set out a process for the school council to follow in selecting a new principal. The council may select the new principal from a list of qualified persons recommended by the superintendent. The decision of the council is binding. The superintendent completes the hiring process after the council has selected the new principal.

By July 1, 1991, 286 schools from 136 school districts in the state had voted to form school councils (KDE, *Biennial Report*, 1992, p. 9). Schools in forty school districts had not voted to form councils. Local school boards in these districts identified schools to participate. These 326 councils represented 79 high schools, 40 middle schools, and 207 elementary schools (KDE, 1991, p. 2). By the end of the 1991 – 92 school year, there were approximately 420 councils in the state.

During the 1992 meeting of the General Assembly, some legislators expressed concern that the number of councils in operation was smaller than they had expected. This prompted the Department of Education to consider a plan to provide financial incentives to schools that voted to form councils. There was some thought given to the idea that councils would be able to apply for grants ranging from $1,000 to $5,000 to support start-up activities. When the plan was presented to get a reaction from the field, it was postponed because districts felt that it penalized schools that had taken the initiative to go ahead and form their councils. If the number of councils does not grow significantly in the next two years, the Department may explore this option again.

Concurrently, during the 1992 General Session, legislation was passed to prohibit any employee in a school district from serving as a parent representative to a school council. The General Assembly believed that this provision was necessary because the parent representative on many councils in the state was an individual who had children attending the school, but who was also a teacher in another building. The legislature believed that this practice did not enable councils to benefit from the non-educator parental point of view. Parents who were employees of the school system and were seated on a school council prior to July 1, 1992, may serve their one-year term, but may not be reelected to the council.

Council Instructional Decision-Making Responsibilities

KERA lists eight areas where councils may adopt policy. These optional areas include:

(*1*) Determination of curriculum, including needs assessment, curriculum development, alignment with state standards, technology utilization, and program appraisal within the local school board's policy

(2) Assignment of all instructional and non-instructional staff time

(3) Assignment of students to classes and programs within the school

(4) Determination of the schedule of the school day and week, subject to the beginning and ending times of the school day and school calendar year as established by the local board

(5) Determination of use of school space during the school day

(6) Planning and resolution of issues regarding instructional practices

(7) Selection and implementation of discipline and classroom management techniques, including responsibility of the student, parent, teacher, counselor, and principal

(8) Selection of extracurricular programs and determination of policies relating to student participation based on academic qualifications and attendance requirements, program evaluation and supervision

Councils have discretion as to which of these areas they wish to develop policy in. A council could decide to develop policy in all eight areas or none of the areas. Most councils began by developing policy in one or two of the areas specified. As time progresses, it is expected that the councils will assume more and more responsibility for instructional decision making. This is extremely important since policies adopted by the council must be implemented by the principal.

In addition to these eight areas, councils are required to determine which instructional materials shall be provided. School boards are required to provide money to councils for acquisition of these materials. During the first year of the reform, the State Board of Elementary and Secondary Education passed a regulation requiring districts to allocate $75 per student to school councils. Since that time, the State Department has developed a procedure, which they are piloting in several districts, that enables councils to have access to large amounts of money and provides them with great discretion in expending these funds.

Further, councils must determine the student support services that shall be provided to the school. While councils may not transfer or dismiss present school employees, when a vacancy occurs, the council members can decide whether they want to fill the vacancy as it is currently defined or whether they want to fill the position with someone with a different certification to perform different functions. Councils can decide to use the money to acquire additional instructional materials and supplies, or to hire teacher aides. KERA gives councils the authority to decide how to use the resources available to best meet the needs of their school's children.

Since the vast majority of school districts in the state adopted the sample policies developed by the Kentucky School Boards Association, there has been great consistency across the state in procedures for formation of councils, election of officers, and council planning procedures. (See Appendix A for a sample board policy.)

Teacher, Parent, and Principal Roles Change

Once the council was formed and began to function, the roles of everyone involved began to change. Most school councils spent the first year of operation dealing with the "nuts and bolts" of getting organized, receiving training, and developing council bylaws. There was a tremendous demand for awareness and orientation sessions for teachers, parents, and administrators. As councils became more comfortable with the operational aspects of functioning, they began to identify specific areas to work on such as materials acquisition or discipline codes.

Teachers reported that through the work of the councils and the subcommittee structure, they were able to work together as colleagues in solving instructional problems in a more formalized way than they had before. Because of the desire to involve as many teachers as possible in the work of the council, faculty got to know one another better. Some principals found that teachers were far more interested in the details of how the school system operated than they had expected. Teachers wanted access to school and district information. While some teachers appeared to be hesitant about getting involved because they lacked training in this area; once they received training and began to work on solving instructional problems, their confidence level grew and they became enthusiastic advocates for the initiative. Particularly in schools where the administration took a positive, supportive role, teachers reported that the morale of the building improved. However, since most of the work related to the operation of the council took place after the normal school day, it was time consuming. It was not unusual for teachers to report that during the first year of operation, they were spending ten to fifteen hours a week on council business in addition to classroom time.

Parents serving on councils reported the greatest perceived change in their role. While many of the parents elected to the council were already actively involved in supporting the school, their role in the past was typically characterized by fundraising activities, providing coffee and cookies at school-related events, or volunteering in classrooms. Now, parents saw their role expanded, which led to an increased number of parents interested in supporting the school. Parents were encouraged to bring their expertise to the school. For example, parents with expertise in finance, accounting, and higher education were able to bring that knowledge to the school, allowing for a better decision-making process. Parents with expertise in environmental issues were able to suggest cost-cutting measures the school could use to provide more money for instruction.

Principals comfortable with a collegial setting made the transition to chairing a school council with more ease than principals who were used to making decisions on their own. Some expressed relief that the council now shared the responsibility for making instructional related decisions. They reported that there was greater buy-in to a decision before it was made with the new process. In the past, the principal often had to deal with opposition from staff and parents to a unilateral decision. Now, with broad-based involvement in making the decision, there was stronger commitment to making it work. Principals found they could stay involved, but had to "let go" of their decision-making power. Some were more successful with this than others.

Generally, districts reporting the highest percentage of schools voting to form councils were districts where the superintendent and board were perceived by staff as being very supportive of the program. One superintendent in the state, who oversaw sixteen schools, reported that fourteen of his schools had formed councils. In that district, the superintendent had assigned one central office staff person to act as a resource to each council and provide a communication link to central administration and the board. Board members were encouraged to attend council meetings so that the work of the councils and the district board were in support of one another. As the process evolved, the trust factor between the councils and the board increased. Boards became more aware of how district policies might impact the work of the councils and the councils became more aware of their role in developing policies that helped the district achieve its goals and objectives. In the best cases, the councils viewed themselves as extensions of the local board.

Associations Get Involved

With the formation of close to 400 councils in the state, the amount of dialogue about student achievement and creating supportive learning environments among parents, teachers, and administrators increased dramatically. Because councils expressed a need to network and share information and successful practices across councils within the state, a new state association for council members was formed. The Prichard Committee continued to maintain an active, supportive position to councils, and in November, 1991, they published Susan Weston's book, *School-Based Decision Making: A Guide for School Council Members and Others*. This publication was designed to explain the law regarding the formation and operation of councils for the lay audience. The document was reviewed by representatives from all the major education interest groups and was deemed accurate and clearly expressed. This publication became a valuable resource to councils throughout the state and was incorporated into the State Department's handbook for council operations. Written in a question-answer format, the book dealt with such questions as "What is school-based decision making?" "What does a schedule for non-instructional staff need to include?" and "What can be purchased with the school's basic allotment?"

In addition to this publication, the Prichard Committee began an initiative to set up KERA community support groups across the state. The organization has been a strong advocate for the successful implementation of KERA. In the introduction to the school-based, decision-making book, they state,

> School-based decision making offers teachers and principals the freedom and authority to use their professional knowledge and judgment in deciding how to best help children learn in their schools. Parents, who have high stakes in school success, have an unprecedented opportunity for meaningful school involvement. Engaging these parents and professionals in a meaningful way will be the biggest test, but it is also the key to the overall success of education reform in Kentucky. As all players— teachers, administrators, school board members, parents, students and the general public—struggle with the changes put in place by KERA, there will be need for fairness, dialogue, patience and acceptance in facing new roles and responsibilities. (p. iii)

In February, 1991, the Kentucky Congress of Parents and Teachers published *Parent Guidelines* to assist in council formation. This publication included sample forms such as Parent Notification, Nomination Ballot, Voting Ballot, and Eligible Voter Registry Book, to name a few. It provided guidelines for chairing the parent representative election meeting and listed activities for PTA presidents, to prepare them to assist in council formation.

The Kentucky Teachers Association produced a videotape and training materials to assist teachers in preparing for council formation.

No association or organization opposed the concept of shared decision making. Each group attempted to assist the constituency they serve in organizing and implementing this mandated initiative in the best way they could. As the process continues, the dialogue among the various groups is supported by a series of meetings sponsored by the State Department of Education. Every two to three months a voluntary group of representatives from associations, organizations, school districts, consultants, and university representatives come together to share information. These meetings have helped build communication links across organizations and build trust among these groups.

Proposed Budget Allocations for Councils

In March, 1992, the commissioner issued a Program Advisory to all superintendents in the state regarding budget allocations for school councils. The advisory described a mechanism for allocating money to school councils in addition to the $75 per pupil mandated by state regulation. Participation by districts in the suggested allocation process was voluntary, and was meant to serve as a pilot that could lead to the development of a state regulation later on.

Districts who chose to pilot the process had to agree to provide a budget allocation to each school in the district. The allocation would go to schools with councils and also to schools that did not have councils. The primary basis for the allocation during the 1992−93 school year was projected average daily attendance based on actual attendance for the 1990−91 school year.

The first allocation to the school site would provide for the actual salaries of all teaching staff employed in the spring of 1992 plus money for the yearly increment due for the 1992−93 school year and any contractually obligated salary increase.

If the school had a known vacancy, an allocation of 95 percent of the average 185-day salary paid in the school district in 1991−92 (KDE, *Program Advisory*, 1992, p. 1) would be provided. The money provided by this allocation for a vacant position did not have to be used to hire another certified staff person unless that person was required to enable the school to meet class size state requirements. School councils had the discretion to use the allocation for certified staff, classified staff, or any other instructional purpose. This provision did exclude teachers and other certified staff for handicapped children programs.

Application of this provision would act as a deterrent to schools to recommend hiring a new teacher who would qualify for a salary in excess of 95 percent of the district average. During the time this process is piloted, it is anticipated that this provision may be modified to enable a school to recommend the hiring of a seasoned veteran teacher.

An allocation formula for classified staff in non-categorical programs was to be developed at the local district level and applied consistently across the district. Once the money was allocated to the school site, the school council had the discretion to expend the money for classified non-categorical positions, certified positions, or instructional materials. Non-classified categorical positions were defined as secretarial, clerical, aide, and custodial.

In Kentucky, there has been a long-standing concern regarding the number of persons employed by a local school board in this category. Accusations of board members using jobs as a means of assuring their reelection to the board were common. Board members argued that it was unfair for the state to specify the number of persons to be employed in these positions because the needs of every district were different. A small elementary school may need more custodians than a new, larger middle school because of the age of the elementary school. By applying this provision, the parents, teachers, and principal of the school would decide how many non-categorical staff persons were required to serve the building. If the council determined that fewer non-categorical positions were needed, the school could use the extra money for other purposes. Also, a provision to cover the costs of all fringe benefits would be made to the school.

In the new funding formula created by KERA, there is a provision for add-on funds for at-risk students. This add-on is determined by the number of students who qualify for free lunch. "At-risk funds beyond amounts necessary to support the allocation for staffing will be allocated to schools in relation to the at-risk population. Districts may withhold from the school no more than 15 percent of this allocation for district-wide costs and initiatives" (KDE, 1991, p. 2).

The program advisory also set out a number of areas where the district may allocate funds to schools if it so chooses. These areas included staff development beyond the district plan, instructional equipment, and plant operation costs.

The Department projected that, based on the results of the pilot, the state regulation covering allocation of funds to local councils would be modified in November of 1992 to establish guidelines for the 1993–94 school year. Some have suggested that "where goes the money . . . there goes the power." Implementation of these suggested guidelines would certainly shift decision-making power for the expenditure of approximately 70−85 percent of a school district budget to the school council. The State Department has indicated that approximately fifteen districts are piloting these budgeting procedures for the 1992−93 school year. It is predicted that the results of this pilot and the nature of the subsequent guidelines emanating from the State Department may significantly impact the number of councils formed and the nature of the discussions and work of the council.

Since tentative budgets were due to the State Department in May of 1992 and this program advisory was not issued until March, 1992, local councils in the districts that are piloting this model did not have a great deal of time to get involved in the budgeting process. One could speculate that during the 1992−93 school year, councils in these districts would spend an increasing amount of time with budgetary issues.

School-Based Decision Making Nationally

A recent review of the literature on school-based decision making (Malen, Okawa, and Kranz, 1990), done to determine the relationship between SBDM and improved student achievement, produced the following findings.

1. District policy was largely unaffected by the formation of a school council. Schools continued to report that they experienced interference from central administration.

To help curb the possibility of this type of interference, the 1992 General Assembly modified the section of KERA dealing with SBDM to read as follows:

> No board member, superintendent of schools, or district employee shall intentionally engage in a pattern of practice which is detrimental to the successful implementation of or circumvents the intent of school-based decision making to allow the professional staff members of a school and parents to be involved in the decision making process in working toward meeting the educational goals established in KRS 158.645 and 158.6451 or to make decisions in areas of policy assigned to a school council pursuant to paragraph (j) of subsection 2 of this section. (KDE, 1990, KRS 160.345, p. 277)

Any "affected party" who believes that interference has taken place may write to the Office of Educational Accountability and that office will investigate. "A first violation will result in reprimand and a second can result in removal from office" (Weston, 1991).

2. *The issues councils tended to deal with were not directly related to instructional issues, but more often focused on facility concerns, student discipline, and fundraising.*

In the first two years of implementation in Kentucky, councils have dealt with similar concerns. However, the law clearly gives Kentucky's councils decision-making authority in most areas related to the delivery of instruction and holds schools accountable for the results of those decisions. The strong accountability component of Kentucky's statute may produce different results here.

3. *The principal continued to be the most dominant force on the council.*

Based on informal discussions with council members, this finding is consistent with the Kentucky experience.

4. *Power relationships within the school community did not change. The traditional balance of power in favor of the professional educators was maintained.*

While parents have indicated that those serving on councils feel more involved in the decision making of the school, the very makeup of the councils in Kentucky tends to reinforce maintenance of power positions.

5. *The variation in levels of expertise of council members was not addressed through training.*

Since there has been a statewide initiative by all the major associations and the State Department to address the training needs, this finding may not be as applicable in Kentucky. However, the length of term for council members may necessitate the development of various levels of training as new members are elected and old ones continue in their positions. Since no council member may serve more than three years, adequate training will be a continuing need for all council members.

6. *After councils had been in operation for a time, the morale of the group seemed to drop. Part of this was attributed to the amount of time devoted to being a council member.*

It is too soon to tell if this will be an outcome in Kentucky. However, many new councils reported that members were spending as much as ten to fifteen hours a week on the job in the first year of operation. Since councils are prohibited from meeting during the school day, this means that members are giving up evenings and weekends to perform council business.

7. *School programs continued to operate much as they had in the past.*

Again, most Kentucky councils have been in operation for a little over a year, and it is too soon to determine the long-term impact on the quality of school programs.

8. *Councils did not tend to generate very much innovation.*

Time will tell if this is true for Kentucky.

9. *Student achievement was not affected by the formation of the council.*

Since Kentucky is undergoing a transition from a standardized, norm-referenced state assessment system to an authentic assessment system, the state will not be able to determine whether schools with councils did better than schools without councils. That kind of comparative data will not be available until 1994. At that time, a thorough analysis of the relationship between councils and student achievement will surely be made.

Regardless of the results thus far, the concept of SBDM appears to be sweeping the nation. Initially embraced on a school district by school district basis, more state legislatures are beginning to mandate some form of participatory decision making through statute.

Lawler (1987, p. 38) identified ten advantages of shared decision making (Bailey, 1991, p. 27).

(*1*) Work methods and procedures: Less resistance to new methods may result, and the problem-solving process may produce innovations.

(*2*) Attraction and retention of employees: Improvement results from increased satisfaction and involvement.

(*3*) Staffing flexibility: Increased flexibility results from cross-training and teamwork.

(*4*) Service and product quality: Higher motivation and better methods increase quality.

(5) Rate of output: Higher motivation and better methods increase the rate of output.

(6) Staff support level: More "self-management" and broader skills reduce the staff support level.

(7) Supervision: More "self-management" and broader skills reduce the need for supervision.

(8) Grievances: Better communication and an improved union-management relationship reduce the number of grievances.

(9) Decision-making quality: Better input and decision-making processes improve the quality of decisions.

(10) Skill development: Problem-solving as well as technical skills are developed.

Whether the adoption of school-based decision making in the educational setting can produce these same results is yet to be seen. Lawler (1987) does acknowledge that moving to a shared decision-making process requires training, time, and strong leadership.

Bailey (1991, p. 43) contends that "principals in the twenty-first century will be the boss, but they will not be bossy." In his book, *School-Site Management Applied*, he describes the role of the principal in the Fort Worth Schools. Fort Worth has had school-based decision making for several years. A principal in this system is seen as the leader of a learning community and the leader of a management team that is comprised of representatives from the major constituent groups, teachers, students, and parents; and the principal and the management team are responsible for the site-based program.

Herman (1990) suggests caution before jumping on the bandwagon of school-based decision making. He developed a checklist for schools to use to determine if they are ready to move in this direction. The questionnaire includes such questions as "Do you really believe in shared decision making?" and "Are you willing to take full responsibility (accountability) for your decisions?" Van Meter (1991) echoes the call for caution and reinforces the need for a clear understanding of the role and functions of the council. Many educators in Kentucky are not sure whether they want to jump aboard. Since schools do not have to have councils until 1996, there is still time for careful analysis, deliberation, and perhaps some documented research analyzing whether student achievement is enhanced by the decision making of school councils.

The Kentucky experience with this initiative may determine the role of school-based decision making in public schools in the twentieth century.

REFERENCES

Bailey, William J. 1991. *School-Site Management Applied.* Lancaster, Pennsylvania: Technomic Publishing Co., Inc.

Harvey, Elizabeth, J. D. 1991. *Reaching New Heights: A Guide to the Implementation of School-Based Decision Making under the Kentucky Educational Reform Act.* Frankfort, Kentucky: Kentucky School Boards Association.

Herman, Jerry. 1990. *School-Based Management: A Checklist of Things to Consider.*

Kentucky Department of Education. 1990. *Kentucky School Laws.* Frankfort, Kentucky: Banks-Baldwin Law Publishing.

Kentucky Department of Education. 1991. *Kentucky Education Reform Act: 1990 Implementation Report,* Frankfort, Kentucky.

Kentucky Department of Education. 1992. *Biennial Report: 1989–91,* Frankfort, Kentucky.

Kentucky Department of Education. 1992. *Program Advisory: School Finance SBDM Allocation,* Frankfort, Kentucky.

Lawler, Edward. 1987. *High Involvement Management.* San Francisco: Jossey-Bass.

Malen, B., R. T. Ogawa and J. Kranz. 1990. "What Do We Know about School-Based Management? A Case Study of the Literature—A Call for Research," in *Choice and Control in American Education, Vol. 2, The Practice of Choice, Decentralization and School Restructuring,* W. Clune and J. Witte, eds. Philadelphia: Falmer Press, pp. 289–342.

Moak, Deborah. 1991. *Kentucky Congress of Parents and Teachers Parent Guidelines.* Frankfort, Kentucky: Kentucky Congress of Parents and Teachers.

Van Meter, Eddy. 1991. "The Kentucky Mandate: School Based Decision Making," *NASSP Bulletin,* 75(532):52–62.

Weston, Susan Perkins. 1991. *School-Based Decision Making: A Guide for School Council Members and Others.* Lexington: Prichard Committee for Academic Excellence.

CHAPTER 5

Seeking Financial Equity: Kentucky's Search for the Grail*

FINDING an equitable method for coping with the disparity in wealth between school systems has been public education's equivalent of the medieval search for the grail: it is a seemingly endless quest. Removing disparities between rich and poor in an essentially democratic, capitalist country confronts a host of putative "rights," such as school district boundaries; the extent of the development of wealth to tax within and outside those boundaries; the entanglement of the individual rights of parents to choose where to live; and for the wealthier, the right to live and send their children to school wherever they choose.

The growing gap between social haves and have-nots was forcefully illustrated in Jonathan Kozol's shattering book *Savage Inequalities* (1992), in which he noted

> There is a deep-seated reverence for fair play in the United States, and in many areas of life we see the consequences in a genuine distaste for loaded dice; but this is not the case in education, health care, or inheritance of wealth. In these elemental areas we want the game to be unfair and we have made it so; and it will likely so remain. (p. 223)

He also notes, "In public schooling, social policy has been turned back almost one hundred years" (p. 4).

THE PURSUIT OF EQUALITY IN KENTUCKY

Kentucky's quest for educational equity began in November, 1985, when the Council for Better Education filed a class action equity suit claiming Kentucky's method of funding education was not equitable

*This chapter first appeared in the July, 1992, issue of the *International Journal of Educational Reform*, Vol. 1, No. 3, Technomic Publishing Co., Inc., Lancaster, Pennsylvania. The article has been updated to reflect action taken by the 1992 Kentucky General Assembly.

(Legislative Research Commission, 1990). The defendants in the case were the governor, the superintendent of public instruction, the treasurer, the president pro tem of the Senate, the speaker of the House of Representatives, and the State Board of Education and its members. The plaintiffs were 66 of the state's 176 school districts, seven boards of education, and twenty-two students, which made up the non-profit corporation, the Council for Better Education.

When District Circuit Judge Ray Corns issued his judgement in October, 1988, he stated in his Findings of Fact that Kentucky's system of funding schools was one of the most severely deficient in the nation (*Council for Better Education v. Collins*, 1988). The case was appealed to the Kentucky Supreme Court (*Rose v. Council for Better Education*, 1989) and an opinion rendered in June, 1989. In declaring the entire educational system unconstitutional, the Supreme Court took the position that the problem was not simply a problem of funding. Rather, the entire system was in need of change. The Court said:

> This decision applies to the entire sweep of the system—all its parts and parcels. This decision applies to the statutes creating, implementing and financing the system and to all regulations, etc., pertaining thereto. This decision covers the creation of local school districts, school boards, and the Kentucky Department of Education to the Minimum Foundation Program and Power Equalization Program.

EVOLUTION OF STATE SUPPORT FOR PUBLIC SCHOOLS

State support for public schools can be traced back to the nineteenth century (Johns, 1971). By 1890, state support accounted for 23.8 percent of school funding (Mort, 1933). Federal support for education did not begin until 1917 with the enactment of the Smith-Hughes Bill (Johns, 1971, p. 1). "Although it was generally conceded that education was a state responsibility under the Tenth Amendment to the federal Constitution, most states during the nineteenth century exercised that responsibility, primarily, by authorizing the levy of local school taxes for the support of public schools" (p. 2). Development of the theory of state school support did not begin until 1905, when Ellwood P. Cubberley wrote a monograph entitled *School Funds and Their Apportionment* (Cubberley, 1905). According to Johns, the conceptualization of school finance can be attributed to Cubberley, who went from Teachers College, Columbia University, to Stanford University, and George D. Strayer, Sr., who stayed at Teachers College. "The conceptualizations of school finance developed by these two men, their students, and students of their students have dominated the thinking on educational finance during the twentieth century" (p. 3).

Cubberley (1905) described the state's responsibility to the appropriation of state school funds as follows:

Theoretically all the children of the state are equally important and are entitled to have the same advantages; practically this can never be quite true. The duty of the state is to secure for all as high a minimum of good instruction as is possible, but not to reduce all to this minimum; to equalize the advantages to all as nearly as can be done with the resources at hand; to place a premium on those local efforts which will enable communities to rise above the legal minimum as far as possible; and to encourage communities to extend their educational energies to new and desirable undertakings. (p. 17)

Updegraff (1922) with his method of financing teacher units, Strayer and Haig (1923) with their concept of "equalization of educational opportunity" and Mort (1924) with his definition of a state-assured program, all focused on defining the state's role as providing a state minimum educational program.

A satisfactory equalization program was defined by Mort (p. 23) as follows:

A satisfactory equalization program would demand that each community have as many elementary and high school classroom or teacher units, or their equivalent, as is typical for communities having the same number of children to educate. It would demand that each of these classrooms meet certain requirements as to structure and physical environment. It would demand that each of these classrooms be provided with a teacher, course of study, equipment, supervision, and auxiliary activities meeting certain minimum requirements. It would demand that some communities furnish special facilities, such as transportation.

State Support for Public Schools Increases

From 1929–30 to 1969–70, the role of state government in financing schools increased rather dramatically. State contributions to schools rose from 17.0 percent to 40.7 percent, while the role of the local community decreased from 82.7 percent to 52.7 percent with about 98 percent of local revenue being derived from property taxes (Johns, 1971, p. 19). According to the U.S. Office of Education, in 1930 Kentucky provided $5,841,000 in state funds to support education. By 1969 that figure had risen to $235,000,000. Twenty-two years later, in 1991, the state contributed $1,469,888,000 to the Support Education Excellence in Kentucky (SEEK) formula (KDE Summary of HB 799, 1990).

Equity Litigation Filed

Beginning in 1968, litigation challenging the legislature's methods of distributing state funds began to be filed. The basis for these challenges was the equal protection clause of the Fourteenth Amendment (Alexander, 1991). In *Serrano v. Priest* (1971), the California Supreme Court ruled ''that unequal distribution of school funds violated the equal protection clauses of both the federal and the California constitutions'' (p. 342). However, in 1973, the United States Supreme Court held that the equal protection clause did not apply to state school financing methods. Cases concerning state school financing equity filed after 1973 were generally litigated through the state court system. Most were confined to state financing formulas.

Kentucky Case Sets Precedent

The Kentucky case is significant and may mark the beginning of a new era in school finance litigation because of the breadth of the Court's decision (Alexander, 1991, p. 343).

> The court's decision led directly to a complete revision of the scheme of school finance and substantial modification in the organization and administration of the public schools. The case caused the legislature to fashion new tax legislation which resulted in increased revenues of over one billion dollars. Without the impetus of the court, it is doubtful that any new tax funds would have been allocated to the public schools. The court provided the legislature with both the nerve and the rationale to raise taxes, equalize school funding, and make other necessary changes.

Up until this time, the legislature had not assumed complete responsibility for the equitable funding of Kentucky's schools. This led the Kentucky Supreme Court to conclude that, ''the General Assembly of the commonwealth has failed to establish an efficient system of common schools. . . . Kentucky's entire system of common schools is unconstitutional'' (*Rose*, 1989).

Kern Alexander (1991, p. 345) summarizes the major points in the decision as follows:

First, the court set the boundaries in the separation of powers between legislative prerogative and judicial responsibility. In so doing, the court asserted a limited but certain judicial role in delineating the affirmative constitutional obligations of the General Assembly to provide for public schools.

Second, the court acknowledged and established the fundamentality of education. The court avoided the legal contortions and grouping that have characterized the question of fundamentality under the federal equal protection clause, and chose instead to frame the fundamentality of education as a simple and obvious fact.

Third, the court gave form and substance to the education provision of the Kentucky Constitution and firmly established its importance as a standard to which the legislature must adhere.

Fourth, the court defined the foundational nature of public schools as common schools and set forth the implications of the constitutional intent for legislation.

Fifth, the court showed a willingness to interpret substantively the details of the education clause of the Kentucky Constitution by holding that an "efficient system" of public schools required equality of opportunity.

Finally, the court justified the appropriateness and efficacy of striking down the entire state system of education, rather than merely invalidating selected offending school funding statutes.

In rendering its decision, the Supreme Court focused considerable attention on the adequacy and equity of funding (Legislative Research Commission, 1991). The Court stated that "the total local and state effort in education in Kentucky's primary and secondary education is inadequate and is lacking in uniformity" (*Rose*, 1989, p. 26). Table 5.1 describes the disparities in key financial indicators prior to the reform. As shown on the table, the property wealth per pupil ranged from a low of $39,138 to a high of $341,707. Local revenue per pupil ranged from $80 to $3,716. Money for teaching supplies ranged from $8 to $259 per pupil. The number of teacher aides ranged from 0 to 40.7 per 1,000 students.

Dr. John Augenblick (1991), in a report prepared for the Kentucky Department of Education, describes the state's funding system prior to KERA as follows:

> The flawed school finance system reviewed by the court was an amalgam of several components: (1) the Foundation Program, which had evolved from the Minimum Foundation Program enacted in 1954; (2) the Power Equalization Fund, created in 1976; and (3) a variety of other programs

Table 5.1. 1989 – 90 Pre-KERA Disparities.

	Low	High
Property Wealth per Pupil	$39,138	$341,707
Levied Equivalent Tax Rate	22.9	111.9
Local Revenue per Pupil	$80	$3,716
State Revenue per Pupil	$1,750	$2,753
Av per Pupil Expenditure		
For Administration	$31	$356
For Instruction	$1,499	$3,709
For Teaching Supplies	$8	$259
Av Administrator Salary	$32,017	$56,691
Av Teacher Salary	$21,718	$30,379
Av Certified Salary	$24,102	$32,268
Staff per 1000 Pupils		
Classroom Teachers	49.5	84.7
Librarians	0	7.7
Guidance Counselors	0	4.5
Teacher Aides	0	40.7
Total Certified Staff	60.4	104.1

designed to provide support for the special operating and capital needs of school districts. One of the problems of these components, particularly the Foundation Program and the Power Equalization Fund, was that they did not operate in the way such programs are intended to operate. A foundation program is characterized by several features: (1) the state determines an amount of revenue that each district is guaranteed to obtain through a combination of state and local resources; (2) the state determines a uniform tax effort that every district must make; and (3) state aid becomes the difference between the amount of revenue guaranteed and the amount of revenue generated locally at the uniform tax effort. Kentucky's Foundation Program used an elaborate procedure driven by numbers of personnel eligible to be reimbursed and a statewide salary schedule to determine the revenue level guaranteed to each district. However, there was no requirement that school districts make a contribution to the program. Therefore, the allocation of state aid was not sensitive to the wealth of districts but became, in essence, a ''flat grant'' that provided about the same amount of support per pupil for all districts, regardless of their fiscal capacity.

A power equalization program is a very specific form of a ''reward for effort'' approach under which school districts determine the amounts of revenue they want to obtain and state aid is allocated in a way that is sensitive both to the relative wealth of the districts and their tax effort.

Power equalization implies that every district will have precisely the same ability to generate revenue per pupil per unit of tax effort and requires that funds be ''recaptured'' from districts in which wealth is so great that their ability to generate revenue exceeds what the state guarantees. Under Kentucky's Power Equalization Fund, school districts were required to make a 25 cent property tax effort but state aid only assured an equivalent ability to generate revenue up to about half that rate. In fact, at the level at which it was operating, the Power Equalization Fund behaved as if it were a foundation program because a common tax effort was required rather than allowing tax effort, and state aid, to vary based on school district choice. Also, the Power Equalization Fund had no recapture provision.

Because the Foundation Program and the Power Equalization Fund did not provide sufficient revenue for school districts, most districts supplemented state aid with local funds derived in large measure from local property taxes and from permissive taxes districts were permitted to impose under legislation originally enacted in 1966. The revenue generated locally was dependent on two factors: the wealth of each district and the tax effort of each district. Some of the poorest communities in the state made the lowest tax effort while some of the wealthiest communities made the highest tax effort resulting in wide disparities in the local revenue used to supplement state aid.

Task Force Sets Goals

In designing a new school finance system, the Task Force on Education Finance Committee developed a list of objectives.

The new school finance system should:

- be more sensitive to the disparity in wealth that exists among the state's school districts
- assure consistency across school districts in the determination of property wealth
- correct the structural problems in the old system
- provide an adequate base of revenue for every school district
- permit some flexibility in the tax effort of school districts and be sensitive to differences in tax effort
- either require or encourage some of the poorest districts in the state to raise their tax effort
- be more sensitive to the special needs of school districts, particularly those related to the number of pupils enrolled in special education programs, and to the needs of pupils considered to be at-risk of failure in school

- assure that revenue disparities across school districts are limited and that whatever disparities are permitted would be related to the needs of the districts or their willingness to tax themselves
- provide funds for capital outlay and debt service that are sensitive to the wealth of school districts
- provide more flexibility to school districts to spend funds in ways they feel to be appropriate and, consistent with the recommendations of the Curriculum Subcommittee
- encourage districts to develop new approaches to paying professional employees based on more factors than simply their training and experience
- be evaluated periodically to assure that it remains "efficient," providing an adequate level of resources and maintaining an appropriate level of equity

KENTUCKY'S NEW FUNDING FORMULA

The new state finance system is made up of four distinct parts: the SEEK formula, Capital/Debt, Teacher Retirement, and Other Programs. Combined, these initiatives increased state funding for education during the 1990-91 fiscal year by 25.1 percent (Augenblick, 1991, p. 22). However, discussion will focus on the SEEK formula. HB 940 created the Support Education Excellence in Kentucky (SEEK) formula. Augenblick describes the formula as a "tiered" school finance system. It is composed of three parts: an adjusted base guarantee, Tier I, and Tier II.

Adjusted Base Guarantee

This is a foundation program that "specifies a guaranteed level of per pupil revenue ($2,305 per pupil) in Average Daily Attendance (ADA) for 1990−91" (Augenblick, p. 12). This base was established by determining an average for prior statewide spending, and full funding of previously enacted state programs, which includes $100 per pupil for capital outlay. The base of $2,305 is the only amount in the adjusted base guarantee that is constant across all districts. The base is then adjusted for transportation costs and for the number of exceptional children and at-risk students. Transportation costs are fully funded using the existing state formula. The exceptional children adjustment is a weighted calculation based on the number and type of exceptionality. The at-risk factor is based on the number of students in the district who qualify for free lunch. In 1990–91, each at-risk student generated $346 (the base times a factor of .15). To determine the amount of state money per student generated for the adjusted base, add the transportation, exceptional children, and at-risk factors to the base and divide by the number of students in the district. The only figure that remains constant across districts is the base. Additionally, money generated by the number of exceptional children and at-risk children does not have to be spent on these populations. How the district expends money generated by the SEEK formula is up to the district as long as the district meets federal regulations. This policy is in keeping with the outcome-based philosophy behind KERA and greater decision-making autonomy at the school site and district level. It is also related to the outcome requirements of KERA and on increasing the "proportion of successful students."

Expending money generated from the SEEK program did lead to changes and concerns. For example, the previous state formula provided special education teacher units. The state had never funded enough units to meet the district's needs. In the past, special education units paid for special education teachers. Under the new system, the base included full funding for identified exceptional children. This change has caused concern among the special education community because some people believe that districts will use the money generated by identified exceptional education children to fund other programs. Since exceptional children programs are highly controlled by state and federal regulations and statutes, the concerns seem unwarranted; however, districts are being closely monitored regarding this issue.

Tier I (LRC, p. 6)

Tier I is the second component of SEEK. This is an optional component that allows local school districts to generate additional revenue of up to 15 percent of the adjusted base guarantee. School districts whose per pupil property wealth is less than 150 percent of the statewide average per pupil property wealth ($225,000 for FY 1990–91) receive state equalization funds. This component provides that any district whose wealth is less than 150 percent of the statewide average can generate the same revenue per pupil if they make the same tax effort above the 30 cents required. Districts may participate at any level up to 15 percent. The decision is one for the local school board, and the levy is not subject to a recall by the voters.

Prior to 1990−91, the range in the local district-levied equivalent tax rate ranged from a low of 22.9 to a high of 111.9 (LRC, p. 3). The General Assembly appropriated $20 million to fund Tier I. It was insufficient. In 1990−91, 169 districts participated in Tier I (Augenblick, p. 21). State aide for Tier I had to be prorated at 40 percent. Districts complained about the inadequate funding and the legislature responded by assuring districts that every attempt would be made to fully fund Tier I during the 1992−94 biennium.

The fact that the number of districts participating in Tier I exceeded expectations is being perceived as a very positive indicator on the part of local communities to more vigorously support the reform effort.

Tier II (LRC, pp. 6-7)

Tier II, also optional, is the third component of SEEK. Tier II allows districts to generate additional revenue up to 30 percent of the amount generated by the adjusted base guarantee and Tier I. These funds are not equalized by the state, and school districts must obtain voter approval in imposing additional taxes within Tier II. Tier II has the effect of placing a cap on the amount of revenue a local school district can raise, thereby maintaining some control over the disparity in per pupil revenues that might be available in local school districts. The disparity in revenues cannot exceed 49.5 percent (1.15 × 1.30) in districts with similar needs.

The amount of additional funding that can be achieved through Tier II, like Tier I, is dependent upon the adjusted base guarantee. This, in effect, provides an incentive for every district in the state−not just the less wealthy−to be vitally concerned about the base guarantee.

Table 5.2 illustrates how the SEEK calculations might look in two Kentucky school districts−one with low per pupil wealth and one with high per pupil wealth.

In this illustration, District A has a per pupil assessment of $39,100 while District B has a per pupil assessment of $341,700. Both districts have the same equivalent tax rate of 53.9. Both districts receive the same SEEK base of $2,305. The add-on for the at-risk, exceptional child, and transportation is different for each district based on the formula described above. Notice that the required local effort of 30 cents generates $117 per pupil in District A and $1,025 per pupil in District B. The amount generated through local effort is deducted

Table 5.2. Example of SEEK Calculation for Two School Districts.

	District A	District B
District Characteristics		
per Pupil Assessment	$39,100	$341,700
Equivalent Tax Rate	53.9	53.9
SEEK		
Base	$2,305	$2,305
At-Risk	$308	$92
Exceptional Child	$370	$357
Transportation	$204	$146
SUBTOTAL	$3,187	$2,900
Required Local Effort—$.30	$117	$1,025
State Adjusted Base per Pupil	$3,070	$1,875
Tier I State	$351	0
Tier I Local	$74	$646
Total State Aid per Pupil	$3,421	$1,875

from the subtotal, leaving a state-adjusted base of $3,070 per pupil in District A and $1,875 in District B. District A receives additional state funds through Tier I and both districts receive additional local funds through Tier II. The result provides District A with total state aid per pupil of $3,421 and District B with total state aid per pupil of $1,875. Over time, the application of this new formula is expected to achieve financial equity among Kentucky districts.

The Facilities Support Program of Kentucky (FSPK) was created to provide additional fiscal support for school construction. It required that districts levy an additional 5 cents in order to participate in FSPK and the School Facilities Construction Commission. "The 5 cent levy is equalized at 150 percent of the average per pupil property wealth. Like Tier I, FSPK is designed to guarantee that districts receive the same revenue for a similar levy — without regard for the property wealth of the district" (LRC, pp. 25–26). The 5 cent requirement was levied by 174 of the 176 districts during 1990–91.

In addition to SEEK and FSPK, teacher retirement was fully funded. Also, a number of categorical programs, such as the Preschool program, Extended School Services, Gifted and Talented, and Professional Development were funded. A summary of the 1989–90 and 1990–91 funding levels and the percent of increase are given in Table 5.3.

Table 5.3. Quintile Characteristics for 1989 – 90 and 1990 – 91.

	Lowest	Second	Third	Fourth	Highest
Quintile Characteristics			**1989 to 1990**		
1—Number of Districts	54	43	40	33	6
2—Number of Pupils	113,817	116,108	112,657	106,026	120,846
3—Average Property Wealth per Pupil	$73,100	$107,837	$140,804	$180,740	$281,361
			1990 to 1991		
1—Number of Districts	52	47	40	32	5
2—Number of Pupils	111,145	116,953	116,778	104,084	118,441
3—Average Property Wealth per Pupil	$79,632	$116,116	$150,964	$197,468	$171,127

INTERVIEW WITH TOM WILLIS

In August, 1991, Tom Willis, LRC budget analyst, was interviewed by the author regarding the initial implementation of the new funding formula. Exerpts of that interview follow.

Betty: Are we achieving financial equity in Kentucky?

Tom: The big question is "What is equity?" It depends on how it is defined. People are defining it differently. Some define equity as a dollar amount. Personally, I think we are moving toward equity however it eventually gets defined.

Betty: What about instructional equity?

Tom: I think that if you look at the big inputs, we are moving toward it. However it is ultimately defined, the legislature is hoping to achieve it in five years. That is the projected implementation period for the SEEK system. I guess you could assume that the legislature intends to have the system fully implemented and "equitable" by 1996.

Betty: What were the major problems in designing the system?

Tom: Politically or otherwise?

Betty: Both!

Tom: On the political side, we ended up with a minimum guarantee of 8 percent. Every district had to receive what might be termed a significant amount of money. That was the political side of trying to achieve equity. In reality, we will never achieve real financial equity as long as we have the guarantees.

Betty: Do you think there will be enough money going into "economically deprived" districts during the first few years to enable them to document that they have been more effective because of the increase in money?

Tom: One of the bigger problems is that the amount of new money generated at the local level is tied to property assessments. Getting accurate property assessments may take as long as three or four years.

Betty: Why?

Tom: Well, the property valuation agent (PVA) is an elected official in Kentucky. Also, in many counties, the PVA doesn't have any staff to assist in the mandated revaluation process. They don't have the staff to get out and look at every piece of property. During the last General Session, there was a separate set of bills that put considerable money in the Revenue Cabinet to hire additional staff for PVAs.

Betty: Do you think that eventually, underevaluation of property won't be as much of a problem?

Tom: It shouldn't be. In all honesty, statewide, it's not as much of a problem as it's perceived to be. While it may be pretty easy for a news reporter to go out and find an elected official whose house is assessed at $30,000 but worth about $300,000, put that in the paper, and give the impression that it's a statewide problem, the number of counties where this sort of thing might happen is relatively small.

Betty: Every time I talk to someone about finance, they always mention the fact that salary increases for the first year were substantive. If districts continue giving large salary increases, will that cause a problem later on?

Tom: Salaries are a continuing growth expenditure. I think that what they are saying is that most of them can support a 10 – 15 percent increase the first year. They are going to get into trouble if they give increases in excess of what the state is providing in new funds in later years.

Betty: I think the KERA implementation is going well. Do you agree?

Tom: It's doing a whole lot better than many people expected.

Betty: How did the legislature generate the support for the tax increase?

Tom: Well, it was obvious up-front that there had to be some additional money. The question was how much money and from day one, there was never any talk about dealing with this without dealing with the money issue at the same time. True, there was some pork, but that was inevitable.

Betty: I've read all kinds of suggestions about how much of the tax increase actually went to support K − 12 education. Do you know?

Tom: The leadership of the Democratic side says that 94 percent went into education. Of that amount, 75 percent was for elementary/secondary education. It all depends on who is supplying the figures and how the calculations are made. The bottom line is that, so far, it appears to be working.

EQUITY ANALYZED

In an effort to assess the degree to which equity was being achieved by the new funding mechanism, Dr. John Augenblick undertook a comparative study of 1989 − 90 and 1990 − 91 funding and staffing levels. (For a full explanation, see Augenblick, 1991.) The 176 school districts were divided into wealth quintiles. Each quintile included approximately 20 percent of the student population. Data from the Augenblick report was synthesized by the Legislative Research Commission and included in their December, 1991, report to the legislature. Three tables selected from that report have been presented here to show the degree to which equity is being achieved in funding Kentucky education. The funding formula is expected to evolve over a four-year period. In his initial study, Augenblick used a correlation coefficient for the analysis of equal opportunity. Dr. Augenblick explains that, "the correlation coefficient ranges between 1.00 and − 1.00. A strong positive correlation suggests that as one variable increases, the other does also. A strong negative correlation suggests that as one variable increases, the other decreases. A correlation near zero suggests that there is no systematic relationship between the two variables" (Augenblick, p. 30).

Table 5.4 shows the pupil weighted averages for equivalent tax rates by wealth quintile. In 1989−90, districts in the lowest quintile had an average equivalent tax rate of 29.41 cents. In 1990−91, the rate had increased to 43.7 cents. Debt service for the districts in the lowest quintile for 1989−90 was 3.51 cents. By 1990−91, this had risen to 6.61,

Table 5.4. Pupil Weighted Averages for Equivalent Tax Rates by Wealth Quintile.

Equivalent Tax Rates (in cents)	Lowest	Second	Third	Fourth	Highest	State-wide
1989 to 1990						
Current Operations	29.41	31.02	32.33	39.18	63.94	39.46
Debt Service	3.51	4.78	2.67	4.86	4.85	4.14
TOTAL	32.92	35.81	34.99	44.04	68.79	43.6
1990 to 1991						
Current Operations	43.7	41.86	45.86	48.5	64.57	48.99
Debt Service	6.61	7.15	4.24	5.22	6.05	5.86
TOTAL	50.31	49.02	50.11	53.72	70.62	54.85

demonstrating the increases in local tax effort among districts in the lowest quintile. The spread in equivalent tax rates in 1989−90 between the lowest and the highest quintile was 35.87 cents. The spread in 1990−91 was 20.31 cents demonstrating the movement toward equity.

Table 5.5 compares the pupil weighted averages for revenue by wealth quintile for 1989−90 and 1990−91, and shows the coefficient of variance. Comparing the lowest quintile with the highest quintile between the two years, a substantial increase in local and state revenue per pupil for districts in the lowest quintile is seen. Federal revenue for districts in the lowest quintile remained about the same. While revenue increased in all three categories for districts in the highest quintile, the increase was not as dramatic. The spread in total revenue per pupil in 1989−90 from lowest to highest quintile was $1,199. The spread in 1990−91 had dropped to $861.

Table 5.6 shows the pupil weighted averages for expenditures by wealth quintile. All categories show increases for all wealth quintiles. Per pupil expenditure for instruction across all quintiles rose by $352 per pupil. This category reflects teacher salary increases that averaged over 10 percent across the state. Transportation costs per pupil rose from $200 to $250. Fixed charges also saw a substantial increase. All available or related data will have to be compared over several years before patterns and trends can be identified. At this point, it can be said that the approximately $500,000,000 in new money received by school districts in 1990−91 was used in all major categories of the budget. (See Appendix B for the conclusion of Augenblick's report, which includes ten issues and recommendations for improving education in Kentucky.)

Table 5.5. Pupil Weighted Averages for Revenue by Wealth Quintile:
1989 – 90 and 1990 – 91.

	Lowest	Second	Third	Fourth	Highest	Statewide
1989 to 1990						
Local Revenue						
per Pupil	$290	$436	$587	$895	$1,985	$851
Coeff. of Var.	.525	.376	.328	.299	.167	.779
State Revenue						
per Pupil	$2,352	$2,270	$2,221	$2,176	$2,125	$2,228
Coeff. of Var.	.056	.048	.045	.050	.048	.061
Local-State						
per Pupil	$2,642	$2,706	$2,808	$3,070	$4,110	$3,079
Coeff. of Var.	.079	.083	.072	.099	.086	.200
Federal Revenue						
per Pupil	$545	$394	$321	$289	$276	$365
Coeff. of Var.	.287	.261	.289	.538	.173	.420
Total Revenue						
per Pupil	$3,187	$3,099	$3,129	$3,359	$4,386	$3,444
Coeff. of Var.	.081	.083	.067	.119	.088	.170
1990 to 1991						
Local Revenue						
per Pupil	$397	$588	$818	$1,145	$2,162	$1,028
Coeff. of Var.	.271	.299	.194	.230	.104	.639
State Revenue						
per Pupil	$3,045	$2,859	$2,686	$2,470	$2,348	$2,682
Coeff. of Var.	.056	.052	.054	.061	.058	.109
Local-State						
per Pupil	$3,442	$3,447	$3,505	$3,615	$4,510	$3,710
Coeff. of Var.	.047	.062	.059	.082	.063	.129
Federal Revenue						
per Pupil	$584	$423	$370	$314	$478	$435
Coeff. of Var.	.309	.278	.279	.508	.354	.401
Total Revenue						
per Pupil	$4,026	$3,871	$3,874	$3,929	$4,987	$4,145
Coeff. of Var.	.062	.072	.068	.099	.084	.131

Table 5.6. Pupil Weighted Averages for Expenditures by Wealth Quintile.

	Lowest	Second	Third	Fourth	Highest	Statewide
1989 to 1990						
Administration	$86	$79	$70	$77	$118	$86
Instruction	$1,894	$1,933	$1,992	$2,158	$2,714	$2,145
Attendance	$24	$24	$21	$20	$24	$23
Health	$5	$3	$3	$3	$5	$4
Transportation	$211	$195	$194	$169	$226	$200
Operation of Plant	$190	$194	$201	$218	$340	$230
Maintenance	$87	$91	$90	$109	$152	$105
Fixed Charges	$100	$86	$99	$98	$145	$106
Total Current Expenditures	$2,592	$2,604	$2,670	$2,847	$3,723	$2,898
1990 to 1991						
Administration	$96	$98	$88	$86	$129	$100
Instruction	$2,306	$2,313	$2,379	$2,466	$3,006	$2,497
Attendance	$26	$27	$25	$21	$27	$25
Health	$7	$3	$5	$3	$6	$5
Transportation	$272	$253	$240	$210	$257	$247
Operation of Plant	$217	$211	$225	$228	$364	$250
Maintenance	$108	$107	$135	$112	$131	$119
Fixed Charges	$130	$118	$123	$125	$164	$132
Total Current Expenditures	$3,162	$3,131	$3,220	$3,252	$4,084	$3,376

TOUGH ISSUES TO BE CONSIDERED

While progress toward equity appears to be underway, it is still too soon to proclaim success in achieving equity in school funding in Kentucky. The formula is expected to evolve over the next few years with the inclusion of weighted formulas for vocational education and special education. The state is undergoing a five-year reassessment of property values mandated by the General Assembly, and some tough issues are still hanging in the wings waiting to be addressed. One of them is whether the more ''affluent districts'' will permit equitable funding to be achieved.

''The lesson of California is that equity in education represents a formidable threat to other values held by many affluent Americans. It will be resisted just as bitterly as school desegregation'' (Kozol, 1992,

p. 222). Provisions of the reform package provided minimum increases of 8 percent the first year and 5 percent the second year of the biennium, for all districts. Projections for 1992–94 indicate that one in four school districts may receive no new state money (*Lexington Herald*, Feb. 15, 1992, pp. 1 and 10). While these figures do not reflect cuts outside the basic funding formula or adjustments for changes in student enrollment, they are clouds on the reform horizon. If these projections become reality, they will quickly translate into program and staff reductions. In the early stages of the latest national recession, Kentucky was not hit as dramatically as other parts of the nation. However, as the recession lingered, the impact has been felt in the state coffers, resulting in state budget cuts. The attitude of our large urban districts in Jefferson County and Fayette County was strong support for reform when it was initially enacted. Now that it seems clear that these districts, where some of our most powerful legislators reside, may feel they have been penalized for building effective educational programs that produce results, the future is questionable. The cry prior to the 1992 meeting of the General Assembly was for the governor and the legislature to find the money to provide appropriate increases for all districts, not just the poorest. The condition of the state economy made that impossible during 1992.

EDUCATION BUDGET, 1992–94

The 1992 General Assembly made every effort to continue to fund KERA implementation at levels consistent with the predictions made in 1990 when the bill was first passed. Legislators point to the fact that Tier I of the SEEK formula was fully funded at an additional cost of $56 million for the first year of the biennium. The Kentucky Teachers Retirement System gained $11.39 million and Health Insurance grew by $20.8 million for 1992–93 (*KASA Hotline Newsletter*, April, 1992).

Educators talk about the reduction in the amount of money for Rewards and Sanctions, Technology, and Extended School Services. Money for Rewards and Sanctions and Technology was held in escrow during the 1990–92 biennium. The Rewards and Sanctions escrow account will be used in 1994, the first year sanctions and rewards will be given. In reducing the amount of state funds deposited in this account during 1992–94, the legislature argued that the state economy would support a greater contribution in 1994. The Technology money budgeted in 1990–92 is still being held in escrow because of a delay in getting program approval for this initiative. Since the program implementation has been delayed, a reduction in the state budget contribution does not result in a decrease in the funds available. At $66.5 million, the Extended School Services' 1992−94 budget is less than projected but more than was spent during the 1990−92 biennium (*Perspectives*, Spring, 1992). The Kentucky Association of School Administrators' newsletter (April, 1992) indicated that while two-thirds of the districts in the state would receive increases in state funds for the 1992−93 school year, sixty districts would receive no increases (p. 2). Other programs which enjoyed funding increases included Professional Development, Family and Youth Services Centers, and the Preschool program.

There was an overall 2 percent state budget increase for 1992−93 in the amount of $34.6 million and a 5 percent increase for 1993−94 of $104.2 million (*Perspectives*, Spring, 1992, p. 2).

FUTURE RAMIFICATIONS

The future political ramifications of the current district funding levels are still unknown. When the constituencies of legislators in districts receiving no new funds make their feelings known at reelection time, Kentucky legislators will be forced, once again, to stand the high ground in order to maintain movement toward equity. Many will find themselves between the ''rock'' of local opinion, and the ''hard place'' of the Supreme Court decision to achieve equity in funding schools.

With increases of 20 to 40 percent in their annual school budgets, will our poorest school districts be able to produce and sustain high levels of student achievement? Some critics of education have long held that money was not the problem in many of our schools, so money will not be the solution. The Supreme Court took the position that the problem was the ''entire'' system of education, which included money. KERA provided the programmatic initiatives and the money to produce the changes required, which should enable *all* children to learn at significantly higher levels. The analysis of how these new monies were spent during the first year indicates that much of it was spent on salary increases. Only time will tell whether these salary increases coupled with the other programmatic initiatives can produce the desired outcome. Much of it depends on the success of the comprehensive professional development programs currently underway. The programmatic initiatives in KERA are believed to be sound. Whether teachers and administrators can learn the skills necessary to deliver the intent of these programs quickly enough to produce demonstrated, dramatic increases in student achievement is not yet known. Teachers and administrators in Kentucky are working hard to meet the goals, to learn the skills, and to implement the comprehensive array of new programs.

Part of the present problem is juggling the number of new initiatives to be implemented. Whether educators will be able to sustain the effort they are currently maintaining over a long period of time, without becoming disillusioned, is not known. The stress and anxiety factor among many professionals is presently quite high. The current budget crunch is not helping. Many believe that the next two years will tell the story. If educators can begin to see the fruits of their labors, we stand a chance of maintaining this effort over the long haul. If budget shortfalls, ineffective professional development plans, diminished parental support, and unrealistic workloads persist, the ''miracle'' of KERA is in jeopardy.

Most assuredly, the horizon looks cluttered with obstacles. However, significant progress has been made. Three years ago, no one dreamed Kentucky would become a leader in systemic change in education. The state has many believers who have faith that the progress made to date will be sustained. Time will tell.

REFERENCES

Alexander, Kern. 1991. ''The Common School Ideal and the Limits of Legislative Authority: The Kentucky Case,'' *Harvard Journal on Legislation*, 28(2).

Augenblick, John. 1991. ''An Evaluation of the Impact of Changes in Kentucky's School Finance System: The SEEK Program, Its Structure and Effects,'' report to the Kentucky State Board of Elementary and Secondary Education, August.

Council for Better Education v. Collins, Kentucky, 1988.

Cubberly, Ellwood P. 1905. *School Funds and Their Apportionment*. New York: Teachers College, Columbia University.

Johns, Roe. 1971. ''The Development of State Support for Public Schools,'' *Status and Impact of Educational Finance Programs*, R. L. Johns, K. Alexander, and D. Stoller, eds., Gainesville, Florida: National Education Finance Project.

Kentucky Association of School Administrators. 1992. *KASA Hotline Newsletter*, 21(4).

Kentucky Department of Education. 1990. Summary of House Bill 799.

Kozol, Jonathan. 1992. *Savage Inequalities*. New York: Jossey Bass.

Legislative Research Commission. 1991. *Office of Education Accountability: Annual Financial Report* (December).

Lexington Herald Leader. 1992. ''One in Four School Districts to Get No New State Money,'' Feb. 15, pp. 1 and 10.

Mort, Paul R. 1924. *The Measurement of Educational Need.* New York: Teachers College, Columbia University.

Mort, Paul R. 1933. *The National Survey of School Finance: State Support for Public Education.* Washington, D.C.: The American Council on Education.

Prichard Committee for Academic Excellence. 1992. *Perspectives,* 3(Spring).

Rose v. Council for Better Education, Kentucky, 1989.

Serrano v. Priest, California, 1971.

Strayer, George D. and Robert Murray Haig. 1923. *The Financing of Education in the State of New York, Vol. 1,* report of the Educational Finance Inquiry Commission. New York: Macmillan Co.

Updegraff, Harlan. 1922. *Rural School Survey of New York State: Financial Support* (unpublished).

CHAPTER 6

Primary School

ONCE upon a time, there was a place . . . a magical place. It was bright and clean. Children who came to this place were happy. They felt safe! The adults in this place loved children . . . accepted them for what they were . . . nurtured them . . . protected them . . . helped them grow. Both children and adults worked hard, and most importantly, worked together. Mutual respect between the children and the adults grew over time. They protected each other. They supported each other. They celebrated together.

This place seemed to provide children with a window to the world—a world filled with ideas, adventure, and excitement. Parents stood in awe as they watched their children grow and learn in this place. For the children, each day seemed more exciting than the last as they explored a new country, or concept, or idea. For the children entering this place, it was like looking through a giant kaleidoscope, each new pattern more exciting than the last . . . bringing more questions, more ideas. The teachers guided the children toward answers to these questions. It was easy for everyone to see the children growing, learning. One only had to sit and talk to a child for an understanding of what had been accomplished.

The children remained curious, excited, and confident. The teachers remained caring, supportive, and respected. When the children left this place, there were tears from the children, the parents, and the teachers . . . and smiles for what lay beyond.

Everyone understood what was being accomplished in this place. The spark of curiosity within each child became a blazing fire, an eternal light to burn throughout the life of the child. The child grew to believe in him/herself; the child gained an attitude of confidence and of self-reliance; a deep, abiding love of learning; and a respect for the adults and the other children in this place—a place called primary school.

This vision for what primary school could be was created by the

Kentucky Department of Education (KDE) between April, 1990, and July, 1991. It was embodied in the KDE publication, *The Wonder Years*, and carried forward by the reorganized KDE in the draft program advisory and draft action plan distributed in March, 1992. The program was built upon the statutory requirement, KRS 158.030 (2), which states,

> "Primary school program" means that part of the elementary school program in which children are enrolled from the time they begin school until they are ready to enter the fourth grade. Notwithstanding any statute to the contrary, successful completion of the primary school program shall be a prerequisite for a child's entrance into fourth grade. The State Board of Elementary and Secondary Education shall establish, by regulation, methods of verifying successful completion of the primary school program pursuant to the goals of education as described in KRS 158.6451. (KDE, 1990, p. 232)

Although initially there was some question as to whether kindergarten was part of the Primary School program, the statute clearly stated that any child who was five years old on or before October 1 of a given year was to enter primary school. Kindergarten, in the state of Kentucky, is mandated as a half-day program, instead of whole days, five days a week.

Before passage of the bill, the United States had no statewide examples that could serve as models for the development of this program. However, the statute stated that the "ungraded primary program . . . shall be implemented by the beginning of the 1992−93 school year."

Responsibility for the design of the program was given to a Department of Education matrix team. Matrix teams (Steffy, 1991) were used to develop the initial implementation strategies for most of the programmatic initiatives in KERA. Membership on these teams was made up of Department staff who had an interest in a particular programmatic initiative with work on the teams being completed after their normally assigned work. For example, the chair of the matrix team responsible for the conceptual design of the primary school program, Linda Hargan, served as the associate superintendent for exceptional children. Her duties as associate superintendent were demanding and encompassed more than a forty-hour week. Nevertheless, because of her dedication and belief in the philosophical basis of the primary school, she took on the additional responsibility of chairing the team for developing the Primary School program.

Similar stories could be told of the other matrix team chairpersons. This early work, accomplished between the passage of the bill in April, 1990, and the reorganization of the Department on July 1, 1991, was completed by employees from the "old" Kentucky Department of Education. This work included the design and implementation of the Preschool program, assistance to the Cabinet of Human Resources in the creation of the Youth and Family Services Center program, development of the SEEK formula, design of the Extended School Services program, delivery of awareness level professional development, and initial training for school-based decision making. In addition, development of the new state curriculum standards was underway several months prior to the passage of the bill. Other initiatives, including formation of the Professional Standards Board, creation of a new State Board for Elementary and Secondary Education, and implementation of a statewide Principal Assessment Program, began soon after the bill was passed and before the reorganization of the Department.

Under the direction of the new commissioner, Department of Education employees have developed a comprehensive performance assessment system, designed a Regional Service Center network, designed a statewide technology system, created a process for state approval of professional development, restructured the State Department of Education, and formalized the action plan for implementation of the Primary School program. Development of this program offered a unique set of challenges. In the spring of 1990, initial activities focused on identifying primary school models within the state, nation, and the world; conducting regional awareness sessions to explain the law; and compiling the research base upon which the program would rest. Two resources were identified early in the development of the program: the reissued book by John Goodlad and Robert Anderson, *The Non-Graded Elementary School* (1987); and the work being done in British Columbia on the creation of a mandated primary program. The Goodlad and Anderson book was first published in 1959. In the Introduction to the 1987 edition, these authors state

> Nongrading never became a movement as such, nor did it ever succeed in weakening the strangle-hold of the publishing industry, whose fortunes were (and are) geared to selling complete sets of textbooks for each grade level. Whatever their many virtues as resource materials for pupils and their teacher, textbooks nurture conformity and tempt teachers to cover material whether or not it is appropriate for the wide range of individual differences among pupils. (p. xi)

Successful, nationwide implementation of non-graded schools did not take place for a number of reasons. Some of the most often cited reasons include the heavy burden on teachers for record-keeping and a lack of acceptance on the part of parents for a system that did not enable parents to easily compare one child with another. These issues remain stumbling blocks that will have to be addressed in the design of Kentucky's Primary School program.

When deciding to implement non-graded schools, two important decisions during the early design of the program helped with initial statewide acceptance by teachers. First, the matrix team purposefully involved a wide range of practitioner advisory groups in the design of the program. Ideas were shared with these advisory groups and modifications in the program were made based on their input. Accompanying advisory group input was a conscious attempt to inform the public about the emerging design of the program through presentations at conferences, statewide professional development utilizing the Kentucky Educational Television Network, and periodic publications and conferences by the Department of Education. In addition, the Department provided small grants to about sixteen school sites that wanted to implement the pilot program. These two initiatives, consensus building among groups and school pilot sites, enabled the matrix team to design a solid foundation for the program. The work of the pilot sites has continued to be instrumental in providing educators with models for how the program could be developed and implemented.

The Primary School Position Statement published in *The Wonder Years* (1991, p. 8) states,

> An appropriate primary program for all children recognizes that children grow and develop as a "whole," not one dimension at a time or at the same rate in each dimension. Thus, instructional practices should address social, emotional, physical, aesthetic, as well as cognitive needs. The primary program flows naturally from preschool programs and exhibits developmentally appropriate educational practices. These practices allow children to experience success while progressing according to unique learning needs and also enables them to move toward attainment of the educational goals and capacities of the Kentucky Education Reform Act in an environment which fosters a love of learning.

The Position Statement goes on to identify seven critical attributes of the program. These critical attributes (p. 9) have become the foundation of the program. Table 6.1 identifies the attributes and lists descriptors for each.

Because of the comprehensive nature of this important program, the Department decided to implement the program in three stages. The first stage took place during the 1990–91 school year and was called Explora-

Table 6.1. Critical Attributes of Kentucky's Primary School Program.

Developmentally Appropriate Educational Practices

- Integrated curriculum
- Active child involvement, interaction, and exploration
- Use of manipulative/multi-sensory activities
- Balance of teacher-directed and child-initiated activities
- Varied instructional strategies and approaches such as whole language, cooperative learning, peer coaching/tutoring, thematic instruction, projects, learning centers, and independent learning activities, etc.
- Flexible groupings and regrouping for instruction based on interest, learning style, problem solving, skill instruction (short term), and reinforcement, random, etc.

Multi-Age/Multi-Ability Classrooms

- Heterogeneous grouping
- Flexible age ranges
- Family groupings

Continuous Progress

- Students progress at own rate as determined by authentic assessment
- Promotes social, emotional, physical, aesthetic, cognitive development
- Success oriented
- Non-competitive
- Documentation of pupil progress through anecdotal records, observations, portfolios, journals, videotapes, computer disks, etc.
- Non-retention/Non-promotion

Authentic Assessment

- Occurs continually in context of classroom involvement
- Reflects actual learning experiences
- Emphasizes conferencing, observing, examining multiple and varied work samples, etc.
- Documents social, emotional, physical, aesthetic, and cognitive development

Qualitative Reporting Methods

- Descriptive, narrative, ongoing
- Reflect a continuum of pupil progress
- Varied formats such as portfolios, journals, videotapes, narratives, etc.

Professional Teamwork

- Securing regular time for planning/sharing
- Varied instructional delivery systems such as team teaching, collaborative teaching, peer coaching, etc.
- Regular communication among all professional staff (PE, Music, Art, Special Education, Gifted, Chapter I, etc.)

Positive Parent Involvement

- Home/School partnerships
- School/Community partnerships
- Continuous information exchange

tion. This was a time for districts to implement awareness activities that would enable faculty to gain an understanding of the changes necessary to move from the traditional elementary concept of schooling to the "success oriented" Primary program. During stage one, districts were encouraged to engage in the following activities: reading, attending conferences, visiting resource schools, sharing and discussing information and generally finding out about primary school. To provide guidance to districts beginning this process, the Department prepared a series of hypothetical implementation plans that could be used as models (see Figure 6.1). Each model addressed the critical attributes of the program and listed suggestions for curriculum, organization, instruction, learning environment/collaboration, learning environment/assessment, and learning environment/parent involvement. Each model describes activities that could take place during orientation, during initial implementation, and during full implementation.

The second stage, called Orientation, dealt with preparation for the change. This stage took place during the 1991–92 school year and included,

> Applying information gained from the Exploration stage to district, school, and individual considerations of Philosophy, Curriculum and Instruction, Organization, Assessment, and the Learning Environment for Primary School. During Orientation, studies of the district curriculum should be made in order to align it with the Curriculum Framework and the Valued Outcomes at the fourth grade level. Assessment strategies and the Continuous Assessment Program should be re-examined as well. District decision makers and School Councils (where they are in place) should be involved in these processes. (p. 14)

Districts were told that during the spring of 1992, they would have to develop an action plan for each school describing how the district intended to achieve full implementation of the Primary School program by the beginning of the 1995–96 school year.

The final stage was Implementation. Implementation was described as a "process, not an event" and was designed to take place over a period of time, depending on the level of expertise at the school and the nature of the students. During the 1992 legislative session, the Department's design for a gradual implementation of the program was questioned by key legislators. A bill was introduced in the Senate to mandate *full* implementation by 1993–94. The filing of this bill brought swift, strong reaction from the field. Most felt the implementation of the program was moving ahead at an acceptable pace, given all of the demands of KERA.

Below are three examples of hypothetical plans (A, B & C) from the beginning of the implementation stage through several years. Each program is different in its own way within the framework of the primary program. Each program is addressing the critical attributes but different strategies and procedures are being used to implement an exemplary primary school program by 1995-96. There will be many other variations of many different approaches within the framework of the primary school. There may even be different techniques happening within the same building. Strategies identified may become a part of a school Action Plan.

PLAN A

	Orientation	Implementation		
		92-93	93-94	94-95
Curriculum	All subjects are taught separately	Several interest centers are designed to extend and enhance the daily curriculum/ Center time occurs for a block of time in the afternoon after most content/ skills have been introduced/ Centers change throughout the year, activities in each center changes weekly	Centers expanded to include all content areas and are kept throughout the year/ Extra centers are incorporated and changed throughout the year/ Activities change weekly, support the curriculum, and are open-ended to allow for varying ability levels/ Center time block is increased	Open centers: students move between centers and small group instruction/ Centers expanded to include all the arts/ Children involved in planning designing and evaluating activities/ Students make most of their own choices/ Activities are performance based
Organization	One teacher teaches the classroom	One teacher teaches in the classroom and guides center flow and activities	Two teachers combine classes (of two different years in school)/ About 1/2 of children stay with their last year teacher Activities and subject matter are presented to entire group/ Small groups are used for skill building/ Teachers team teach, plan and support each other through the day	Family grouping continues/ Older students work with new students to understand the routines and expectations The two teachers work as one
Instruction	Textbooks are used for each subject with field trips, experiments and specific activities added to the science and social studies curriculum/ Some math manipulatives and real items are used for math	Basal readers used for core of instruction/ Good literature and print rich environment abound Special area teachers and aides assist in management and flow of center traffic	All textbooks used as reference and supplemental materials Students assigned to cooperative learning groups quarterly	Cooperative learning groups are a vital part of the integrated day Extensive resources available for students' use (globes, maps, reference books, a wide variety of real items, etc.)

Figure 6.1. Sample Phases in Implementing Primary School. Source: KDE, The Wonder Years, 1991.

121

PLAN A

| | Orientation | Implementation | | |
	92-93	92-93	93-94	94-95
Learning Environment/ Collaboration	Children with special needs (special education classes, speech, Chapter I tutoring, gifted education, etc.) are pulled out of classroom during the day	Some collaboration with tutoring and speech/ Other programs still pull-out but teachers planning together more/ Librarian helps to secure a variety of quality literature for classroom use and helps regularly with reading center	Collaborative model started with other special needs students/ Special area teachers help with ideas for centers/ Portable computer lab available for all students	Speech and Chapter I teachers continue, modify and perfect collaborative model to meet needs of students and styles of teachers/ Collaborative model used but some pull-out programs are still needed for some children/ Special area teachers, including the librarian and computer teacher, work with the classroom/ Also involved in setting up and maintaining particular centers and related activities and instruction
Learning Environment	Every student has his/her own desk and is expected to work on his/her assignments	Materials are available and accessible to students/ Children are allowed to move, choose centers and to talk with peers/ Centers are arranged around the room in many different ways/ Work areas vary with particular centers/ Tables are used for large and small teacher - directed instruction	More tables and comfortable areas for learning are set-up throughout room/ Students actively involved in their own learning	Classroom environment changes to accommodate centers and activities available/ Children are responsible for their own learning
Assessment	Letter grades are given and reports cards sent home quarterly/ Children are retained when not meeting defined expectations	Starts keeping portfolios and other samples of work performance (authentic assessment)/ Work performances broken down into skills that generate fourth grade outcomes/ Skills listed as a continuum/ Uses report card but changes evaluation to read: steady progress, improving and needs more time/ No retention/ Family grouping - will keep about 1/2 of students next year	Moves to progress report with narrative descriptions of progress/ Continues with portfolios/ Begins with anecdotal record keeping/ No retention/no promotion/ Family grouping continues/ Skills continuum generated for each center and correlated with authentic assessment	Authentic assessment and qualitative recording methods driven by developmental appropriate curriculum/ Children initiate audio and video taping of performances and projects/ Family grouping continues
Learning Environment/ Parent Involvement	Parents asked to participate on field trips and party days/ Parents requested to attend conferences when problems arise	Parents asked to help in the classroom on a regular basis/ Parent/teacher/student conferences established for all students/ Emphasis is placed on what a child does well	Parents form a special council to help with school-based management for next year/ Parents actively involved/ Three parent/teacher/student conferences held yearly	Parents are active members of school based management council/ Parents work with local businesses to secure more computers/ Narratives sent home regularly/ Conferences held every quarter

Figure 6.1 (continued). Sample Phases in Implementing Primary School. Source: KDE, The Wonder Years, 1991.

PLAN B

	Orientation	Implementation		
		92-93	93-94	94-95
Curriculum	Content areas taught traditionally Language arts supplemented with daily journal writing and literature based reading Math manipulatives are added to the math curriculum ACES (Activity Centered Elementary Science) is being adopted Three computers added to classroom Writing and editing emphasized	Children from two grades work together Whole language approach being started/ journaling, process writing, independent reading, etc./ Language is integrated to include parts of all content areas/ Mini-skill groups used when needed Specific programs are used when they fit into the curriculum (they are not forced, nor do they drive the curriculum) Math taught without the use of workbooks by using manipulatives and "Math Their Way" approach Social studies, science and math ability grouped for skill study Programming is emphasized in technology One more new computer added Charts developed to assist teachers in adequately addressing fourth grade outcomes	Integrated curriculum Broad based themes are used (and changed four times per year/ Topical themes are used that support the broad based theme and are changed when the children are ready to tackle a new topic/ These themes generate the "connections" that integrate the curriculum and make it real to the students. Reading and writing are demonstrated daily Curriculum is performance based Children are involved in planning and evaluating the themes, the class's progress and their own progress/ Group meetings are held daily Librarian and special area teachers are invited into the classroom to help with group planning/ All areas are incorporated into the themes/ Literature, art, music and PE are included throughout the day/ Most technology is taught in class, not the lab/ More computers are added to classroom setting Skills continuum organized to assure fourth grade outcomes are addressed	Developmentally Appropriate Curriculum in place Continuously fine-tunes curriculum and desired knowledge base for attainment of performance outcomes
Organization	Multi-age groupings of two or more age spans, forming several classes in a "pod" 5 year olds (First year students) come in for buddy reading Some ability grouping for content area. Students move from teacher to teacher and are regrouped throughout the day/ Children involved with all teachers and have contact with every student in the pod (through the regrouping) for a "family" feeling PE, music, art, creative writing and field trips are multi-ability grouped	Family grouping is used/ Children stay in same homeroom/ New students enter into the class when openings are left by outgoing students/ Students heterogeneously grouped for entire language arts block/ First year students involved with buddy reading and special projects	Family grouping is ongoing/ Children are in charge of helping new students feel comfortable in this situation The entire pod is heterogeneously grouped (except for special skill groups on an ad hoc basis) First year students are in class half their school day	Grouping and regrouping adjusted throughout the year to meet children's needs First year students involved for most of the day Family grouping continues

Figure 6.1 (continued). Sample Phases in Implementing Primary School. Source: KDE, The Wonder Years, 1991.

PLAN B

	Orientation	Implementation		
		92-93	93-94	94-95
Instructional/ Teamwork	Teachers specialize in specific content areas but plan the curriculum together / Pod teachers have approximately 1/2 hour planning time together daily / Teachers read and attend workshops on whole language/ All staff development is geared towards this area	Teachers plan together and start facilitating learning rather than teaching / Teachers feel like real "team" and work together for the "whole" program / Staff development emphasis is on theme development and integrated curriculum / Daily team planning time is essential	Teachers facilitate the day and they observe and conference regularly with students They ask questions for high level thinking skills to be developed / Staff development emphasis is on Gardiner's seven intelligences and how to incorporate them into next year's curriculum / Teachers are excited about learning and plan to develop new strategies every year	Teachers start charting activities and strategies that address each of the seven intelligences / Emphasis is on providing equal opportunities for all intelligences. / Creative ideas are being pursued to ensure planning time with all teachers (including special area and needs teachers)
Learning Environment/ Collaboration	Collaborative model for all special needs population put into effect/ Extra planning and adaptation to meet all children's needs are necessary	Special needs teachers and pod teachers plan and work together/ Careful observation of students is performed by all "pod" staff	Collaborative model working smoothly / Teachers, aides, and students work well smoothly	Special needs children are developing high self-esteem
Learning Environment	Children sitting at desks/ Desks grouped when appropriate/ Tables provided for group times / Reading corner designated	Tables bought and bean bag chairs donated / Carpet squares laid down in corners / Some desks still available / Space provided for each child's belongings / Children move around as they learn	Children may work where they feel most comfortable/Classroom arrangement changes daily / Free selection of materials and work stations available to all students / A continuous low hum fills the room / Children stay actively involved and busy / Cooperative learning groups used for certain activities / Shelves and supplies at children's level	Students take responsibility for their classroom / Classroom environment guided by curriculum and instruction

Figure 6.1 (continued). Sample Phases in Implementing Primary School. Source: KDE, The Wonder Years, 1991.

124

PLAN B

	Orientation	Implementation		
		92-93	93-94	94-95
Assessment	Each child has his/her own daily plan, developed by the pod teachers/ Each child has his/her own portfolio/ Teachers carry clip boards and jot down notes as needed (anecdotal records) Report cards are changed to progress reports	Teachers and students write daily plans together during their bi-weekly conferences They plan (at the beginning of the week) and review (at the end of the week)/ Students file their own papers in their portolios/ Evaluation is authentic and performance based Daily plans, anecdotal records, and portfolios are used in parent conferences (The progress report is no longer used)	Students write their own plans Students consult and conference with teachers regularly	Children are given responsibility for their own learning and for evaluating themselves/ Conferencing occurs regularly with peers and teachers Performance "matches" outcomes
Learning Environment/ Parent Involvement	The school chooses to implement school based decision making/ Parent Council is formed Parents welcome in the classroom/ Parents invited to participate in any way they can Parents asked to conference twice a year	Parents ionvolved in reading and writing with children during class time Parents help to raise money for multiple sets of good literature books and new computers Parents asked to conference three times per year/Weekly narratives go home	Parents working to buy more math manipulatives and computers for classroom Students included in parent/teacher conferences	Parents actively involved in classrooms and as support personnel Parents initiate community based involvement with area businesses/ Grants are written for more comfortable furnishings and to expand the multiple intelligences research to be used in the following years

Figure 6.1 (continued). Sample Phases in Implementing Primary School. Source: KDE, The Wonder Years, 1991.

125

PLAN C

	Orientation	Implementation		
		92-93	93-94	94-95
Curriculum	Units/themes for science and social studies Manipulative math Faculty starts developing their own curriculum framework including desired outcomes, goals and standards for student performance	Continues integrated social studies, science and math/ Supplements the basal reader with literature based instruction (throughout year moves away from basal teaching) School's outcomes are incorporated in KERA's outcomes Framework is integrated with curriculum and instruction strategies	Theme based instruction expands to incorporate literature based reading and other content areas Curriculum and instructional strategies are driven by the performance outcomes	Theme-based integrated curriculum in all content areas (including whole language) Student's knowledge and performance directly linked with expected fourth grade outcomes
Organization	Self-contained classroom	Mixes two age groups for social studies and science (about 1 1/2 hours per day) multi-age/multi-ability Starts Cooperative Learning	Starts family groupings (keeps most students from last year) adds in new second year students to have at least two age groups in team Multi-ability grouping continues in social studies and science and now in reading and language Cooperative Learning Groups used regularly	Multi-age/multi-ability all day Includes first year students for about an hour per day - each student becomes a member of a cooperative learning group
Instructional Teamwork	Shares ideas and materials mainly with one other teacher/ Collaborates on themes with the one teacher/ Makes time to work together Works closely with librarian to get books and materials relative to the science and social studies themes/units Asks for input with special area teachers related to themes/units	Team planning of themes being taught in social studies and science - 2 age groups (multi-ability) Secures planning time once a week Librarians, along with special area and special needs teachers, start incorporating the themes into their own instructional time/ These teachers are asked to be involved in planning when possible	Total team teaching with one other teacher in two adjacent rooms/ door open all the time/ teachers and students move from room to room depending on activities Secures daily planning time Special area teachers take multi-age groups Librarian moves toward "open library time" with classrooms having special skill classes on an ad hoc basis	Adds a third teacher to their team and works together closely with kindergarten teacher Daily planning continues Collaborative model used for special area teachers Art, Music, and PE valued and incorporated throughout the day

Figure 6.1 (continued). Sample Phases in Implementing Primary School. Source: KDE, The Wonder Years, 1991.

126

Many educators felt that speeding up the full implementation might jeopardize the entire program.

The events planned between April, 1990, and June 30, 1991, by the Department of Education, to design and implement the program between April, 1990, and June 30, 1991, are summarized below (KDE, 1991, *Implementation Report*, pp. 101–104).

PROCESS

(*1*) April–May–June, 1990
- literature review, compilation of resources on primary schooling and non-graded education
- development of training materials, handouts, and transparencies for "awareness level" training at regional meetings
- organization of a "study group" within the Department of Education
- delivery of regional meetings to central office personnel
- delivery of awareness training for KDE staff
- development of list of resource personnel in universities and local school districts
- meeting of study group to organize action plan for primary school initiatives
- continued research/identification of model programs, parameters of existing models, expansion of bibliography and other resources
- sessions held with resource person from Vermont
- involvement of thirty local school districts in creating a list of principals from ungraded elementary schools
- development of brochure to be used for public information
- expansion of study group to include university and local district persons from across the state
- presentation to Kentucky Association of School Superintendents on primary school
- meeting with KDE study group to share materials, update and develop plans for primary school activities
- Kentucky Education Television telecast for principals
- initial development for primary school training institutes in October

(2) July – August – September, 1990
- meeting with KDE study group to finalize "Principles" and "Survey of Existing Practices"
- presentation on primary school to elementary educators at Eastern Kentucky University
- distribution of "Principles" for ungraded primary schools and "Ungraded Primary Program Survey" to all elementary buildings
- development of materials for August regional meetings
- establishment of dates and sites for primary institute
- bringing together in-state practitioners to explore primary school concept and to gather input from practitioners on preliminary plans for primary school initiative
- completion of parameters for model school sites for staff development activity in 1990–91
- finalization of *Primary School Initiative: Preliminary Plans 1990–91*
- presentation on primary school to administrators of Ohio Valley Educational Cooperative
- sessions at regional meetings
- workshop on primary school for all elementary teachers in Bardstown
- mailing to all elementary building principals and central office staff inviting participation in Primary School Institute
- first meeting with staff development site contact people
- presentation on primary school to representatives from colleges of teacher education
- mailing to superintendents inviting participation with staff development sites
- arrangements for Primary School Institutes – facilities, consultants, printing, etc.
- second planning meeting for Institute
- presentation on primary school at Western Kentucky Chapter I Conference
- presentation on primary school at Kentucky Social Studies Conference
- pre-registration due for October Training Institute
- interviews to determine content for November *Ed News* issue featuring primary school
- development of a database program to manage assignment of 2,500 participants in Primary School Institute

(*3*) October — November — December, 1990
- arrangements for Primary School Institutes — facilities, consultants, printing, etc.
- primary school presentation at Southern Elementary School in Lexington
- primary school presentation at National Association of Colleges of Teacher Education in Lexington
- primary school presentation to teachers at Spalding College in Louisville
- development of a slide presentation for opening at Primary School Institute
- primary school update to superintendents at KEDC
- primary school presentation to Jefferson County curriculum group
- Primary School Institutes in Louisville
- press conference on primary school
- third meeting with staff development projects
- *Ed News* featuring primary school
- presentation at Southeast Regional IRA Conference
- presentation at Murray State University for higher education representatives and teachers from local districts
- presentation at Bethany House for parents and representatives from social services agencies
- presentation at Prichard Committee Conference
- regional meetings for institutes on higher education (IHEs)
- fourth meeting with primary school staff development sites
- meeting of KDE primary school study team and staff development site coordinators to develop forms and coordination of directives and resources within KDE

(*4*) January — June, 1991
- compilation of new listing of materials/resources/sites
- identification of subgroup of statewide committee to formulate key issues for resolution regarding primary school
- meeting with early childhood and elementary education higher education personnel
- meeting to synthesize statewide philosophy or framework for Kentucky primary schools
- ongoing meetings with staff development sites
- meeting with statewide PTA organization to plan strategies for informing parents about primary school

- meeting sponsored by University of Louisville to address teacher training issues regarding primary school
- identification of subgroup of statewide committee to work on intensive public relations campaign for parental awareness
- development of regulations on operational procedures for primary schools
- development of materials, radio and TV spots, etc, for public relations campaign
- ongoing meetings with staff development sites
- regional meetings
- beginning of public relations campaign
- planning Primary Institute II
- regulations passed by State Board for Elementary and Secondary Education on operational procedures
- Primary Institute II—statewide conference to present findings, share materials developed, etc., from staff development sites

As the program evolved, a number of policy issues surfaced. These included the following:

(*1*) Role of kindergarten—must it be included? How can half-day programs be effectively included, particularly afternoon sessions?

(*2*) What does "implementation" mean in the statute? How much multi-age grouping is required? Can we start slowly and build?

(*3*) Need for state-level identification of consistent framework or philosophy for "ungradedness." What does the term mean?

(*4*) Teacher certification issues—particularly regarding 1−8 certification and "K" only certification

(*5*) Building-level organization plans that are inconsistent with the K−3 block. K−1, K−2, etc.

(*6*) Flexibility in use of state textbook dollars to be used for more developmentally appropriate materials in primary schools—manipulative, etc.

(*7*) Potential conflicts between primary school effective teaching practices and the direct instruction model embedded in the Kentucky Internship Training Program

(*8*) Coordination with federal programs—effective collaborative models for Chapter I, Special Education, Gifted programs

(*9*) Massive need for teacher training—inservice and preservice levels—and very few qualified resource people in-state to do training

(*10*) Public information/parent awareness and training on developmentally appropriate practices. When should state-level campaigning begin?

(*11*) Development of the regulations (which should be flexible) establishing the procedures for an ungraded primary program to guide districts during this developmental phase

(*12*) Establishment of the criteria for successful completion of the primary school, including guidelines for decision making relative to gifted and handicapped children

(*13*) Class size issues—Can they be waived in a building that doesn't yet have a school council?

(*14*) Planning time for teachers in the primary school

During the time when the Department was undergoing reorganization until the time when the position of division director for Early Childhood was filled, these policy issues were being addressed. This Division is responsible for both the Primary program and the Preschool program.

By September, 1991, the new division director for Early Childhood arrived at the state capitol. Work continued on the development of the program through the winter of 1992. By mid-March a draft program advisory and draft action plan were in the final review process (*Program Advisory*, 1992). Each school in the state offering primary school was required to complete a Primary Program Action Plan and send it to the State Department by May 31, 1992.

The Plan required schools to describe how they would fully implement the program over a three-year period. Assurances had to be filed with the Plan and required the signature of the building principal, a teacher representing all staff, and a representative of the parents. If the school had a school council, the Plan had to be submitted to the council for approval by May 15, 1992. Those signing the Plan assured the State Department that:

(*1*) They have analyzed the curriculum and instructional techniques, class organizational patterns, assessment techniques, criteria of the learning environment, level of parent involvement, and instructional resources that exist within the school.

(*2*) A comprehensive action plan has been developed.

(3) The action plan reflects a progression toward full implementation of the critical attributes by 1995–96.

(4) All special needs children have been addressed.

(5) Personnel involved in action plan development included primary teachers, intermediate teachers, special education teachers, parents, elementary principals, school counselors, assistants/aides, music teachers, school council members, Chapter I teachers, art teachers, physical education teachers, librarians, and other support staff.

In addition, those signing the Action Plan assured the state that the Plan was completed in full and that copies of the summary were available to teachers, parents, and all those involved with primary students (KDE, 1992, *Program Advisory*, pp. 15–16). For the purpose of developing the Plan, KDE prepared a Matrix Chart (*Program Advisory*, p. 5) which consolidated the seven critical attributes into four key planning factors: the learning environment, developmentally appropriate curriculum, assessment, and educational partnerships (see Figure 6.2).

To assist in designing a response to each of the four key planning factors, the Department provided a list of questions to consider in developing the Plan. Schools were not required to answer these questions on the forms, but they were encouraged to use them to guide their discussions.

QUESTIONS TO CONSIDER

Learning Environment

(1) How does an integrated curriculum affect the environment?

(2) Do any of the other quality indicators affect the environment? How? Is this reflected in your plan and summarized on this form?

(3) How will your classrooms be arranged?

(4) What type of schedule will be followed?

(5) How will classes, children, and teachers be organized?

(6) How will multi-age/multi-ability classrooms evolve?

(7) How will flexible groupings with flexible age ranges be organized?

(8) How will all special needs children be accommodated?

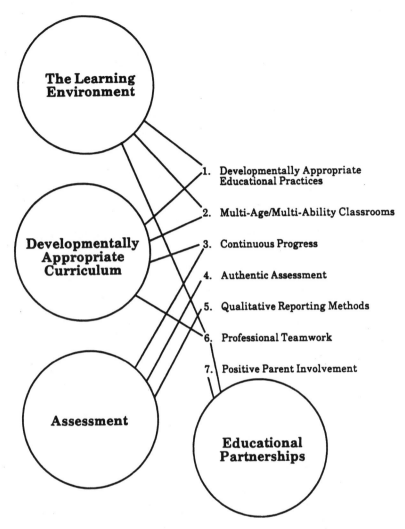

Figure 6.2. Matrix Chart of the Seven Critical Attributes. Source: Kentucky Department of Education, 1992.

(9) What materials and equipment will be needed?

(10) How will teachers have common planning time?

Developmentally Appropriate Curriculum/Instruction

(1) What approaches will be used?

(2) What strategies will be used?

(*3*) What materials will be used?

(*4*) How will curriculum be integrated?

(*5*) Does the curriculum reflect a global community? Is it multi-cultural and non-sexist?

(*6*) What instructional techniques will be used to deliver the curriculum?

(*7*) How may instruction vary?

(*8*) When will children be grouped and regrouped?

(*9*) How will children be grouped and regrouped?

(*10*) Is there a balance of individual, small group, and large group activities?

(*11*) Does the curriculum and instruction allow for a wide range of abilities?

(*12*) How will continuous progress affect your curriculum? Your instruction?

(*13*) Does the documentation and record keeping system of progress reflect the curriculum, techniques, and strategies?

(*14*) Is the curriculum aligned with Kentucky's goals and valued outcomes?

(*15*) How will special needs students be accommodated or included?

Educational Partners

(*1*) How will teachers work together?

(*2*) What types of collaboration will be used?

(*3*) How will parents be involved?

(*4*) How will the community be involved?

(*5*) How will teachers secure common planning time or other communication measures?

(*6*) How will the school regularly communicate to parents, community members, and other district schools?

(*7*) Are you including all personnel involved with primary students in some type of group planning? How often? What creative methods could assist you in obtaining some whole group planning?

(*8*) How will preschoolers (public, private, and Head Start) be transitioned into the Primary program?

(*9*) How will fourth-year students be transitioned into fourth grade?

Assessment

(*1*) Does the assessment reflect Kentucky's learning goals and outcomes?

(*2*) Is the assessment authentic?

(*3*) Is the assessment performance-based?

(*4*) Does the assessment reflect continuous progress for all children in all five domains (social, emotional, physical, aesthetic, and cognitive)?

(*5*) Is the whole child assessed in all five domains?

(*6*) Does the assessment reflect the curriculum, strategies, and approaches?

(*7*) Is the child involved in self-evaluation?

(*8*) Are all staff members who render services to a child involved in his/her assessment in all five domains?

(*9*) Are parents involved in the assessment?

(*10*) What qualitative recording methods will be used?

(*11*) Are parents regularly informed of their children's progress through authentic assessment? (KDE, 1992, *Program Advisory*, pp. 9, 13, 17, and 21.)

Each year, by June 1, schools must submit a program evaluation form describing what worked, what didn't work and why, and what adjustments were made.

Preparation for the implementation of this statewide program has been comprehensive, has continued throughout the reorganization of the Department; and has evolved over time based on the feedback provided by an elaborate state network of competent Kentucky educators. The vision of those who crafted KERA was for the development of a learning environment that was success oriented, where all children could learn at their own rate and in their own way. The work that has been completed thus far has positioned the state to achieve this objective.

Currently in Kentucky, approximately 20 percent of the children entering fourth grade have been retained. The cycle of school failure has already begun for these youngsters. Imagine a future where children are exposed to a learning environment where they succeed for the first four years of school.

Kentucky educators have attempted to describe that environment around the seven critical attributes. Appendix C describes what this environment would look like.

Over the next three years, teachers, parents, and administrators working in Kentucky's Primary program will attempt to make the dream come true. The program has been well planned, is based on research, and has been designed with the involvement of a large constituency of Kentucky educators. The pilot sites have become strong advocates for the program. Many other districts have initiated their own pilot primary programs. Generally, feedback from these pilots has been very positive. Teachers who were initially skeptical about the program have become strong supporters of the program. Teacher testimony about the success of the program is commonly heard across the state. As a result of the initial acceptance of the program, teachers at the middle and secondary levels are beginning to think about how the critical attributes of this program could be embraced at a higher level. This outcome is exactly what was envisioned by the creators of the legislation.

Imagine what it would be like to receive students from the Primary program who had experienced four years of a success-oriented learning environment and who could demonstrate skills at high levels of proficiency. This demonstration of student achievement would be captured in the student's portfolio and would be available to parents, teachers, and other students for review.

> In every task the most important thing is the beginning . . . especially when you deal with anything young and tender.
>
> —Plato, *The Republic*

From all indications so far, the Kentucky Primary School program has had a good beginning.

EXTENDED SCHOOL SERVICES

Since all children do not learn at the same rate and in the same way, the legislature included a provision in KERA to provide additional learning time beyond the regular school day for those students who might need it. This program, combined with primary school, would provide young children with a success-oriented learning environment for the first four years of schooling. While the program would not be limited to students in primary school, it does supplement that program. KRS 158.070 (7) states, '' Schools shall provide continuing education for those students who are determined to need additional time to achieve the outcomes defined in KRS 158.6451, and schools shall not be limited to the minimum school term in providing this education. Continuing education time may include extended days, extended weeks, or extended years'' (p. 217). The program became known as Extended School Services (ESS). A decision to change the name from Continuing Education to Extended School Services was made during the summer of 1990. Continuing education has traditionally been used to describe adult education programs.

This initiative enabled districts to offer after-school, before-school, evening school, weekend school, and summer school programs.

The legislative intent behind this initiative was to enable teachers to identify students who were beginning to fall behind in any content areas at any time during the school year. Once identified, the teacher, school, or district would have the funds to design and implement an intervention strategy that would enable students to be successful. The program serves students who may fall behind in class, are at risk of being retained, are at risk of failing to graduate and are low performing. School districts began the program as early as November 1, 1990.

Statutory language did not specify the nature of the program or the mechanism for the distribution of the funds. The State Board for Elementary and Secondary Education was charged with developing regulations establishing the criteria for program design and the distribution of money. This program was generously funded by the legislature. In the first year of the biennium, $27 million was allocated. This allocation rose to $53 million during the second year. However, due to the recession causing a shortfall in state funds, the program was cut by over a third in the spring of 1992. For the 1992 – 94 biennium, $66.4 million has been allocated.

When the program began in 1990, the initial allocation was estimated to be sufficient to provide approximately one-third of the students in the state with ten additional instructional days. During the development of the reform package, there was quite a lot of discussion about extending the school year for all students. Some argued that not all students needed additional time in school. Consequently, this program was created to provide additional time for those students who might need it the most.

Development of this program raised some very interesting issues. First of all, the program was supposed to support the students' attainment of the goals specified in KRS 158.6451. When the program was designed, state curriculum standards had not been developed. The seventy-five valued outcomes were not approved by the State Board until

December, 1991. Secondly, districts put pressure on the Department of Education to distribute the money at the beginning of the 1990 – 91 school year, five months after the bill passed. The regulation stating the criteria for the allotment was prepared during June, 1990. Both the regulation and the reporting system established by the Department gave districts tremendous freedom to design the program any way they chose. Because of the diversity in program design and implementation, it has been difficult to assess the impact of the program. The formula for distributing the money was based on district average daily attendance and on student need. Districts were free to design programs in any way they thought would best meet the needs of students. Further, districts were not mandated to serve a particular type of student with these funds and districts could choose which students to serve and how to best serve them.

ESS Program Evaluated

As might be expected, this program is very popular. In an effort to determine the effectiveness of the program, the University of Kentucky was awarded a contract to evaluate the initial implementation. The program evaluation report was filed with the Department on January 31, 1992, addressing six questions (pp. 3 – 4).

(1) Who participated in the program and what type of programs were created?

(2) Were the goals of the program achieved?

(3) How did programs compare with one another?

(4) Were certain programs more successful than others?

(5) Were sufficient funds available and were they being used equitably?

(6) What barriers prevented children who needed service from obtaining that service?

Information was obtained from qualitative data collected by the Department, through telephone interviews with program coordinators and from focus group meetings held around the state. In addition to educators providing the services, participants in these meetings included parents, regular teachers, and principals. The report included information about program implementation through the fall of 1991.

From January 1, 1991, to December 30, 1991, over 156,000 students were served by the program (p. 7). This represents approximately 25 percent of the students enrolled in Kentucky schools. Nearly 50 percent of the students served were from grades Kindergarten through fifth. During the spring, summer, and fall of 1991, more male students received services than female students. In the spring and fall terms, after-school programs accounted for almost 90 percent of the preferred program design model. Saturday programs and before-school programs made up the rest.

Since there are a number of federally funded programs, such as Chapter I, Special Education, and Migrant programs, there was interest in determining the number of students participating in the ESS program who also qualified for services through federally funded initiatives. It was determined that during the spring term, approximately 28 percent of the students receiving ESS services were also receiving Chapter I services (p. 10). During the summer, that percentage fell to 1 percent and then increased to 6 percent during the fall of 1991. While students identified as requiring special education services made up over 7 percent of those served in the spring of 1991, this number dropped to less than 1 percent during the summer and continued at less than 1 percent during the fall. The category with the largest increase appeared to be children who met the federal definition of migrant. In the spring of 1991, less than 1 percent of the students enrolled were also in this federally funded program. This figure rose to 28.6 percent in the summer and 25 percent in the fall. Another category of students that rose significantly was the number enrolled in the state-funded Remediation program. This program provides extra money for establishing transitional classes for students who are not quite ready for the next elementary grade. By fall of 1991, 22 percent of the children receiving ESS services fell in this category. During the 1992 General Session, funding for this state program was eliminated because of the creation of the primary school.

The four categories of Migrant, Chapter I, Special Education, and Remediation students accounted for 54 percent of the students enrolled in ESS in the fall of 1991. It is assumed that the other 46 percent were students who did not qualify for other funded assistance. Table 6.2 shows the primary type of assistance provided during the three sessions (University of Kentucky, 1992, *Evaluation*, p. 11). Tutoring and direct instruction were the most common services provided.

Regarding whether the students were able to meet the goals established for them, the study revealed

> The achievement gap was closed, students who were in danger of being retained or failing to graduate on time were able to move ahead to the

Table 6.2. Primary Type of Assistance Provided.

Assistance	Spring 1991	Summer 1991	Fall 1991
Tutoring	45,626 (76.7)*	6,359 (19.0)	52,748 (86.0)
Counseling	422 ($<$1.0)	161 ($<$1.0)	520 (1.0)
Therapy	34 ($<$1.0)	41 ($<$1.0)	0
Study Skills	2,219 (3.7)	1,438 (4.3)	1,336 (2.0)
Direct Instr.	9,708 (16.3)	25,307 (76.0)	4,409 (7.0)

*Parenthetical numbers indicate percentages.

next level, and students who were in danger of falling behind were able to sustain their present level of performance, especially over the summer. (pp. 14−16)

Additional findings from the study indicated that it was difficult to compare the effectiveness of programs because of the idiosyncratic nature of each district, self-reported student self-concepts appeared to improve, and parents were "overwhelmingly positive" about the program. District administrators consistently expressed a desire to keep the program as flexible as possible. Nevertheless, the legislature has grown increasingly interested in documented evidence of the effectiveness of the program. Because of this legislative need, the record keeping required by the State Department has substantially increased for the 1992−93 school year.

If the program is working effectively, it is anticipated that the legislature will place the $66.5 million currently supporting the program into the general SEEK formula in 1994. In order to justify this move, they need documented evidence of program effectiveness.

Based on the results of this first study, the University of Kentucky was given a continuation grant to complete a longitudinal study of students in the program. A sample of 500 students will be compared before and after receiving ESS services in areas such as achievement scores, attendance patterns, attitudes toward school, and classroom behavior. By comparing the sample with eligible, non-participating students, the study will also measure the effect of ESS on successful transition to work, involvement in crime, income level, and single parenthood, to name a few.

Some critics of the program have suggested that changes are needed in instructional strategies during initial teaching, rather than providing additional services after the student has shown signs of difficulty. Theoretically, if the critical attributes of the Primary program are implemented, the need for these services will be diminished. Still, there are children who need the "gift of time" that this program can provide.

Over the next four or five years, both the Primary School program and Extended School Services will be closely monitored to determine whether they have achieved the dream envisioned by the creators of KERA.

REFERENCES

Goodlad, John and Robert Anderson. 1987. *The Non-Graded Elementary School*. New York: Teachers College Press.

Kentucky Department of Education. 1990. *Kentucky School Laws*. Frankfort, Kentucky: Banks-Baldwin Law Publishing.

Kentucky Department of Education. 1991. *The Kentucky Education Reform Act: 1990 Implementation Report*, Frankfort, Kentucky.

Kentucky Department of Education. 1991. *The Wonder Years*, Frankfort, Kentucky.

Kentucky Department of Education. 1992. *Program Advisory: Action Plan for KERA's Primary Program*, Frankfort, Kentucky.

Steffy, Betty. 1991. "Matrix Management for a State Department of Education," *National Forum of Applied Education Research Journal*, 1:6–12.

University of Kentucky. 1992. *Evaluation of Kentucky Extended School Services*, Lexington, Kentucky.

CHAPTER 7

Creating a Level Playing Field

Children are like snowflakes.
At first they appear to be alike,
But on close examination they are all different.
Focus on their similarities,
But understand their differences.

—Berger, 1991

ALL children do not arrive at the school house door equally prepared to learn. The legislature believed that a half-day preschool program for four-year-old, economically disadvantaged children and three- and four-year-old children with handicaps would help to improve the ability of these children to be successful in school. According to Kentucky Department of Education (KDE) records, approximately 39 percent of the 54,000 four-year-old children in the state are estimated to be at risk of educational failure. As defined by KERA, at risk of educational failure means any child who qualifies for free lunch. In addition, 10 percent of the three- and four-year-old children in the state could have handicapping conditions.

Harold Hodgkinson, director of the Center for Demographic Policy, states that about one-third of the nation's children are at risk of school failure even before they enter kindergarten (*Kappan*, September, 1991, p. 10). Multiple causes can be cited: about one-fourth of all preschool children have lived in poverty since 1987; about 350,000 children are born to mothers addicted to cocaine each year; the stereotypical family unit made up of a working father, two children, and a mother who does not work currently accounts for about 6 percent of U.S. households; one-fourth of all pregnant mothers receive no medical attention during the first trimester of pregnancy, and the number of child abuse and neglect complaints received tripled between 1976 and 1987.

It appears that the problem is not solely a Kentucky problem and it was not directly caused by the schools. In fact, the problem is so endemic that its solution has become part of President Bush's *America 2000* plan. One of the six goals of *America 2000* is "All children will enter school ready to learn."

CURRENT STATUS

The vision of the KERA Preschool Programs is a comprehensive early childhood educational delivery system which provides developmentally appropriate practices to children, integrated services to families, and interdisciplinary and interagency collaboration among organizations serving young children in Kentucky. (KDE, 1991, *Preschool Final Report*, p. 1)

At the beginning of the 1991−92 school year, all 176 school districts in the state had operational preschool programs. Of the estimated 54,000 four-year-olds, approximately 21,000 are eligible for the program. In 1990−91, 64 percent of the eligible children were served by either the state-funded program or Head Start. Head Start funds supported 7,811 children and KERA funds supported 5,659 children. In 1991−92 it is estimated that 83 percent of the eligible children will be served (p. 13).

THEORETICAL BASIS FOR PROGRAM

In a KDE publication entitled *Kentucky Preschool Programs: Overview of Child Development*, the theoretical work of Erik Erikson, Piaget, Arnold Gessell, B. F. Skinner, Albert Bandura, Walter Mischel, Roger Barker, and Urie Brofenbrenner is used as the basis for the state's Early Childhood program. Nine developmental principles were identified from a review of this literature (p. 3):

(1) Development in the early years is significant to attaining potential future development.
(2) Development is affected by maturation and learning.
(3) Development is predictable; emergence of skills occurs in a sequence. However, tempo or rate at which skills develop may vary.
(4) Development is directional. According to Gesell, development proceeds from head-to-toe (cephalocaudal) and from center part of body to outer parts (proximodistal).

(5) Development is interrelated; for example the refinement of visual skills and change in the shape of the eyeball affect the development of fine motor skills as well as attention to detail.

(6) Development is qualitative as well as quantitative. As the number of skills and patterns of behavior develop, the quality of skill becomes more refined.

(7) Development is influenced by opportunities to exercise skills or patterns of behavior through repetition.

(8) Development is continuous; may be exhibited in growth spurts and may be affected by external or internal changes.

(9) Development occurs in stages characterized by themes and patterns of behavior (Helms and Turner, 1978; Peterson, 1987; Santrock and Yussen, 1988). During the critical developmental phase of this program, technical assistance was provided by KDE staff and through five Early Childhood Regional Training Centers.

In utilizing these principles to develop Kentucky's Preschool program, the Department publication (p. 7) addressed the difference between chronological age and developmental age and the impact of individual differences caused by special needs and the environment on the growth of the child. It was noted that a child with a chronological age of four may exhibit development age differences from two to seven depending on the skill being assessed. The traditional factory school model tends to penalize children with developmental age characteristics below, and sometimes above, the chronological age. Because environmental effects, such as child abuse, dysfunctional family, or special needs may significantly impact the physical and psychological well-being of children, teachers have a responsibility to develop trusting relationships with children; demonstrate care and genuine concern for the welfare of children; enhance their self-esteem; create a friendly, accepting environment; provide materials and experiences suitable for the children's developmental level and cultural background, and recognize and validate parents as primary educators.

THE STATUTE

157.3175 Preschool education program; grant allocation; program components; exemption

(1) Beginning with the 1990−91 school year, it shall be the responsibility of each school district to assure that a developmentally appropriate half-day preschool education program is provided for each child who is four (4) years of age by October 1 of each year and at risk of educational failure. Any school district which can show a lack of facilities to comply with this section may apply for an exemption to delay implementation until 1991−92. All other four (4) year old children shall be served to the extent placements are available. The State Board for Elementary and Secondary Education, upon the recommendation of the chief state school officer, shall adopt administrative regulations establishing the guidelines for the program. Administrative regulations shall establish eligibility criteria, program guidelines, and standards for personnel.

(2) "Developmentally appropriate preschool program" means a program which focuses on the physical, intellectual, social, and emotional development of young children. The preschool program shall help children with their interpersonal and socialization skills.

(3) Funds appropriated by the General Assembly for the preschool education programs shall be granted to local school districts according to a grant allotment system approved by the State Board for Elementary and Secondary Education. Children who are at risk shall be identified on the federal school lunch program eligibility criteria for free lunch. Appropriations shall be separate from all other funds appropriated to the Department of Education.

(4) The chief state school officer shall receive and review proposals from local school districts for grants to operate or oversee the operation of developmentally appropriate preschool education programs. Districts may submit proposals for implementing new services, enhancing existing preschool education services, or contracting for services. In designing a local early childhood education program, each district shall work with existing preschool programs to avoid duplication of programs and services and to avoid supplanting federal funds.

(5) Each program proposal shall include, at a minimum:

(a) A description of the process conducted by the district to assure that parents or guardians of all eligible participants have been made aware of the program and of their right to participate;

(b) A description of the planned educational programming and related services;

(c) The estimated number of children participating in the program;

(d) Strategies for involving children with disabilities;

(e) Estimated ratio of staff to children with the maximum being one (1) adult for each ten (10) children;

(f) The estimated percentage of children participating in the program who are at risk of educational failure;

(g) Information on the training and qualifications of program staff and documentation that the staff meet required standards;

(h) A budget and per-child expenditure estimate;

(i) A plan to facilitate active parental involvement in the preschool program, including provisions for complementary parent education when appropriate;

(j) Facilities and equipment which are appropriate for young children;

(k) The days of the week and hours of a day during which the program shall operate;

(l) A plan for coordinating the program with existing medical and social services, including a child development and health screening component;

(m) Assurances that participants shall receive breakfast or lunch;

(n) Program sites which meet state and local licensure requirements;

(o) A plan for coordinating program philosophy and activities with the local district's primary school program; and

(p) An evaluation component.

(6) Programs shall reflect an equitable geographic distribution representative of all areas of the Commonwealth. (KDE, 1990, p. 193)

Section 157.318 authorizes the use of regional training centers for preschool and early childhood education authorized and funded through Public Law 99-457 for peer to peer training, consultation, and technical assistance, and Section 157.317 authorized the formation of the Kentucky Early Childhood Advisory Council. The Advisory Council included one member of the state board and sixteen members, appointed by the governor, representing the following agencies or groups: preschool teacher, public school teachers, elementary school principals, parents, child care providers, community education, the Interagency Task Force on Family Resource Centers and Youth Services Centers, the Head Start Association, the Head Start director, the Head Start program, the Infant/Toddler Coordinating Council, the Department of Health Services, the Department for Social Services, the Department for Social Insurance, the colleges of education, and the colleges of home economics. The role of the Advisory Council is to advise the chief state school officer on the implementation of early childhood education programs.

In addition, Section 157.226 provided for preschool programs for children with identified disabilities who are three or four years of age. This program became effective with the 1991–92 school year. Required attendance was not mandated. Parents could choose whether or not they wanted their children to participate in these programs.

COMPONENTS OF THE MODEL

The Kentucky Preschool Model is designed to be universal, comprehensive, inclusionary, and collaborative. The components are described in the recorded proceedings of the Early Childhood Collaboration Forum held in Shakertown, Kentucky, in May, 1991 (p. 1). The Forum was held as an opportunity for various groups that had been impacted by the legislation to come together and discuss concerns and explore issues that had surfaced in program implementation.

(*1*) Universal
- mandates availability of preschool services to all four-year-old children in Kentucky who are at or below 130 percent of poverty
- mandates availability of services to all preschool children ages three through five with handicaps, regardless of income level
- encourages preschool programs and support services for other children

(*2*) Comprehensive
- focuses on family approaches via Family Resource Centers to promote health and social service coordination, family literacy and child care as well as preschool education
- includes a family component in all preschool programs

(*3*) Inclusionary
- implements preschool services for all children in a mainstream setting, including children with gifts and talents, with disabilities and with special needs
- is supported by a nationally recognized innovation model of personnel development and credentialing: Interdisciplinary Early Childhood Education (I.E.C.E.)

(*4*) Collaborative
- encourages cooperation among fund sources and agencies for blended funding to meet mutual goals of preschool service provisions
- develops a partnership across all preschool agencies through the Early Childhood Advisory Council
- supports an interagency model for planning transition with families

Some of the issues that had surfaced during the first year of implementation included the role of private day care providers; the need to enhance collaboration across agencies serving eligible families and children; the need to see that the provisions of the memorandum of agreement with Head Start were implemented, the need to avoid the duplication of services and the need to honor the parent's choice of program provider. Resolution of some of these issues led to changes in the statute during the 1992 General Session and an expanded memorandum of understanding with Head Start. Statutory changes strengthened the requirements for districts to work with local agencies and service providers to create as many placements as possible for children who qualify for services. The local district program application was required to include a sign-off provision to ensure that local districts had held meetings with the major providers in the community and these providers were involved in the design of the program. During the first two years of the program, there were persistent accusations that a few local school districts designed and developed the program without consultation with community service providers. The legislature felt that this problem was serious enough to correct through legislation.

MEMORANDUM OF UNDERSTANDING

Program implementation required the development of a memorandum of understanding between the Kentucky Department of Education and the federally funded Head Start program to avoid concerns about supplanting. Federal law prohibits the use of state money for programs with federal funding. Since there was not enough federal Head Start money to serve all the eligible children in the state, this was not considered a supplanting issue. Initially, there was concern that Head Start agencies would transfer their money to serve three-year-old children and use the state funds to serve the four-year-old population. If that had happened, no new four-year-old children could have been served. The state money would have simply replaced the federal funds. The memorandum of agreement addressed this issue in addition to interagency cooperation, certification, and program standards.

A second memorandum of understanding was required to address facility requirements. Prior to KERA, four-year-old day care programs officially operated under the direction of the Cabinet for Human Resources. Facility requirements for these centers are different from facility requirements for K−12 schools. This memorandum of understanding expanded the K−12 facility requirements to the Preschool program if the program operated on school grounds.

The initial memorandum of understanding with Head Start was modified and the agreement was extended to 1994. The new agreement addressed the expectations for the Kentucky Department of Education and Head Start in the areas of program standards; communication and collaboration; finance related to both state funds and federal IDEA funds, and conflict resolution procedures. This updated agreement was signed by the president of the Kentucky Head Start Association, the Commissioner of Education, the regional administrator for the Administration for Children and Families and the Kentucky coordinator for the Head Start Collaboration Project.

FUNDING

The funding allocation for the four-year-old preschool program and the three- and four-year-old program for children with identified disabilities was combined. The funding allocation for fiscal year 1991 and 1992 was $18 million for the first year and $36 million for the second. The substantial increase the second year was based on the involvement of more children and the inclusion of three- to five-year-old handicapped students the second year. Since the actual amount of money required the second year was less than budgeted, the program allocation for 1992 – 94 was $33 million the first year and $37 million the second. These funds should be sufficient to cover the costs of the program. The program is estimated to be currently serving 84 percent of the eligible four-year-old children in the state and 60 percent of the eligible children with disabilities.

The funding formula for the 1990 – 91 school year included the allocations shown in Table 7.1.

Districts developed their grant proposals and budgets using estimated figures of the number of children who would be eligible. Proposals were approved based on projected figures and the budgets were modified to reflect the actual enrollment in the program as of December 1. During the second year of the program, the regulation governing the program was changed to indicate that if a child was eligible for the program at the beginning of the school year, the child would not be dropped from the program if his/her eligibility status changed.

During the first year of the program a total of 5,659 children were served with state funds. Of the $18 million available, $14,331,290 was expended, $35,000 was encumbered and $3,633,710 was carried over.

Table 7.1.

Basic grant/child	$1,730	(half of the SEEK/student amount plus an at-risk amount)
Transportation add-on (optional)	200	(did not cover all costs)
Support services add-on	200	
Initial program start-up	400	
TOTAL	$2,530	

The State Department was designated $200,000 for personnel and $100,000 for operating expenses.

The Kentucky Department of Education Early Childhood Matrix Team Final Report for 1990−91 included additional financial data.

DISTRICT BUDGETED AMOUNTS AND PERCENTAGES OF TOTAL EXPENDITURES BY CATEGORY

Data from financial reports submitted by the 130 school districts providing services for the four-year-old, at-risk students were analyzed relative to percentages of expenditures in major cost categories. The findings are summarized in Table 7.2.

COMPARISONS OF COSTS OF KERA PRESCHOOL PROGRAMS WITH COSTS OF OTHER PROGRAMS

The following sources (reported in KDE, 1991, *Final Report*) were utilized for cost comparisons with KERA Preschool programs: national statistics from a study conducted by the United States General Account-

Table 7.2.

Cost Category	Amount Budgeted	Percent of Total
Administration	$ 177,051	1.13
Instructional Staff	4,266,850	27.27
Pupil Transportation	1,864,367	11.92
Instructional Materials	369,995	2.36
Social Services	109,145	.70
Contractual Services	2,463,451	15.74

ing Office on preschools accredited by the National Association for the Education of Young Children (NAEYC), information from the Kentucky Cabinet for Human Resources on Title XX funding, and Head Start data.

KERA

The KERA funding allocation to school districts per child for 1990–91 was $2,530. The average daily costs based on the required minimum of 175 school days (2.5 hours per day) was $12.17.

NAEYC

The GAO study examined costs for 265 full-day preschools accredited by NAEYC. Because those facilities closely resemble the KERA Preschool programs in terms of quality and services, their costs can be compared to the KERA Preschool program. The average yearly per child costs in NAEYC accredited programs was $4,200. (This figure does not include in-kind contributions by the facilities, which would raise that amount to $4,794 in terms of real costs.) The average daily costs based on 260 in-class days (full days) would be $16.15 per child.

Title XX

The reimbursement rate for children participating in Title XX child care funding from CHR is approximately $9.00 per day (full day). No health screening, social services, etc., are required, so programmatically, there are differences.

Head Start

The approximate annual allocation per child for Head Start programs in 1990–91 was $2,438. Based on an average of 144 days (length of day varies) the average daily cost per child would be $16.93. Services are very similar to KERA funded programs, but include more extensive health and social services and generally are in session 3.5 hours or longer (*Final Report*, p. 15).

Given the increase in the number of districts participating in the program the second year and the addition of mandated services for the three- and four-year-old children with identified disabilities, the $36 million allocation for the second year of the program, while considered adequate, is not deemed to be excessive. The program is projected to serve approximately 4,500 three- and four-year-olds with disabilities. For funding purposes, these disabilities have been categorized as Less Intensive, Moderately Intensive, and Most Intensive. Funding for children with Less Intensive disabilities has been set at $2,516, Moderately Intensive disabilities at $5,827 and Most Intensive disabilities at $10,710 (*Final Report*, p. 14).

PROGRAM IMPLEMENTATION PROCESS

(*1*) April—May—June, 1990
- planned for KERA regional meetings
- mailed Child Count Survey to districts
- had preliminary meetings with Head Start personnel (regional and national) on how to interface the two programs
- met with Legislative Research Commission staff to define General Assembly intent
- outlined regulations in rough draft
- disseminated "Guide to Effective Early Childhood Programs"
- disseminated interim policy on certification to districts
- received Council on Teacher Education and Certification approval to continue development of Early Childhood Certification Model to submit to the new Professional Standards Board
- conducted additional awareness sessions for principals
- returned Child Count Surveys to the Department
- finalized grant allocation system
- developed program proposal
- finalized regulations (reflects closure on issues with Head Start, Cabinet for Human Resources, Transportation, Buildings and Grounds, School Food Service, etc.)
- held technical assistance meetings for grant application process
- distributed "Guide to Effective Early Childhood Programs" which was developed by the Department and "Preschool Interagency Contracting: A Technical Assistance Guide"

(*2*) July—August—September, 1990
- presented regulations to State Board for Elementary and Secondary Education
- prepared program proposals by districts
- provided consultation to districts in preparing proposals

- reviewed and approved 130 proposals
- notified districts regarding proposals and allocation
- provided technical assistance to districts initiating programs

(3) October — November — December, 1990
- provided technical assistance to districts initiating programs as needed
- designed computer program to record data regarding program
- named Early Childhood Advisory Council members
- distributed forms for December 1 enrollment count and financial report
- processed enrollment counts and made allocation adjustments
- began site visitations
- set up site visitation schedule for January through April
- evaluated two Regional Training Centers for possible model programs
- prepared newsletter for January dissemination and included publicity and starting dates on the guided observations, mentor network, self-study, and video exchange
- began photo portfolio for use in informational presentations and brochures
- arranged interviews for Head Start Collaboration Project
- developed a public awareness campaign for spring, 1991

(4) January to July, 1991
- disseminated newsletter
- contacted NAEYC accredited programs for possible use as model sites
- began recruiting mentor network
- finalized procedures and forms for mentor network, video exchange, guided observations, and self-study
- established an agenda for meeting of Early Childhood Advisory Council and finalized arrangements
- continued program visitations
- evaluated RTCs for possible model sites
- set production schedule for technical assistance booklets and video of exemplary programs
- analyzed program data
- developed 1991 — 92 proposal forms
- held regional training for proposals for non-participating 1990 — 91 districts
- revised regulations and memorandum of understanding

  – initiated discussions with universities regarding the design of a longitudinal study on the effects of the program on later school performance
  – began proposal review process

PROGRAM IMPLEMENTATION INTERVIEW

Debbie Schumaker was the unit director for Early Childhood in the Kentucky Department of Education in 1991. She has been involved in the design and implementation of major state initiatives in early childhood education for many years. Before the Department restructuring, she was co-chair of the Early Childhood matrix committee and she was the director of the Early Childhood Division in the Office of Exceptional Children. This interview was conducted on August 7, 1991.

Betty: I guess this program, more than any other, is the "star" of KERA, and that is nice to hear. In your opinion, why was it such a successful implementation?

Debbie: Well, I think there were a number of technical things done well, but, more to the point, there was a great deal of excitement in attitudes. When the General Assembly said they were going to establish preschool, school districts really took it on wholesale and wanted it to work. I think it was a matter of everyone who was involved, wanting this piece to be the very best it could be. There was a general statewide attitude that this was going to be wonderful for children. When you put that kind of attitude in combination with everybody trying hard to make sure everything works smoothly, technically, that's why it worked.

Betty: I think part of it had to do with the fact that we had a Division of Early Childhood in the Office of Exceptional Children and we had the network of Regional Training Centers around the state. Lots of people have told me that it would not have been as successful an implementation without those centers.

Debbie: That's correct! We in the Department had been working since 1986 to implement a network of support for early childhood education. Certainly not at the magnitude of the Preschool program, but pieces were ready and could be expanded upon. That is the technical aspect that is the network that built that positive attitude. Everyone wants this piece to work, to be a showcase, so that when you go into a district this is the program they showcase.

Betty: It's nice they all have these programs to showcase this year. Some of the other programs are getting bad press and some of them are floundering. The technology program was supposed to be a showcase but they have not been able to get that one off the ground. The school-based decision making is not as widely subscribed to as the legislature had hoped. So, this is the one that they are all turning to saying, "Here, this is a program created by KERA."

Debbie: Everybody sees it working. Everybody, even those who were not charging forth with a great deal of enthusiasm . . . when they saw the results, and saw the differences with the families, they were convinced. One of the most successful components of the program is working with the families. All preschool services are not just for children in the classroom. Rather, you are working with the total family, health, and social services. We believe that is going to have a long-term impact.

Betty: Parent involvement is a really important piece of this program, and I wondered how that was going.

Debbie: Very positive! Some districts didn't believe that home visits or other parent components were critical. But the proof was there when parents began saying that they really believed in the program. These parents will move up to the primary program and I think we will see some differences in the school/community relationship at the primary level because of this program . . . some different expectations.

Betty: That was really the intent behind the parental involvement in this program and the Family Resources/Youth Service Center program. Parents would become involved in the school community in a positive way and eventually you would have schools, parents, and the community working together to improve the educational system.

Debbie: Absolutely! A key component of the reform act was that there was an understanding that the schools cannot do it by themselves. We can improve curriculum. We can do any number of things that we, as educators, know are important; but, the key to success is with the family and the support of the family and all of the dynamics that go along with that.

Betty: How is the program evolving? What are the nuances in terms of the changes which you have seen?

Debbie: In terms of the program, I think we are seeing improvement in the quality of the programming. Very frankly, school districts jumped in, hired personnel and just started. Now that they are breathing a little more calmly at this point, they are really looking more closely at their self-study, program improvement, and evaluation. That area is coming along. They are understanding more about the parental involvement component. The area that has changed the most is the understanding that this is not strictly a school district program. The program is also very much a community program. Last year, when we first started, many districts were very surprised that we were talking about the importance of Head Start involvement. Funding other agencies was not something the school districts did. This year, that relationship and the involvement of Head Start has pretty much been established. Certainly, there are local glitches, but the understanding is there. The issue that did not come up during the legislative session was the issue of the private providers and private day care programs and what was going to happen with their relationship with schools and the use of contracting with that sector of the community system. Certainly, between that and the new child care block grants, which will extend services to some of the same children, the private day care situation has become an issue. That's what we are really dealing with now. What is the relationship between all of those components and how do we work together? It's a real issue to be resolved, and it won't be resolved in a year. But, five years from now, I'll feel very good about it.

Betty: The issue that surfaced in a rather volatile way was the private providers. Is that still there, but not as strong as it was before? Are districts working with the private providers?

Debbie: Some districts are. There is a greater awareness. We have certainly worked more closely with districts on their proposals. We have tried to convey that we are developing a system that doesn't include just school districts, but is a system for children and families. We are not there yet. That issue is not resolved. It will be before the General Assembly during the next General Session.

Betty: Are there other areas that will come up during the next session?

Debbie: There are two areas that will come up and be hotly debated. The first area is collaboration. The good news is that the General Assembly feels that the Department has taken a very strong position in terms of encouraging the collaboration and working with people in a technical way to operate the program. Because of the way the legislation is worded, however, we are not in a position to say that a district is required to contract or with whom they must contract. Besides collaboration, the second area that came up through questioning when we testified before the education curriculum subcommittee was the question, ''What about the children who are not income eligible or who do not have developmental delays?'' They make up about half of the four-year-old population.

Betty: So you estimate that about half of the four-year-old children in the state are eligible for the program?

Debbie: Close. When we look at the numbers of children for this current year, 1990−91, combine our figures with Head Start, we served almost two-thirds of the at-risk, eligible children. We did this in our first year of start-up. This represented almost one-fourth of all the four-year-olds in the state. This coming year, 1991-92, when we look at the expansion of the program, with all of the districts having the program and the expansion of services to preschool children with handicaps, we are projecting that we will be serving 80 percent of the eligible children. We will not be at full implementation even this year. But we are projecting that between a third and a half of all the state's four-year-olds will be involved in the program within the next few years.

Betty: What would it cost to serve all of the four-year-old children in the state?

Debbie: The projection to serve all four-year-olds is an additional $70 million and that assumes that Head Start will continue to serve approximately half of the eligible at-risk children. We also assume that not all children will choose to participate in the program. This is not a required program. Parents have a choice whether their children participate or not. So, to serve all four-year-olds, we are talking about a significant increase in state dollars. Certainly, we want to do that, but the General Assembly may not be able to afford to expand the program to serve all four-year-old children at this time.

Betty: Has transportation surfaced as an issue again?

Debbie: Yes, it has been less of the crisis this year than it was for us last year. But, there are several areas we are trying to work on and improve. One is in terms of financing. With the funding formula, there is simply a $200 add-on per child to cover transportation costs. It is not part of the regular district transportation formula. The real costs of transporting these children will vary based on the geography of the district, the equipment available, the schedule, and other factors of size and density, etc. What we have done is to conduct a survey to find out what it does cost to transport these children. For instance, in rural, western Kentucky, districts are using a third of their preschool budget for transportation. If you look at the add-on, it should be a tenth of their budget. The extra money that is needed for transportation is coming out of teacher salaries and materials for instruction. It is very problematic. It is not the feeling at the present time that simply making the transportation allowance greater, say $300 for everyone, is the correct way to go. So, we are attempting to find out what the real costs are so we can devise a method to equitably distribute the money to cover transportation.

Betty: One way to deal with that is to include the transportation costs as part of the regular district budget and not have it included as part of the preschool program budget.

Debbie: We talked about that, but one concern is that the regular transportation reimbursement is based on average daily attendance and the Preschool program is not financed on average daily attendance. That has been the glitch. That is why we are doing the survey. We are trying to determine just what the actual costs are and decide how we can fix it. There is a problem there, but there haven't been any simple, straightforward solutions. As a matter of fact, much of the cost of transportation is covered out of the regular formula. If the children are on the regular bus, we are not paying for the driver; we are not paying for the mileage; we are not paying for the vehicle, we are not paying for any of the vehicle upkeep costs. We are only paying for the monitor to be there. How to pay for the monitor and the safest location for the preschool children are located on the bus are the key issues right now. It seems that the districts that have a separate preschool bus run do better economically because they have only one monitor. (Author's note: State regulations require that any bus carrying preschool children must have a monitor aboard to assist the children in getting on and off the bus, see that they are safely delivered to a responsible adult, and to oversee their safety while they are riding the bus.) If a district can operate a preschool run, it is generally able to break even or close because they are paying just the driver and monitor. In rural districts, if they are having to have a monitor on every one of their school buses, it is costing a fortune. So, if you are running forty buses, each with a preschool youngster on it, you are paying forty monitors.

The other area which we are studying at the request of the state board is the actual vehicle and the design specifications required to safely transport young children. This is an issue of national concern. There are no national standards for school buses for children under five. Kentucky is working on those specifications. So, once again, Kentucky is leading the way. We have young children on those buses right now, and we need the right kind of buses to safely transport them.

Betty: I know you are developing a Request for Proposal to evaluate the effectiveness of the implementation of this program. What are you looking for in the request?

Debbie: For KERA, there is an overall evaluation being planned by the Department. Since some of the pieces have come on-line first, like the Preschool program, we are designing an RFP to answer some very specific questions that have been asked by the Legislative Research Commission, the General Assembly, the Office of Policy and Management, the Office of Educational Accountability, and the governor's office. They want to know how the program is going and what needs to be changed. They want us to get someone from the outside to look at this program and tell us whether we are on target. The design of that third party evaluation has just gone out for bid. We should have a contractor on board soon. The product they produce will be a two-year report on the program. Particular areas they will be looking at are cost factors, double checking what we're perceiving with an outside view of what is happening. They will be looking at the implementation from a broader base than we are. Perhaps there is another way to do this. We want the contractor to set up what we would ultimately look at as a longitudinal design and the long-term benefits of the program. That data will not be available for five to ten years. We need to start collecting appropriate information now so that a longitudinal study can be conducted. We are also looking for impact data, not just in child performance, but in overall program impact. What are the changes in families, in child rearing practices, and in health services? We are hoping to collect some, what you might call, "softer" data.

Betty: Has the transition in the Department had an impact on your program?

Debbie: Long term, I think it will be a much smoother operation. Staff was on two different floors, which required an elevator transfer. Since we are all housed together, the communication is good. For the Preschool program, that has been very beneficial. Geographic proximity in the reorganization has done quite a bit. In the short term, having unfilled, open positions has created some problems with approvals. With so many open positions, the new people are overwhelmed. But that is going to resolve itself.

Betty: Is teacher certification still an issue?

Debbie: The certification piece is closer. I've briefed the appropriate committee of the Professional Standards Board. It has not gone before the full board, but they are studying it. Their target is to be working with a regulation soon, so that something formally authorizing the teacher preparation programs to go ahead and produce a university preparation program in interdisciplinary early childhood education sometime after January, 1992. So, in terms of getting through the procedures, we are very close. The universities have been sitting there chomping at the bit and are very much ready. We also have an internship committee that has been working on making sure that the existing intern program provides the adequate support for first-year teachers working in the preschool setting. We are looking at it more as a training issue. The research upon which the whole intern program is based comes primarily out of middle and secondary programs. We do have common teaching behaviors, yet, how you look at it may be different.

Betty: I know you are still getting other states looking at what you have done to develop this program. If you were starting all over again, what advice would you have for a group of legislators from another state about the design of the program? What about timelines? What about money?

Debbie: First off, I strongly feel that money drives the system. We are assuming they want a quality program. They should look at adequately supporting it. If they cannot adequately serve all the children they would like to serve, then serve those they can adequately fund. Don't dilute the program monetarily. Secondly, in Kentucky, we had some flexibility because we were further behind in the development of preschool. We didn't have any certification in this area and that gave us flexibility to design a new credentialing program. We could also bridge the existing Head Start program and with the state Preschool program and we were open to doing some things that are not possible in some other states. So, it would be a matter of looking at what the other state's situation is and turn that situation into an advantageous one. The particular area that I would recommend they look at is the relationship between Preschool and the Childcare block grant. I don't think legislators are considering these as separate programs. KERA was implemented right before the child-care component came in, therefore, there is more emphasis on ''preschool'' than ''childcare.'' States beginning their programs now are going to deal with a different set of dynamics.

Betty: So, your focus was more on readiness and preparing four-year-old children to be successful in the school.

Debbie: The fact that the Preschool program is part of education reform in this state gives it a unique flavor. It really had to do with the timing of when we came in more than anything else. I would be concerned, in other states, if they started bringing this in as part of education reform. If the reform wasn't as broad-based as Kentucky's with the Family Resource Centers, and health and social services. They could develop a very academically oriented program. They might get kindergarten pushed down to the preschool. We are having an important impact on the kindergarten program. Because of the preschool program and the primary program, kindergarten is making some major changes in the state. It is not easy for those kindergarten teachers who have been more traditional in their orientation towards what the kindergarten program should be.

Betty: Were there any particular national associations or organizations which you utilized to help develop the program?

Debbie: Yes, as a state agency, we have access to three different technical assistance networks. Two of them are more targeted toward the handicapped program, but they have taken such a broad base since in many states, that is the only mandated preschool program. We tap into the National Early Childhood Technical Assistance Center. Through the Center, we will be meeting with a team from the Ohio Department of Education. They have a similar, integrated preschool and kindergarten program. They are bringing in some people to help us look at monitoring or self-study, to discuss how can we make sure these are quality programs. We are very excited about that. Secondly, we have the Regional Resource Center network which can help state departments get together and compare notes. Of course, everyone wants to know what Kentucky is doing. I know we are ahead, particularly in the design of preschool handicapped programs. Other states appear to be having more difficulty with the contracting issue. The third agency which has been most helpful is the Appalachian Educational Laboratory (AEL). They are sponsoring, along with Head Start, an early childhood transition forum. They will be looking at how programs like Primary, Head Start, Even Start, and Preschool are put together and coordinated at the local level. AEL will also be doing a pilot study relative to the parent involvement and materials for home visits.

Betty: Have we continued to maintain our positive relationship with Head Start? Do we have a new, signed memorandum of agreement?

Debbie: It's not signed yet. It has gone through widespread review.

When this one gets signed everyone will know what is in it. I think that has been very positive. We will still be dealing with some issues to be sure we are not supplanting Head Start funds. There are also some isolated cases of perceived lack of coordination between Head Start and the local school district, but it is much better.

Betty: It is still amazing to me that we were able to get this program started so successfully. Everyone was intent on making it work. By the time issues started to surface, the agreement was signed and we were moving ahead.

Debbie: This time, it is a different situation. Now we are dealing with Head Start program expansion, not just how to avoid supplanting existing Head Start funding. How we use the new money is the question now.

Betty: Are there any pieces of that legislation you would like to see changed, either in the regulations or the legislation itself? If you were doing it all over again, what changes would you make?

Debbie: Oh, yes! In the statute, there was a single count date for funding the Preschool program, December 1. I would change it to be an average enrollment for several months or something like that which would allow a balancing out of children coming in and out of the program. Second, will be a great deal of discussion in the next General Session about whether to require districts to contract as first choice. We will be following that very closely. The system is designed to allow local decision making to assure quality and so we need some checks and balances if contracting is required. It would be very problematic if that happens. I am hoping that we can more clearly define what is meant by collaboration. The present statute requires that districts plan with these other agencies, but they are given an option on the outcome of the planning. The problem seems to be in dissatisfaction with the outcome of the planning on the part of some private providers. That issue will be hotly contended. I honestly don't know the answer, but the statute needs to have clearer language.

Betty: Is there anything else you would like to say?

Debbie: It is very important to be sure there is a quality technical assistance support system. Although it is not directly attached to KERA, we have over a million dollars out there supporting technical assistance for this program. You don't do this with zero administrative costs. Technical assistance is a major issue, especially when teacher training programs are not solidly established in this area. In many other programs you have people coming out of the university system basically trained.

That's not the case for us right now. So, in the first five to ten years, technical assistance and the right kind of professional development is essential to the success of the program both at the administrative level and the teacher level. Anyone who considers doing it without some kind of major support is doomed. We had four years of experience with establishing the technical assistance network. The other area which is going to have a tremendous impact on us is performance-based assessment. Many of the characteristics preschool is trying to develop in a child are not skill-based such as access to health and social services and family involvement. These come under the goal of removing barriers to learning. Rather than looking at whether the child is "ready" for kindergarten, we need to be looking at whether kindergarten is ready for the child. A strong, developmentally appropriate primary program is critical, one which is able to adapt to meet the needs of *all* incoming five-year-old children. Certainly, we are working to have children ready before the formal schooling process, but we don't have good, valid measures to assess this readiness. It is really scary to look at kindergarten academic readiness skills as the measure of our success.

PRESCHOOL—THE FUTURE

It is estimated that the 1992−93 school year will see even greater numbers of at-risk children participating in this program. Evaluation data concerning program effectiveness has been collected but it is still being analyzed. Still, in the hearts and minds of many Kentucky educators, the field is a little more level—perhaps not much, but a little. It is yet to be determined whether the "jump start" of preschool is enough to keep the trust, curiosity, and passion to "know more" we see blazing in the eyes of the young alive, nurtured, and glowing after three or four years of formal schooling. If it isn't, we must find another way, a better way, to serve the young. When they step off the bus for the first time and enter this place called school, they bring with them innocence and vulnerability. Our first responsibility is to respect their status and—using our wisdom and knowledge—lead them through the wonderland of learning. It is not to destroy their personhood, to frighten them, or make them ashamed. For this program to be successful, it is not the children who must change, it is us.

REFERENCES

Early Childhood Collaboration Forum, Shakertown, Kentucky, May 29, 1991.

Hodgkinson, Harold. 1991. "School Reform vs. Reality," *Phi Delta Kappan* (September): 8–27.

Kentucky Department of Education. *Kentucky Preschool Programs: Overview of Child Development*, Technical Assistance Paper no. 1.

Kentucky Department of Education. 1990. *Kentucky School Laws.* Frankfort, Kentucky: Banks-Baldwin Law Publishing.

Kentucky Department of Education. 1991. *Final Report: Kentucky Education Reform Act Preschool Program*, Frankfort, Kentucky.

Kentucky Department of Education. 1991. *The Kentucky Education Reform Act: 1990 Implementation Report*, Frankfort, Kentucky.

CHAPTER 8

Linking Parents, Schools, and Agencies

What happens to a dream deferred?
Does it dry up
Like a raisin in the sun?
Or fester like a sore —
And then run?
Does it stink like rotten meat
Or crust and sugar over
Like a syrupy sweet?
Maybe it just sags
Like a heavy load.
Or does it explode?
                    —Langston Hughes,
                    A Dream Deferred

IS the promise of an equal educational opportunity for all children a myth, something we talk about but we know does not exist? Is it true only for children who come from families who know how to provide a home environment that is educationally supportive? For children climbing off the bright yellow school bus on their first day of primary school, it is not a myth. In their hearts it is real. In a short time it becomes a "dream deferred" for far too many of them.

A critical component to the success of any education reform is the ability of the reform to better connect, in a positive way, families and teachers, schools and communities, the human service bureaucracy and the educational bureaucracy. It is quite common in our present school systems for secondary teachers to have little contact with middle school teachers, or for middle school teachers to have little contact with elementary teachers. It is equally common for people working in juvenile justice agencies to have little contact with people working in health services, and for people in health services to have little contact with people in social insurance. Linking human service agencies with each other and with the schools to impact the educational success of children is the objective of the Family Resource/Youth Services Center (FRYSC) initiative in the Kentucky Education Reform Act.

In 1990, the Children's Defense Fund published *Children 1990: A Report Card, Briefing Book and Action Primer*. It included the portrait of Kentucky shown in Table 8.1.

Clearly, the children in this state and across the nation are increasingly in need of a system that coordinates social services and educational services in new and creative ways. The creators of KERA were mindful of the needs of children and families and recognized that the foundation for success in schools begins with conception. It begins with proper prenatal care, which includes good nutrition and adequate medical attention and continues through the preschool years. It does not begin at age five, when the child steps off the school bus. It begins five years earlier. In order for the child's success in school to be sustained through the years, it requires continued parental support and active involvement in the schools, positive communication between the school and the family, continued high levels of nutrition and health services, adequate emotional and financial support for the student and the family, and a learning environment focused on student academic success and high levels of intellectual growth. The schools cannot do it alone. The human service agencies cannot do it alone. They must learn to work together.

Nationally, many attempts to build these linkages are underway. The Education and Human Services Consortium is a loosely connected alliance of twenty-two organizations interested in connecting comprehensive services for children and families. This alliance includes the National School Boards Association, the Center for the Study of Social Policy, the American Public Welfare Association, The National Governors' Association, and the National Alliance of Business to name just a few. The purpose of this consortium is "to encourage conversation and constructive action among those who share a common interest in the same group of families and children" (*What It Takes*, 1991, p. 4). In

Table 8.1.

1. 67.4% of ninth graders receive their high school diploma four years later	
State Rank: 39	National Average: 71.1%
2. 23.6% of children under 18 live in poverty	
State Rank: 41	National Average: 20.9%
3. 75.9% of all live births receive prenatal care	
State Rank: 32	National Average: 76.0%
4. 61.1 births per 1000 females are to females between the ages of 15 and 19	
State Rank: 40	National Average: 50.6

1989, the Carnegie Council on Adolescent Development published a report of the Task Force on Education of Young Adolescents entitled, *Turning Points: Preparing American Youth for the 21st Century*. This report calls for communities to identify their "human and economic wealth" and find ways to link this wealth in sustained partnerships with schools (p. 70).

In *Joining Forces: A Report from the First Year* (Levy, 1989) the National Association of State Boards of Education identified four purposes: to foster dialogue among systems, to collect and disseminate information on successful examples of collaboration, to assist states in the development and evaluation of collaborative approaches and to foster supportive action at the national level (pp. 17–18).

In July, 1989, The National Center for Family Literacy was established in Louisville, Kentucky. The purpose of this Center is to promote family literacy. Its goal is to "plant the seeds for a comprehensive national assault on the inter-generational cycle of underachievement."

The Family Resource Coalition has a mission to "build support and resources within communities that strengthen and empower families, enhance the capacities of parents, and foster the optimal development of children and youth" (*Family Resource Coalition Report*, 1990, p. 19). The Coalition views its role as one of supporting community-based linkages among all human service, economic, and education resources. Many groups are represented on its board of directors, including the Michigan State House of Representatives, Swiss Bank Corporation, Association of Junior League, National Futures Association, National Black Child Association and the Casey Family Program. The Coalition has developed a "Checklist of Family Support Principles" (p. 7) to guide the delivery of services to families.

(*1*) Are services provided in the most family-friendly, non-stigmatizing environment, and, whenever possible, in the home?

(*2*) Are symptoms, needs, and stresses reframed in a non-blaming way as family and community system issues and problems?

(*3*) Are family-centered services provided in culturally and gender- and age-responsive ways?

(*4*) Are families empowered to reframe their problems as goals to be addressed, and to select from skill-oriented, emotionally supportive, and resource-based options for their solution?

(*5*) Are services provided as early as possible to minimize further risk and harm, or must families be pushed to escalate their problems, hurting themselves and their children, in order to become eligible for services?

(6) Are families treated as partners – given their expertise regarding their problems and preferred solutions – and do policy makers and providers promote a no-reject service ethic, so that family needs drive tailor-made services?

(7) Do services supplant or reinforce family strengths and capacities?

(8) Is there congruence between families' demands for certain kinds of services and the problem-solving tools used by the service providers?

(9) Are families forced to relapse frequently to secure boosters and long-term supports?

(10) Are families provided with a case manager who honors their preferences in the case plans, coordinates service plans, and reduces the contradictory approaches used by providers?

(11) Is the service provider perceived as an enabler, capacity builder, and advocate, or as a prescriber and dictator of case plans?

(12) When case plans fail, is failure attributed to the family, or to the case design, interventions, and their timing?

(13) When family members are separated from one another (e.g., parent in mental hospital or jail, child in group care), are aggressive supports and policies in place to keep all members of the family as involved as possible to accelerate reunification when appropriate?

(14) Are policies and services provided in intergenerationally supportive ways, tapping talents of elders and enabling family care-givers to provide supports equitably across generations?

(15) Do policy makers and managers of services define responsibility for family support as multi-agency, multi-system, and multi-sector, involving the media, schools, corporations, labor, neighborhood and civic associations, and churches, as well as park, recreation, libraries, and the array of health, human, and law enforcement services?

(16) Are public and private sector policies screened for their impact on families?

(17) Are successful family support initiatives evaluated for their cost-effectiveness or even budget-neutrality?

(18) Are family support initiatives used as tools for system-wide

reform or are they designed as additives, creating more service proliferation and coordination problems?

(*19*) Do administrators model some of the same empowering approaches with their staff as they use with families?

(*20*) Do educational institutions provide training and preparation to service providers in the fields of education, social work, health care, law, law enforcement, and other human services, consistent with family and community capacity-building principles?

(*21*) Are key policy and service design decisions treated as opportunities to move the system toward family support principles and practices?

The expectation for the quality of service delivery embodied in these principles would challenge any agency or institution dealing with families. Yet, these principles provide a vision for the caliber of services to be delivered by Kentucky's FRYSC.

Thus the Family Resource/Youth Services Center initiative in the Kentucky Education Reform Act is such an effort. It is considered by some to be the most comprehensive, statewide, legislated initiative to be mandated in statute and supported with state funding.

STATUTE

156.497 Interagency Task Force on Family Resource Centers and Youth Service Centers: formulation of five-year plan; implementation

(1) There is hereby created an Interagency Task Force on Family Resource Centers and Youth Service Centers which shall consist of sixteen (16) members appointed by the Governor. The sixteen (16) members appointed shall include one (1) representative from each of the following agencies or groups:

(a) Department of Education;

(b) Department for Employment Services of the Cabinet for Human Resources:

(c) Department of Health Services of the Cabinet for Human Resources;

(d) Department of Mental Health and Mental Retardation Services of the Cabinet for Human Resources;

(e) Department for Social Services of the Cabinet for Human Resources;

(f) Department for Social Insurance of the Cabinet for Human Resources:

(g) Justice Cabinet;

(h) Governor's Office;

(i) Workforce Development Cabinet;

(j) Parents;

(k) Teachers;

(l) Local school administrators;

(m) Local school boards;

(n) Local community mental health – mental retardation programs;

(o) Local health departments; and

(p) Local community action agencies.

(2) The task force shall be appointed and begin to meet immediately upon July 13, 1990, to formulate a five (5) year implementation plan establishing family resource and youth service centers designed to meet the needs of economically disadvantaged children and their families. The secretary of the Cabinet for Human Resources shall call the first meeting, at which time the task force by majority vote shall elect a task force chair to serve a one (1) year term. A new chair shall be elected annually thereafter, and the chair may succeed himself. The Cabinet for Human Resources shall provide adequate staff to assist in the development and implementation of the task force's plan.

(3) The plan developed by the task force shall include a five (5) year effort to implement a network of family resource centers across the Commonwealth. The centers shall be located in or near each elementary school in the Commonwealth in which twenty percent (20%) or more of the student body is eligible for free school meals. The plan developed for the centers by the task force shall promote identification and coordination of existing resources and shall include, but not be limited to, the following components for each site:

(a) Full-time preschool child care for children two (2) and three (3) years of age;

(b) After school child care for children ages four (4) through twelve (12), with the child care being full-time during the summer and on the days when school is not in session;

(c) Families in training, which shall consist of an integrated approach to home visits, group meetings, and monitoring child development for new and expectant parents;

(d) Parent and child education (PACE) as described in KRS158.360;

(e) Support and training for child day care providers; and

(f) Health services or referral to health services, or both.

(4) The plan developed by the task force shall include a five (5) year schedule to implement a network of youth service centers across the

Commonwealth. The centers shall be located in or near each school, except elementary schools, serving youth over twelve (12) years of age and in which twenty percent (20%) or more of the student body are eligible for free school meals. The plan developed for the centers by the task force shall promote identification and coordination of existing resources and include the following components for each site;

(a) Referrals to health and social services;

(b) Employment counseling, training, and placement;

(c) Summer and part-time job development;

(d) Drug and alcohol abuse counseling; and

(e) Family crisis and mental health counseling.

(5) The task force shall complete its implementation plan for the program prior to January 1, 1991, and local school districts shall develop initial plans for their family resource centers and youth services centers by June 30 of each year thereafter until the centers have been established in or adjacent to all eligible schools.

(6) A grant program is hereby established to provide financial assistance to eligible school districts establishing family resource centers and youth services centers. The Cabinet for Human Resources shall promulgate administrative regulations to establish criteria for the awarding of the grants. In no case shall a school district operate a family resource center or a youth services center which provides abortion counseling or makes referrals to a health care facility for purposes of seeking an abortion. The grant applications shall be reviewed by the task force, which shall make its recommendations to the secretary of the Cabinet for Human Resources.

(7) The task force shall continue to monitor the family resource centers and the youth services centers, review grant applications, and otherwise monitor the implementation of the plan until December 31, 1995, at which time the task force shall cease to exist. During its existence the task force shall report at least annually to the secretary of the Cabinet for Human Resources, the Governor, and the Legislative Research Commission.

(8) Members of the task force may be reimbursed for actual expenses for attending meetings and for other actual and necessary expenses incurred in the performance of their duties authorized by the task force. The expenses shall be paid out of the appropriation for the task force. (KDE, 1990, p. 178)

FUNDING

The first year of the program was designated as a planning year and $125,000 was allocated for this purpose. These funds helped pay the salary of two consultants assigned to the project, expenses for the task force, and some travel. The secretary of the Cabinet for Human Resources and his principal assistant took responsibility for the development of the program. The secretary was quite aggressive in securing additional foundation funding to support this program. The allocated $125,000 was insufficient to cover the initial costs of the program and this amount was supplemented with funds from the current operating budget of the Cabinet for Human Resources and the Department of Education.

The level of funding for the first year of program implementation was $9.5 million. This amount was projected to be sufficient to cover one-fourth of the centers. Additional funds would be provided each year until all qualifying schools had operational centers. These monies were supplemented by grants from the Casey Foundation, Cities in Schools, and the National Center for Community Education (*FRYSC Status Report*, 1991, p. 8). Funding for 1992 – 93 is $15.9 million and funding for 1993 – 94 is $26.4 million. Since this is $3 million per year less than had been projected, it may mean that the full implementation of this program will take six years rather than five.

Center funding was calculated at $200 per eligible child with a minimum of $10,000 and a maximum of $90,000. The average center received $75,000. These monies were to be used to secure the services of a "bridge" person. This individual had the responsibility of coordinating an integrated service delivery system between the schools and the human service agencies serving the school/district.

NUMBER OF CENTERS REQUIRED
EXCEEDS EXPECTATIONS

The level of state funding for this initiative was predicated on the assumption that approximately 500 schools would qualify for the program. It was expected that the funding would increase in increments of $9.5 million for each of the next four years until $36 million per year was allocated to the program and all eligible schools had operational programs.

When the task force first met, it authorized the Cabinet for Human Resources to conduct a survey of school districts to determine how many schools would qualify. All 176 districts responded to the survey. Using FY 90 data, districts reported that 174 districts representing 1,031 schools would qualify for the program (KDE, 1991, *Implementation*

Report, p. 35). Of the 1,031 qualifying schools, 769 were eligible for Family Resource Centers, and 262 were eligible for Youth Services Centers. There was a large variation among the percent of eligible children within these schools. As Figure 8.1 depicts, in eight elementary schools in the state, over 90 percent of the students qualified for free meals. In 318 elementary schools over 50 percent of the students qualified for free meals.

There was also great variance in the number of children eligible for free lunch within qualifying schools. As Figure 8.2 shows, twenty-six schools had more than 450 children who qualified for the program. Only 259 of the state's 1,366 schools had less than 100 students qualifying for free meals.

FRYSC GUIDING PRINCIPLES

In designing the program, four of the principles adopted by the Curriculum Committee of the Task Force on Education Reform were followed (*Executive Summary*, pp. 15 – 17).

All children can learn and most at high levels. For all children to learn, barriers to learning must be removed. The traditional educational paradigms must be altered to meet the complex and changing needs of children, youth and families. School-based and school-linked services must extend beyond those typically conceptualized as educational and include increased attention to physical, social, emotional, and vocational needs as well as the acquisition and integration of basic skills. Parents must be part of the development of these services through opportunities for input and leadership roles. Respect for all persons, including parents, youth and children, should be enhanced to help assure that the goal of achieving an education is successful.

Creation of an atmosphere that empowers the participant (consumer) to acquire the competencies necessary to meet the needs and achieve the goals of attaining an education. The role of the Family Resource Center or the Youth Services Center is to support and strengthen the family's and the individual members' problem solving and nurturing abilities. Such an approach presupposes working in equal partnership with all members of a family to resolve identified problems and when appropriate to enhance family functioning. Interventions should focus on building and strengthening informal support networks as well as making appropriate use of professional support systems. Assistance should be made available to families in a manner that is flexible, individualized, and responsive to the family members.

Develop an interagency focus. Traditional service delivery models within both education and human services will have to be altered to meet the

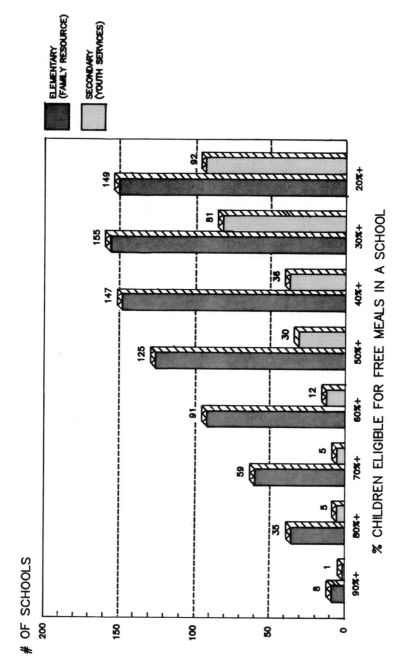

Figure 8.1. *Family Resource and Youth Services Centers. Schools Qualifying for Assistance/Percent Students Eligible for Free Meals. Source: Cabinet for Human Resources (FY '90 Statistics).*

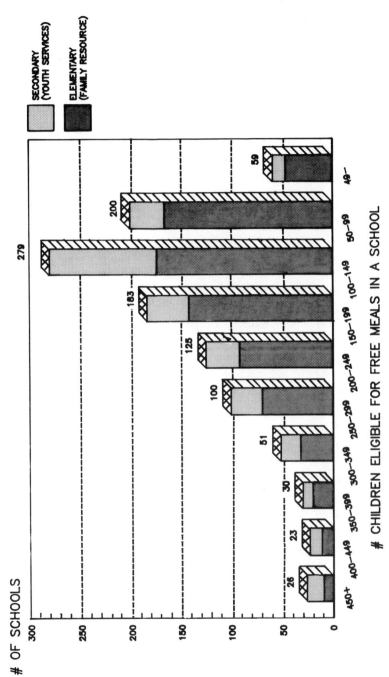

Figure 8.2. *Family Resource and Youth Services Centers. Schools Qualifying for Assistance/Number of Students Eligible for Free Meals. Source: Cabinet for Human Resources (FY '90 Statistics).*

177

complex and changing needs of children, youth and their families. Education and human service systems must join forces and develop the capacity for providing a coordinated, multi-system response to these needs.

Assure community ownership. The Centers should reflect the unique needs and character of a community (in an urban setting this is likely to be the neighborhood). To that end, the planning, design, and governance of each Center should have strong community input and on-going guidance.

PLAN OF ACTION

A five-year implementation plan for establishing the Centers was developed by the Interagency Task Force on Family Resource and Youth Services Centers (pp. 18–34). The plan addressed local community planning and involvement, program specifications, necessary state level support, and the financing strategy for the Centers.

Each community is required to prepare an inventory of the services already available to support children and families. The state Task Force had compiled a statewide listing of services. This list was used to assist local communities in preparing their local inventory. Not all state services are available in every community and some communities have developed local services and programs that are not available statewide. In addition to the inventory of formal programs and services, each local community was directed to compile a list of informal services currently available within the community. These could be programs like church-sponsored day care or medical assistance provided by service organizations. The final part of the inventory was to identify where unmet needs existed in the service delivery mechanism of the community.

Each community was required to develop a community advisory board that was representative of the services the Center planned to deliver. One-third of the advisory board had to be made up of parents from the eligible school(s) served by the Center. The characteristics of the parent representatives were supposed to mirror the characteristics of the community in terms of racial composition and socioeconomic level. In addition, the board for a Youth Services Center must include at least two youth representatives and two student representatives. Additional members of the board could include community representation, teachers, classified staff, administration, and school board members.

Program specifications were developed to provide a framework for the development of the Centers. Since the services available within each community and the needs of each community were different, the specific program design for each Center was expected to be different. However, once a Center was established, the services of the Center would be available to all children, youth, parents, and families who live in the community served by the Center. The services were not available only to the families of children qualifying for free meals. The Task Force did specify that non-public schools could not qualify to establish a Center, but the children living in a community who attended a non-public school could receive services.

The Task Force reinforced the concept of local community flexibility in the design of the program. This flexibility was provided to enhance local community ownership for the success of the Center. By enabling local communities to design the services to be delivered by the Center, the task force acknowledged that local communities had a better understanding of their needs.

The Task Force did provide a listing of the type of goals that should be incorporated into the local plan. These are in keeping with the statutory mandate that the Centers "meet the needs of economically disadvantaged children and their families." The goals for Family Resource Centers are:

(*1*) To promote the healthy growth and development of children, by assisting families to identify and address any home or community barriers to a child's success in school

(*2*) To assist families to develop the parenting skills that can promote the full development of children

(*3*) To ensure that families have access to and are connected with appropriate community resources and receive from those resources the help that they need

(*4*) To encourage social support linkages and networks among families, thereby reducing isolation and promoting family involvement in community activities

The goals for Youth Services Centers are:

(*1*) To promote young people's progress toward capable and productive adulthood by assisting them to recognize their individual and family strengths and to address problems that block their success in school

(2) To assist young people to make effective use of community resources, including employment and training resources, and health, mental health, and social services resources as necessary

(3) To promote supportive relationships among young people themselves, and among young people, their families, and community resources, in order to develop adolescents' self-esteem and competencies

Given these board goals, the local Center was required to design programs and coordinate existing services consistent with the programmatic requirements of the statute.

The Task Force envisioned that most Centers would be staffed with at least one full-time staff member but acknowledged that staffing requirements would be dependent upon the design of the program. Staffing patterns should be designed to meet the goals of the individual Centers. To assist the local advisory councils, the Task Force identified a listing of job duties for Center staff in order to stimulate thought.

Job duties of FRYSC staff may include:

(1) Design program components to fit community needs

(2) Perform participant needs assessment (child and family)

(3) Outreach for target population

(4) Promote the development of community resources

(5) Evaluate and monitor program components

(6) Act as principal liaison to other agencies

(7) Serve as staff to local advisory body

(8) Assure compliance with state level reporting requirements and evaluation system

(9) Develop/coordinate/facilitate training for staff, both paid and volunteer

(10) Seek additional funding for FRYSC services

Other program specifications included the following: Centers were to be located in or near existing schools; services were to be provided beyond the normal school day and year; a parental consent form was to be developed; the local advisory board should establish a communication link to the district and to the local school council if one exists; a strong training component should be established; and a program tracking and performance evaluation system for the Center should be established.

The framework suggested both formative and summative evaluation of the Center.

Formative:

(*1*) Community needs assessment

(*2*) Process analysis (how the program functions in relation to need, action to address need, and benefits to participants)

(*3*) Participant characteristics

(*4*) Resource analysis

(*5*) Service statistics

(*6*) Participant records

(*7*) Consumer satisfaction surveys

Summative:

(*1*) Outcomes—the effects of the service on people's lives. This should be done at least once a year after the program has been in existence. The information needed will be the goals, objectives, services, and population targeted.

(*2*) Impact evaluation shows effect on the community such as public awareness.

(*3*) Cost-benefit analysis—one program compares cost and benefits in monetary terms.

(*4*) Cost-effectiveness analysis compares different program methods rather than one program's costs and benefits.

(*5*) An overall guide of information should be collected for the first few years of operation. Document and describe services provided, resources used, service delivery mechanisms, organizational processes, participant characteristics, and progress toward meeting program objectives.

While the local community is given considerable latitude in the unique characteristics of the local Center, the program specifications require the sophisticated level of program planning.

State-level support provided by the Interagency Task Force on Family Resource and Youth Services Centers will include the review of grant application and recommendations for grant awards, revision of implementation plan as needed to comply with legislative intent, annual report to the secretary of the Cabinet for Human Resources, and monitoring of the overall network of centers.

State-level support from the Cabinet for Human Resources will include:

(*1*) Coordinating the state-level program through the Department of Education, the Workforce Development Cabinet, the Governor's Office for Policy and Management, and other offices as necessary

(*2*) Promulgating administrative regulations establishing the criteria for awarding of grants to school districts

(*3*) Developing a form for informed parental consent to be utilized in local Centers

(*4*) Providing consultation and quality technical assistance throughout local planning, development and implementation at the district level

(*5*) Facilitating information sharing among Family Resource Centers and Youth Services Centers through regional and state training and conferences

(*6*) Awarding grants through contracts with the school districts to establish Centers based on recommendations of the Task Force

(*7*) Assuring that local staff attend training in program design and development

(*8*) Compiling statewide data on processes, services, and performance outcomes through a statewide reporting and evaluation system

(*9*) Monitoring the activities of the Centers through on-site and semi-annual desk report reviews

(*10*) Examining funding alternatives for Centers and requesting that state agencies commit available existing and new resources to Center development

(*11*) Maintaining relationships with national organizations and other state programs

(*12*) Arranging for the Task Force meetings as required.

The final component of the plan of action dealt with financing the Centers. The "average" Center was envisioned as one that would receive $75,000 to provide a core infrastructure around which other services would be provided. Funding for the Centers was not meant to actually pay for the delivery of services. Rather, it was designed to build the mechanism to coordinate and focus the services currently available within a community.

CURRENT STATUS

One hundred thirty-three Centers serving 232 schools were funded for the 1991−92 school year (see Figure 8.3). These Centers served over 111,000 of the state's estimated 625,000 children. Services provided by the Centers included parent and child education, after-school child care, health services, employment counseling, and job development. The first year of the program, 1990−91, was a planning year. Schools where more than 20 percent of the students qualified for free lunch were eligible for the program. Initially, it was estimated that approximately 500 of Kentucky's 1,350 schools would qualify. Actually, over 1,000 schools met the requirement.

The authorized program design and implementation authority for this program is the Cabinet for Human Resources. As the Kentucky Education Reform Act was being debated in the 1990 General Assembly, the authorized agency moved back and forth between the Department of Education and the Cabinet for Human Resources.

INTERAGENCY COLLABORATION

One very important factor in the successful development and implementation of this program was the close, positive relationship between high-level policy makers at the Department of Education and the Cabinet for Human Resources. These policy makers understood the vital importance of this component to the success of the Reform Act, and made certain that there was solid, sustained cooperation and communication among and within the two agencies in the development and implementation of the program. This sustained collaborative effort withstood the reorganization of the Department of Education and the political transition from one governor to another.

In awarding grants, the percentage and number of children eligible for free school meals in the service delivery area was taken into consideration. Other factors considered in awarding grants included evidence of local initiatives to promote the delivery of services currently unavailable to the area, but included in the legislation; the efforts of the community to contribute to the effective implementation of this program through in-kind services such as transportation, space, personnel, and funding; and an effective evaluation plan. In awarding the first round of grants, there was also an attempt to distribute the Centers among rural,

Center Size/# Eligible for Free School Meals	Number of Centers	Type*	Location**	Number of Schools	SBDM	Number of Children—Free Lunch	Total Number of Children	Funding	Average Funding per Center
Large 300-above	85	45 F 17 C 23 Y	25 U 10 S 3 RS 47 R	165	15	38,562	85,251	$7,020,400	$82,600
Medium 150-299	39	23 F 8 C 8 Y	11 U 4 S 24 R	56	10	9,146	23,010	$1,822,800	$46,800
Small 149-below	9	5 F 1 C 3 Y	2 U 7 R	11	2	1,060	2,982	$212,600	$23,600
Total	133	73 F 26 C 34 Y	38 U 14 S 3 RS 78 R	232	27	48,768 43.89%)	111,243	$9,055,800	$68,100

* F = Family Resource Center; C = Combined Family Resource and Youth Services Center; Y = Youth Services Center

** U = Urban; S = Suburban; RS = Rural Suburban; R = Rural

Figure 8.3. Family Resource and Youth Services Centers, 1991–92. Approved Grant Applications. Source: Cabinet for Human Resources, 1991.

urban, and suburban settings, large and small districts, and to proportionally balance the number of Family Resource and Youth Services Centers.

Since the program was not designed to pay for service delivery, but rather to fund a "glue" or "bridge" position, the Cabinet for Human Resources contracted with the Center for the Study of Social Policy (CSSP) to (1) name other state and federal funding sources which could be used to pay for direct services, (2) identify other federal funding sources such as Medicaid and Title IV-E, and (3) conduct an in-depth study of five school districts to identify entitlement programs that could be used to support this initiative (*Executive Summary*, pp. 38–39).

PROCESS

(*1*) April–May–June, 1990
- regional awareness workshops planned and delivered as a joint effort between the Cabinet for Human Resources and the Department of Education
- policy discussions with representatives from the Legislative Research Commission to clarify legislative intent for the program
- preliminary discussions with district administrators and legislative aides regarding the number of eligible children and the level of funding
- working relationship established with the Department of Education
- the Secretary's office identified as the site of program responsibility for this initiative
- Interagency Task Force on Family Resource and Youth Services Centers appointed by the governor through executive order
- first meeting of the Task Force was held
- establishment of contacts with universities, United Way, and foundations

(*2*) July–August–September, 1990
- meeting with Department of Social Insurance Managers
- meeting with University of Kentucky Interdisciplinary Task Force for Family Resource and Youth Services Centers

— second meeting of Interagency Task Force
— presentation to Kentucky Association of School Administrators
— meeting with Legislative Research Commission and Family Resource and Youth Services Centers (FRYSC) staff to discuss number of eligible schools
— several meetings with Governor's Office for Policy and Management to discuss policy issues and program design
— meeting with Department for Social Services Advisory Council
— meeting to determine subcommittees of Interagency Task Force
— third meeting of Interagency Task Force
— tours of Lexington area programs: Family Care Program, Cardone Centre, Research and Development Center for Child Care and Early Childhood
— visit to Family Resource Center in Cecil County, Maryland
— meeting with Center for the Study of Social Policy and Dr. David Hornbeck
— meetings with Student Assistance Initiative group
— meeting with home economics chairs — state universities
— fourth meeting of the Task Force
— subcommittees meetings; Resource Identification, Program Design, Finance
— fifth meeting of Task Force

(3) October — November — December, 1990
— meetings with subcommittees of Task Force
— presentations to various professional organizations
— meetings with legislators to discuss legislative intent and design of the program
— meeting with the Center for the Study of Social Policy
— sixth meeting of the Task Force
— attendance of Governor's Conference on Children and Youth, Cleveland, Ohio
— attendance of Family Resource Coalition Conference in Chicago
— meeting with representatives from Kentucky Education Association, Kentucky Youth Advocates, Council on Higher Education, Kentucky Association of School Administrators, University of Kentucky

- seventh and eighth meeting of the Task Force
- review of site visit reports submitted by The Center for Study of Social Policy

(*4*) January — June, 1991
- State Implementation Plan submitted to governor and Education Reform Task Force
- Request for Proposals announced and procedures sent to school board and interested parties
- technical assistance provided to school districts in developing proposals
- review of proposals; grants awarded to 134 districts
- local school district implementation plans received

INTERVIEW

This interview is with Ronnie Dunn, Division Manager for Family Resource/Youth Services Centers in the Cabinet for Human Resources. At the time the legislation was passed, Ms. Dunn was principal assistant to the Secretary of the Cabinet for Human Resources. This interview was conducted on August 6, 1991.

Betty: In the past sixteen months, this program has gained an increasingly positive reputation. When the Advisory Council first began to work, there was some concern about whether the program was carrying forward the legislative intent of the General Assembly. Now, that discussion has subsided and we are hearing many more positive comments about the program. Do you agree with that assessment?

Ronnie: Yes, I do! Well, we know of various states across the nation that are doing pockets and portions of what we hope to do in the Centers. We are attempting to do it all . . . statewide. So we know everyone is looking to us during the planning and implementation phases of the legislation to see how we do it. What problems we come up against. How we solve these problems. Can we document that the centers are doing what they should be doing?

Betty: Why do you think they were included in education reform?

Ronnie: I think they were included because David Hornbeck did a good selling job. He is so interested in children. Of course, his total focus is kids, always kids. He puts the kids in front. When you think about it, when you get down to the kids and you consider the needs of those kids before they even walk into the classroom, you have to include the families of those kids. Family Resource Centers are the answer.

Betty: I happen to agree with you. I know when you were first looking at the design of this program you went to Connecticut and New Jersey to look at their programs. Are there other states that are trying to implement this type of program?

Ronnie: San Diego, California, has what they call New Beginnings. It is very similar. Of course, Maryland has the Family Resource Centers. They have six. They are similar to what we are doing, but they are funded at a greater amount, $250,000 per site. It's the same focus, but it's a different way to get there.

Betty: What is the status of the program now? Sixteen months ago, it was words on a page.

Ronnie: Those words have become a state implementation plan. We did criteria for awarding grants. One hundred and thirty-four grants have been awarded. We have training sessions planned for all of the center coordinators. The school districts have been divided among the staff in this office. We are all responsible for districts in specific areas. We are going to get out there and help them establish their centers or, if they were not funded, to beef up their applications so that next year, we can ensure that they will be funded. If they didn't apply for a center, find out why, and encourage them to realize the importance of the center and to realize that now is the time to plan. Even if they planned to ask for funds three years from now, they need to start planning right now.

Betty: So, you are having 134 project directors come into Frankfort for training?

Ronnie: Actually, the training will take place in Louisville and Lexington.

Betty: What type of training is it? Is it one day or two days?

Ronnie: The training is two full days and believe me, it is two full days. We have Judy Carter coming in from the Family Resource Coalition. We have keynote speakers from the legislature to give us legislative intent. There will be speakers from New Jersey and Connecticut and also people from the Brighten Center here in Kentucky. There will be sessions by the Cabinet for Human Resources describing the local programs that are currently operating around the state, which they can access for their centers. All kinds of service providers will be coming together to talk about how they can help.

Betty: Do you intend to have more training after this?

Ronnie: This is the kickoff. For the next training, we are going to send all program coordinators to Flint, Michigan, to receive community coordinator training. The Mott Foundation is going to pay for the transportation, the lodging, and the meals. All we have to pay is a $50 registration fee. It is a whole week of training.

Betty: I know that Dr. Coward has been very aggressive in finding financial support for this program. Are there other examples of this type of supportive funding?

Ronnie: Yes, Cities and Schools gave us a $100,000 grant. This is a national organization that basically does what Family Resource Centers are designed to do by providing services to children, youth, and families. Their focus is on the business community and getting children ready for employment and helping families with employment too. Another foundation that we have received funds from is the Annie Casey Foundation. We have received $175,000 from them to provide training and technical assistance. The training that we are doing this month is supported by those funds. We are now working on a grant from HHS, Health Human Services, in Washington, D.C., for $200,000, for networking. You can not use this money for services. It has to all be used for planning. Our grant proposal is going to be focused on eastern Kentucky. In the Big Sandy area, there were a lot of districts who applied, but their proposals were not strong enough to get funding. So, we are going to be working with the Big Sandy area development districts helping them plan for their centers and implement their centers.

Betty: I know that when the program first got started, there were some rocky times. One of the major problems was that there was not enough funding to support one-fourth of the districts in the state that would qualify for the program. Can you talk a little bit about the number of districts in the state that did qualify for this program and how you worked through all of that?

Ronnie: Initially, it was estimated that 500 schools would be eligible for this program. One of the first things we did was conduct a survey. Based on the information that schools fed back to us, over 1,000 schools would qualify for a Center based on the 20 percent of the student body eligible to receive free lunch. So one-fourth of over 1,300 is a lot more than one-fourth of 500. So, to encourage more schools to apply, we told them that they could form consortia. They did this, and some grants are for three to five schools. The one Center will serve more than one school.

As a matter of fact, of the 134 grants that were awarded, that is over 232 schools. So, that is almost a fourth of the eligible schools. Certainly, we are moving in that direction.

Betty: When you approved a consortia type of arrangement, did you look at the proximity of the schools?

Ronnie: We asked them to demonstrate in the proposal what populations they would be serving, what services would be provided, and how that population would access those services. If they demonstrated to us, satisfactorily, that they would do it, then we did approve the grant.

Betty: As I recall the grant application process, it accommodated all types of situations. Districts did not have to have an ongoing program for coordinating services already operational. On the other hand, districts that had been coordinating service delivery were not penalized. How did you balance that?

Ronnie: Well, we had a point system. I believe this was one of the most apolitical grant award processes I have seen in state government. We made decisions about granting these awards strictly on points. We had volunteers who read these proposals and scored them according to the point structure. The top scores got the money. I think it was that simple. We did get some phone calls from senators and representatives and some area development directors that ask us to give special consideration to specific schools, and Dr. Coward's response to all of that was firm and consistent, ''If they had enough points, they would get funded.''

Betty: I know you were considering using people in the Department as readers when you were first designing the grant review and approval process. In the end you decided not to use Department of Education staff because you wanted a completely unbiased assessment. What was the background of the people you did use to review the proposals?

Ronnie: First of all, they were recommended by members of the Interagency Task Force. So we got people who represented all of the various groups on the Task Force. We got parents, people affiliated with community action agencies, and social workers. We got all kinds of people.

Betty: So, basically, you identified the roles of people on the Task Force and invited others representing those roles to assist you.

Ronnie: That's right, and it worked quite well.

Betty: I know there has been an attempt over the past year to maintain a really close relationship with the State Department of Education. Talk with me a little bit about that relationship. What were the good points about that relationship, what were the bad ones?

Ronnie: It started with the KIDS project back in 1988. The Secretary of Education asked us to go to an academy for dropout presentation. The academy was designed to help us talk about programs that could be designed to integrate services in the schools to reduce the dropout rate in Kentucky. So, he asked people from the Department of Education and the Cabinet for Human Resources to collaborate on this. We didn't know each other at the time. In the spring of that year we went to Virginia, got comfortable with each other, and then in the fall we went to Minneapolis. During these meetings we not only became close friends, we came up with the KIDS program. The secretary had this concept in his mind; he picked our brains for ideas and put a plan together. When we came back to Kentucky, we formed teams and we went out together to school districts. We helped them plan and implement interagency programs. We had common ownership of the program. We worked together to make sure that the programs worked. I think when people at the local level saw State Department agencies collaborating, that transferred to them. We truly became friends and we have maintained that friendship to this day. We became friends not only professionally but also socially.

Betty: I also think it was important that you had top-level policy-setting people in both organizations involved in the design of the program.

Ronnie: That is true. Then when education reform came along, we could quickly see how the Kentucky Integrated Delivery System was really the Family Resource/Youth Services Center program. That concept was there. Then, of course, Dr. Coward, you, and ultimately Dr. Boysen, pushed for collaboration. No one had to push very hard because it was already there and we already knew the benefits of it.

Betty: Talk with me a little bit about the role of the local advisory council. Each local program is required to have one.

Ronnie: I think it is key to the success of the Centers. The advisory council is a local group who knows what the needs of the Center are, and what the culture of the community and the schools is. The members of this advisory council know what services need to be provided. So, it is important for those folks to determine what their Center should look like, where it should be located, who should be the coordinator, how the students will access the services, and how the parents should be involved. Of course, one-third of the council is made up of parents. So, parents are a real key to the success of the Centers.

Betty: If you were advising another state legislature in the design of this type of program, what would you say?

Ronnie: I would hope that I wouldn't have to advise anyone until we had hard data here in Kentucky about what worked and what didn't and that our centers are doing what they were supposed to be doing. I know our centers are going to be good, but I also know that in order to convince someone else, I will need some hard proof. I would sure like to have David Hornbeck sitting right beside me. Of course, I've talked to him and heard him speak so many times since the bill passed that I think he has so much credibility. He cares so much for children.

Betty: Do you think that another state could simply take our statute and enact it in their state and fund it and have it work?

Ronnie: I think so!

Betty: You like the idea of taking one fourth of the districts that qualify and funding a gradual implementation?

Ronnie: Yes!

Betty: How do you feel about the definition for how a school qualifies for the program, that 20 percent of the students qualify for free lunch?

Ronnie: I think that is fine. Ultimately, I would like for every school in Kentucky to have one of these Centers because all children, at some time in their lives, are at risk, not just the economically disadvantaged. Certainly, economically disadvantaged is one way to define at-risk, but all children need these services.

Betty: What is your level of staffing to support this program at the present time?

Ronnie: We are going to have twelve. I am the manager. We have two secretarial positions, and we will have nine people we call family resource analysts. They will provide technical assistance to the schools. They are also involved in providing assistance to the Task Force. We do a lot of different things. My motto here is that nobody says ''That is not my job.'' We all work together to do whatever needs to be done.

Betty: Are they all based here in the capital?

Ronnie: At this point, yes. This is a learning process for all of us. It may be that in the future we would want to regionalize. But at this point, while it is brand new, we need to be together.

Betty: What kind of obstacles have you encountered so far?

Ronnie: There are those shooting at us. Sometimes I feel that we are in a shooting gallery. The Catholic community is one of them. A policy decision was made early that the parochial and private schools would not be eligible to receive this funding. That was based on what we thought was legislative intent. But the Catholic community has let it be known that they will probably be filing suit to enable them to qualify to be eligible for these centers.

Betty: I know that they also raised a question about access to the Extended School Services program.

Ronnie: I know that because of their success with gaining access to the Extended School Services program, that the FRYSC program is their next target.

Betty: Are there others?

Ronnie: Yes, another big problem was child care. The private providers were fearful that this program would take away their business. I do believe that we have been able to allay fears and I don't hear as much about this as I did, although I do think those fears may still be there. The private providers feel that not only the FRYSC but also the four-year-old program are going to run them out of business. They feel the schools will create their own programs within the school system and not involve the private providers. In some cases that is true. I've had school people say to me that the private provider is not delivering developmentally appropriate programs in their Centers. For instance, children sitting in front of a television all day is not a developmentally appropriate practice. Generally, when a child enters the four-year-old program, they are behind the other children and need rather specific readiness, skill development. In some cases, schools feel they can do a better job. These situations need to be reviewed on a case by case basis. I'm telling private providers that if they want to participate in these KERA programs, they are going to have to assure that their programs meet the high standards expected by KERA, and show these school districts that they can do it. I talk a lot about relationship building. You have to build relationships with the schools, you have to trust each other. These schools have a lot of responsibility. In a few years, they are going to have to prove that they have helped these students reach outcomes. They are going to have to trust providers to help them bring the students along.

Betty: As KERA is designed right now, the sanctions and rewards will be applied only to the schools. I have heard some suggest that some type of sanctions and rewards need to be applied to the human service community as well. Do you think that eventually, some type of system of sanctions and rewards will be applied to the human service agencies too?

Ronnie: I don't know. I would hope so. My feeling is that if the families and the children are helped, that is a reward in itself. However, one of the most influential senators in the legislature made the statement that in 1994, if we are in front of them asking for more money to fund more centers, he is going to want to know that if they are not working, if there are still gaps, if there are still waiting lines, how much more money do we need in the Cabinet for Human Resources to meet the needs of children. So, if workers are not paid enough and there is a lot of turnover, then we may have to go back to the legislature in 1994 and indicate that we have this tremendous turnover problem and our workers need more pay. That would be one way to reward staff. I do feel there needs to be a way to reward staff.

Betty: How are you planning to evaluate the effectiveness of the program? Is there an evaluation design in place?

Ronnie: No, there isn't at this point. We understand that the Department of Education is working on an evaluation design. We believe that the FRYSCs need to be a part of that. Until that is in place, we are going to be capturing demographic information about who is served in the centers and what services are provided. What we are most interested in is being able to track who was referred for services in the centers and what type of service they received. If they didn't receive services, then why? What was the reason? We need to be able to go back to the legislature and say, these services were provided, these were not provided and why they were not provided.

Betty: What type of feedback are you getting from the legislature? What are they saying to you about the implementation of the program?

Ronnie: We are getting mixed reviews. There are some constituents who have a fear that the Youth Services Centers are going to be used to provide family planning information. Of course, in the state of Kentucky, this can be done without parental consent. They are aware of this, and they think that having the Youth Center right there in the school is going to encourage more of the young people to access that service. They have talked with their legislatures. When the legislators call us we try to explain that if those parents are involved at the local level, in the design and implementation of the Centers, then if they don't want that service provided, they need to be working with the advisory committee of that local Center. We don't feel, from the state level, that we can say to the local people, you can not do that. Some communities may decide that that is what they need to lower the teenage pregnancy rate.

Betty: Isn't there language in the statute that prohibits Centers from being used to distribute contraceptives?

Ronnie: No, the language says that they can not be used for abortion counseling.

Betty: Is there any typical FRYSC being designed by schools?

Ronnie: No, they are very different. I think this is because the needs and resources are so diverse, community to community . . . the culture, the religious orientation and the extent of the conservative-liberal influences in the community.

Betty: So, utilizing where they are, their own community, their own resources, they have designed a program unique to them?

Ronnie: That's right.

Betty: What kind of funding request are you planning to make for the next biennium?

Ronnie: Well, that is interesting. The funding is in the Department of Education budget. We feel that is the best place for it. The money to award the grants came to us via voucher. We feel it should stay as part of the education budget, because it is part of education reform. So, we are looking to education to go after the expansion request. They have assured us that they will do that. (Author's note: During the 1992 General Assembly, action was taken to place funding for this initiative in the Cabinet for Human Resources.)

Betty: Of all of the agencies outside Kentucky that you have dealt with, which ones have been most helpful?

Ronnie: The Family Resource Coalition and the Center for the Study of Social Policy.

Betty: Tell me about your dreams for this program. You are in a new position. You are in charge.

Ronnie: Well, in four years, I would like to see all eligible schools according to the law right now have Centers in operation helping families and children . . . pulling together all the service providers. When they all have them, there will be no need for this branch. We will all know what we need to know to make them work. So, there may not be a need for us here.

Betty: A short time ago, I had an opportunity to listen to Dr. Hackbart talk about funding programs that were funded outside the SEEK formula and describe the point when they could be folded into the SEEK formula. He suggested a five-year timeline. He felt that you should be able to make a determination within five years whether a program is working. If it is deemed to be successful, then he felt it should be folded into the SEEK formula and made available to everyone. If it isn't working, funding to support it should be eliminated.

Ronnie: That does make sense! The Task Force sunsets in 1995, so they will no longer function after that.

Betty: Has this program had an impact within the Cabinet for Human Resources? Has there been more cooperation and collaboration across the agencies represented within this Cabinet?

Ronnie: Yes, there has been a positive impact within the organization. Personnel in many offices are communicating more frequently and coordinating their service delivery. There were many wonderful proposals that got funded. We are just anxious to get out there and help make them work.

THE DREAM FULFILLED

According to a February quarterly report (*Status Report*, 1992), filed by the Cabinet for Human Resources, 21,129 students, parents, and other family members were served by the Centers from July 1, 1991, to December 31, 1991. There were 118,127 individual contacts reported and 13,558 households were served. State grant expenditures, school board contributions, and community contributions provided an estimated $4,797,697 for the first six months of Center operation.

The dream of linking social services with the educational services of a community is becoming a reality in Kentucky. Perhaps there will be fewer "dreams deferred" among the children in this state because of this program.

REFERENCES

1989. *Turning Points: Preparing American Youth for the 21st Century.* New York: Carnegie Council on Adolescent Development.

1990. "Building Communities," *Family Resource Coalition Report*, 9(2):19.

Cabinet for Human Resources. 1990. *Executive Summary*, Frankfort, Kentucky.

Cabinet for Human Resources. 1991. *Kentucky Education Reform Act: Family Resources and Youth Service Centers Status Report*, Frankfort, Kentucky.

Children's Defense Fund. *Children 1990: A Report Card, Briefing Book, and Action Primer.*

Kentucky Department of Education. 1990. *Kentucky School Laws*. Frankfort, Kentucky: Banks-Baldwin Law Publishing.

Kentucky Department of Education. 1991. *The Kentucky Education Reform Act: 1990 Implementation Report*. Frankfort, Kentucky.

Levy, Janet with Carol Copple. 1989. *Joining Forces: A Report from the First Year*. Virginia: National Association of State Boards of Education.

Melaville, Atelia. 1991. *What It Takes: Structuring Interagency Partnerships to Connect Children and Families with Comprehensive Services*, Education and Human Service Consortium.

Turning Points: Preparing American Youth for the 21st Century. 1989. New York: Carnegie Council on Adolescent Development.

CHAPTER 9

Assault on the Bureaucracy: Restructuring the Kentucky Department of Education**

MOST politicians and the general public hold the view that educational bureaucracies are part of the problem in reforming or improving public education (Elmore, 1991; Lewis, 1989). The scorn heaped upon state education agencies is legion in the field. Such agencies have historically struggled to provide leadership and technical assistance to local education agencies, and to enforce state law and regulations (Goens and Clover, 1991). They have been handicapped by low salaries, the lack of professionalism within the ranks (partly created by political appointments without regard to professional competence or experience), and the lack of adequate funding (Murphy, 1983). The most dramatic ''solution'' to the ''bureaucracy problem'' occurred in Kentucky, where the state education agency was summarily abolished when Governor Wallace Wilkinson signed into law the Kentucky Education Reform Act (KERA).

THE RAZING OF THE BUREAUCRACY

Section 156.016 of KERA states, ''Effective at the close of business on June 30, 1991, all employment positions in the Department of Education shall be abolished and the employment of all employees in the positions shall be terminated." Further, the statute authorizes the Commissioner to conduct a comprehensive study of the Department of Education and reorganize the Department, effective July 1, 1991.

Over time, the Kentucky Department of Education had gained a

**This chapter first appeared in the January 1992 Inaugural Issue of the *International Journal of Educational Reform*, Technomic Publishing Co., Inc., Lancaster, Pennsylvania. The original article covered the period from January 1, 1991, to July 1, 1991. It has been updated to include events up to July 1, 1992.

reputation as an ineffective bureaucracy heavily populated with political appointees who were perceived to be inept, and who had long since "retired on the job." In the eyes of many, the Department was considered to be part of the problem, not part of the solution to educational reform in the Bluegrass State. When the Kentucky Supreme Court decision was rendered, the General Assembly formed a Task Force on Education Reform. This Task Force was made up of representatives from the governor's office and the General Assembly. It did not include the elected and standing superintendent of public instruction or any other Kentucky practicing administrator in the State Department, nor anyone within the education professional associations, nor any educator serving in local school districts. It was the perception of the governor's office and the General Assembly that the conditions in Kentucky schools that led to the landmark state Supreme Court decision were caused by these educators and their predecessors. If there was to be a solution to these problems, the solution would have to come from outside the system.

After the Task Force on Education Reform was named, the current superintendent of public instruction, John Brock, announced his intent to run for United States Senate. This act reinforced the perception that the office of state superintendent of public instruction was used as a stepping stone to higher political positions. Alice McDonald, the previous state superintendent of public instruction, was investigated for the misuse of public funds when she ran for lieutenant governor while still in office.

The Changing of the Guard

KERA not only called for the termination of all present Department employees, it stripped the elected office of the superintendent of public instruction of almost all duties, reduced the salary of the position to $3,000 and established the new position of commissioner of education.

On January 3, 1991, Dr. Thomas Boysen assumed the role of commissioner of education for the Kentucky Department of Education. On his first day as commissioner, he said "he would try to reshape the Department of Education as quickly as possible while ensuring that employees have a fair chance at jobs in the new bureaucracy" (Jennings, 1991, p. B1). He stressed the need for a process that was fair, speedy, humane, and systemic.

While addressing more than 400 state employees that first week,

Boysen predicted the next half-year would "energize us, be fun to live through, and have a happy resolution for every one of us" (Jennings, 1991, pp. A5 and A8).

The new commissioner worked quickly. Early in January he drafted and circulated a transition plan for the Kentucky Department of Education (Boysen, 1991, pp. 1 – 4). The transition plan identified six factors that contributed to the "opportunity, complexity and urgency" of the next six months. These factors were:

(*1*) Change from one chief school officer to another

(*2*) Change from an elected state superintendent to an appointed commissioner who serves at the pleasure of the State Board

(*3*) A newly appointed State Board

(*4*) KERA mandated reforms in curriculum, governance, and finance

(*5*) KERA mandate to reorganize the Department by June 30, 1991

(*6*) The requirement that the new commissioner submit the 1992 – 94 Department biennial budget, through the State Board, to the governor by October 15, 1991

The commissioner proposed engaging in three strategies to address these factors: (1) develop a statewide system for strategic collaboration; (2) conduct an organization design study that included personnel review, compensation, and design components; and (3) begin a strategic planning process.

The first step proposed in the transition process was to form a statewide system for strategic collaboration. This involved gaining the support of the Education Coalition, and the National and Kentucky Business Roundtable, in addition to key legislators and representatives from the governor's office. The Education Coalition was a group of key executives in the state representing a variety of education interests. The Coalition was formed by Superintendent Brock early in his administration. It was considered to be the first formal group with executive director-level representation from Kentucky's major educational interest groups. It included representation from the Kentucky School Boards Association, Kentucky School Superintendent's Association, Kentucky PTA, Kentucky Education Association, Kentucky Chamber of Commerce, the Prichard Committee, Kentucky Non-Public Schools, the Kentucky Department of Education, and others. The commissioner quickly initiated a comprehensive speaking schedule that took him all over the state talking to business leaders, citizen groups, and educators.

Within the first six weeks, the commissioner garnered strong support for strategic collaboration.

Consultants were interviewed and chosen to conduct the organizational design study and lead the strategic planning process. These two activities were conducted to meet the following objectives:

(*1*) Clarify KDE role under KERA

(*2*) Create vision/mission, goals, and priorities

(*3*) Identify Annual Leadership Action Program (MBO system linking strategic plan with each manager's annual plan and evaluation)

(*4*) Review existing design and costs per function

(*5*) Review emerging state agency designs

(*6*) Conduct transition team reviews of seven KDE branches

(*7*) Conduct personnel duties survey

(*8*) Develop alternative organization design

(*9*) Review with key audience

(*10*) Establish organization

(*11*) Review current classification and compensation levels

(*12*) Survey current jobs

(*13*) Establish relationships and levels

(*14*) Conduct compensation survey

(*15*) Establish compensation relationships

(*16*) Set classification and compensation for new organization design

(*17*) Review existing personnel system

(*18*) Evaluate other state agency systems

(*19*) Develop proposed systems

(*20*) Review with key audiences

(*21*) Establish system

(*22*) Make personnel decisions
   – Secretarial, clerical, and technical
      a. Identify number of positions needed
      b. Re-qualification process by examinations, personnel evaluation, and persons to positions they hold
      c. Personnel apply for available jobs
   – Managerial and professional
      a. Identify number of positions needed
      b. Advertise positions to the state and nation
      c. Select personnel

This transition plan was to guide the work of reorganizing the Department over the next six months. The plan was reviewed and approved by the commissioner's administrative cabinet. The cabinet was made up of associate and deputy superintendents. There were two deputy superintendents and eight associate superintendents employed in the Department at the beginning of the transition.

State Merit System Complicates Process

At the time, there was a prevalent assumption that the Department of Education would be removed from the state merit system on July 1. This would enable the commissioner to design a totally new personnel system free of the many constraints attached to the merit system. Under the merit system, new employees could not be paid more than the midpoint of the grade assigned to a specific job classification, no one in the merit system could be paid more than the salary of the governor, and the red tape attached to hiring a merit employee could delay employment for several months.

In the end, the State Personnel Board confirmed that the old Department would be abolished on June 30, 1991; but also stated that the newly formed Department would operate within the merit system. The Personnel Board advised the commissioner that in order to remove the Department from the state merit system, specific statutory language would be required. Because of the constraints attached to this system, the commissioner made an appeal to the governor to add this item to the agenda of a special legislative session held in early 1991. However, the governor decided not to place the item on the "call" stating that there was not enough time to study the issue carefully before legislative action was taken. He suggested that the commissioner plan to support legislative action to establish a new personnel system for the Department of Education during the 1992 General Assembly. Legislation was introduced during the 1992 General Assembly, but because of amendments attached to the bill, it was not passed.

As the discussions regarding the status of Department merit employees continued, other governmental agency employees began to be concerned about losing their merit status. They reasoned that if employees in the Department of Education could be removed from the merit system, then over 30,000 state employees were in jeopardy of losing their status.

The regulations governing the merit system seriously hampered the ability to design an organization with reduced reporting levels, competitive salaries, and flexible project units. This situation was complicated by the fact that the consulting firm doing the organizational study was not familiar with the complexity of Kentucky's merit system and was working within a very short, five-month timeline. The next five months were filled with uncertainty on the part of the employees regarding their status. Rumors became rampant. Mistrust and anxiety grew. Information provided to clarify issues was released and then changed. There was general confusion about who was making decisions and why. This uncertainty permeated the organization at all levels.

Strategic Planning Begins

The strategic planning process began in February with a three-day retreat. The Strategic Planning Team was made up of representatives from the Department, the field, and from groups represented on the Education Coalition. The three-day dialogue was candid and direct. All of those participating felt strongly that the reorganization of the Department was a critical, necessary component to the continued successful implementation of KERA. Expectations for what the Department would be like after July 1, 1991, were high. Participants envisioned a Department of Education where creativity, flexibility, and rapid response to change were commonplace. Paperwork and red tape would be reduced. Work would be focused. Communication with the field and within the organization would be open. Staff would be evaluated honestly. There would be support for risk-taking behavior. Salaries would be increased to attract the highest caliber of staff. These expectations were reflected in the mission statement, belief statement, parameters, objectives, and strategies developed as part of the strategic planning process.

Mission Statement
The New Kentucky Department of Education

The mission of the Kentucky Department of Education, as the national catalyst for educational transformation, is to ensure for each child an internationally superior education and a love of learning through visionary leadership, vigorous stewardship and exemplary services in alliance with school, school districts and other partners.

The work of the strategic planning committee was widely circulated within the Department and throughout the state. The development of action plans to implement the strategies was postponed until after July 1 when it was anticipated that newly hired staff would be in place.

Staff Input Encouraged and Discouraged

During January and February, Department employees were encouraged to share their ideas about Department reorganization. Many employees responded to this invitation. Also during this time, the commissioner took a neutral stand regarding continuing employment of current Department employees. There was some speculation before the commissioner arrived that he would identify certain Department employees to be part of his restructured organization, and would enlist their help and support in guiding the transition. The new commissioner did not do this. Rather, he indicated to present employees that he felt bound by the statute to treat everyone the same. It was made clear that all employees could apply for any jobs in the new organization, but no one was assured of a position. Given the uncertainty of the situation, employees began to explore other employment possibilities. Even when it became clear that some top-level staff were being considered for other positions outside the Department, the commissioner maintained his neutral position.

Early in March, 1991, the commissioner announced the appointment of his new chief of staff. She was a highly respected local school superintendent who had worked previously in the Department. The job was not advertised. By the middle of March, the chief of staff began working three days a week in the Department and two days a week in her local district. She maintained this work schedule until July 1, when she became a full-time State Department employee. The task of managing the logistics of the reorganization was assigned to her.

On March 15, 1991, three important items were released to Department staff: a list of objectives for reorganization, a timeline for selection of KDE staff, and four proposed organization charts.

The objectives of the reorganization were to:

- facilitate achievement of KERA and KDE plan
- consolidate and streamline the organization to improve communication and expedite decision making
- respond to the new position of commissioner of education
- provide for integration of programs across organization lines
- provide for clear position accountability
- establish distinction between service and control/monitoring
- ensure an immediate recognition of priorities of KDE
- establish a service-oriented regional structure to coordinate and facilitate services to local districts

- ensure flexibility to allow State Department to respond to change

The objectives of the reorganization were sound and complied with the intent of the General Assembly. As the reorganization proceeded over the next few months, these objectives guided much of the decision making.

The timeline indicated that the top levels of the new organization design would be finalized by the end of March. These included the deputy commissioner positions and the associate commissioner positions. Division director positions would be identified by April 5, other professional positions, and support staff positions by May 1. All positions would be advertised early in April. Selection would take place between May 16 and 21 (see Figure 9.1).

For a variety of reasons the timelines could not be met. The entire process was much more complicated than anticipated. The timeline for getting job advertisements in the appropriate publications had to be extended because of the lead time required by the various publications. The closing date for job applications had to be extended. The logistics of putting together interviewing teams of personnel outside the Department was complicated. For example, the interviewing teams for support staff included private and public sector representatives. Approximately sixteen three-member teams conducted twenty-minute individual interviews with over 200 Department support staff who applied for continuation of employment. The internal mechanics of receiving and processing hundreds of applications had to be designed and put into place.

Four organization charts were proposed for review (see Figures 9.2–9.5). All four charts dealt with the highest levels of the organization showing the State Board of Elementary and Secondary Education, the commissioner, deputy-level positions and major areas to be included under each deputy. In the end, a variation of alternative A became the

Level	Finalize Org. Decision	Advertise/ Recruit/ Communicate	Screen	Interview	Select
Deputy Comm.	3/29	3/29	4/30	5/15	5/16
Assoc. Comm.	3/29	3/29	4/30	5/15	5/16
Division Dir.	4/12	4/15	5/15	5/30	5/31
Professional	5/15	4/4	5/4	5/15	5/31
Support	5/15	4/4	4/15	4/22	5/15

Figure 9.1. Timeline – Selection of KDE Employees.

basis of the redesign. All four alternatives introduced new terminology for labeling the bureaus: Learning Program Development was the new name for the Bureau of Instruction. While local districts were accustomed to Department reorganization, bureau and office names had been somewhat consistent over the years. The new terminology was designed to signal dramatic change and responsiveness to KERA within the Department. Two of the four proposed organization charts included a deputy commissioner position and two retained the new chief of staff position. Alternatives A and B were the most popular with staff. Alternative C was generally rejected by staff because it appeared to most closely resemble the old Department design. Alternative D was the least popular since it appeared to regionalize most Department services. Top-level management was asked to develop a plan to provide feedback to the commissioner's office by March 25, on the proposed organization designs. The final design was to be completed by March 29. The plan was to finalize the top tier of the organization and then systematically work down, building the organization to reflect the stated objectives.

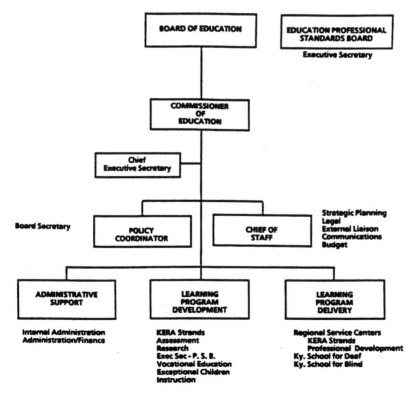

Figure 9.2. Kentucky Department of Education Organizational Chart (Alternative A).

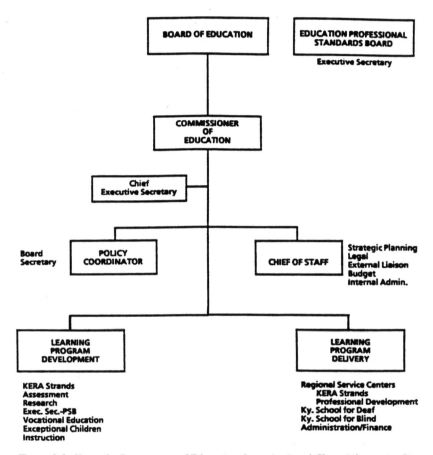

BOARD OF EDUCATION

EDUCATION PROFESSIONAL
STANDARDS BOARD

Executive Secretary

COMMISSIONER
OF
EDUCATION

Chief
Executive Secretary

Board
Secretary

POLICY
COORDINATOR

CHIEF OF STAFF

Strategic Planning
Legal
External Liaison
Budget
Internal Admin.

LEARNING
PROGRAM
DEVELOPMENT

KERA Strands
Assessment
Research
Exec. Sec.-PSB
Vocational Education
Exceptional Children
Instruction

LEARNING
PROGRAM
DELIVERY

Regional Service Centers
KERA Strands
Professional Development
Ky. School for Deaf
Ky. School for Blind
Administration/Finance

Figure 9.3. Kentucky Department of Education Organizational Chart (Alternative B).

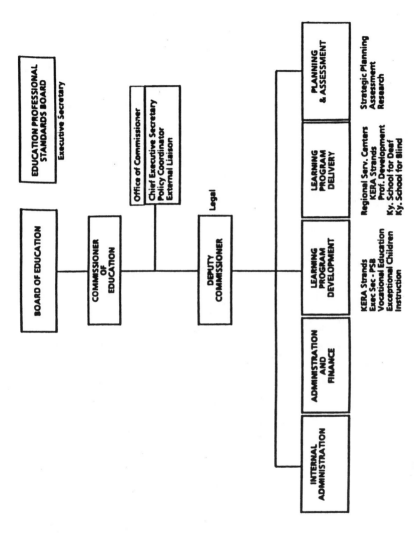

BOARD OF EDUCATION

EDUCATION PROFESSIONAL STANDARDS BOARD
Executive Secretary

COMMISSIONER OF EDUCATION

Office of Commissioner
Chief Executive Secretary
Policy Coordinator
External Liaison

DEPUTY COMMISSIONER
Legal

INTERNAL ADMINISTRATION

ADMINISTRATION AND FINANCE

LEARNING PROGRAM DEVELOPMENT
KERA Strands
Exec Sec - PSB
Vocational Education
Exceptional Children
Instruction

LEARNING PROGRAM DELIVERY
Regional Serv. Centers
KERA Strands
Prof. Development
Ky. School for Deaf
Ky. School for Blind

PLANNING & ASSESSMENT
Strategic Planning
Assessment
Research

Figure 9.4. Kentucky Department of Education Organizational Chart (Alternative C).

209

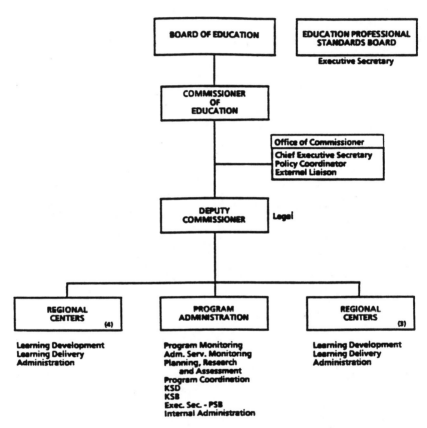

Figure 9.5. Kentucky Department of Education Organizational Chart (Alternative D).

The request for input from staff was appreciated and taken quite seriously. Each office designed a method to solicit input from personnel which included questionnaires, special meetings, and a tremendous amount of dialogue. As requested, each office submitted a written report detailing staff recommendations, suggestions, questions, and comments. Staff anticipated that the process would be repeated as the design for each level of the organization was finalized. Much of the feedback went beyond the initial request and provided staff with an opportunity to raise questions and make comments about the employment process, the creation of Regional Service Centers, and how the rest of the organizational design would look. A few sample responses are listed here.

- How can one screen (4/15) and interview (4/30) people for professional/support positions when the organization design will not be finalized until May?
- When we are selected and told on 5/21, will we know the specific position and our salary? Will we know who our director will be and where we will be located?
- How will upper level personnel interview support and professional personnel? Will they have a choice who they work with and who works for them?
- What is the rationale for each alternative for the organizational design? They seem vague, without explanation.
- How many upper management positions does the plan require?
- How will the lower tier of the organization be designed? Will there be Divisions, Units, etc.?
- How many Regional Service Centers will there be? What type of staff will be needed in the Regional Centers?

Staff Anxiety Heightens and Morale Sags

April was a month filled with heightened anxiety for staff. Personnel system regulations required that merit employees would be informed of their status by May 30. Professional and support staff were classified as merit employees. These two categories accounted for over 90 percent of the Department's staff.

As the timeline indicated, support staff was the first group to be interviewed and selected. Since the organization chart was not finalized at the end of April when support staff interviews took place, applicants interviewed for a job classification without knowing to whom they would report or to which unit, division, or office they would be attached.

Staffing procedures for support staff were announced on April 8. Each employee was asked to complete a Position Interest Form by April 15 indicating whether the employee was interested in continuing to work for the Department. Support positions were not advertised as originally announced so the clerical and secretarial staff did not have to compete with new applicants to retain their positions. Interviews were held at the Civic Center which is within walking distance of the Department building. Interviews lasted approximately twenty minutes. In most cases, staff was notified a day or two before the interview regarding the time of the interview although there were isolated cases of applicants being called late in the evening and told they had an interview the next day. As one might expect, reactions to the interview process varied from joy to tears. The interviews took place in curtained ''rooms'' on the floor of the Civic Center. Most staff appeared to be interviewing for continuation in their present position. It was unclear in the interview process how consideration would be given to those applicants who were seeking advancement or transfer to new responsibilities.

Staffing procedures for professional staff were announced on April 10. These were similar to those announced for support staff although these positions were advertised within the state. A list of position classes was attached to the announcement. Position classes are generic description classifications from the personnel system. For example, the position description for an Administrative Specialist Principal, Grade 12, says, ''Minimum Qualifications: Graduate of a college or university with a bachelor's degree supplemented by three years of professional, administrative, or business experience. Additional administrative, business, research, and/or clerical experience will substitute for the required education on a year-for-year basis. Additional education will substitute for the required experience on a year-for-year basis.''

Both support and professional staff applied for and were interviewed for position classifications, not specific roles within the classification. Although in the actual interview, the candidate's current, specific, job description was available to the interviewers and discussed in the interview, there was no guarantee that the employee would be reassigned to the same responsibility if that responsibility existed in the new organization design. Although all employee job descriptions had been updated in anticipation of this process, the job descriptions had to be designed within the constraints of the personnel system. Even the updated job descriptions did not always clearly reflect the duties being performed.

Department staff obtained additional information regarding the reorganization of the Department from the newspaper ads that appeared beginning in mid-April in several state newspapers, *Education Week*, and *The Chronicle of Higher Education*. The ads requested applications for eleven associate commissioner positions and thirty-one division director positions. These ads were posted in each of the eight elevators of the Capital Plaza office building where the Department of Education is housed. (Posting information in the elevators was the principal communication system employed by the informal network within the Department. Many other state agencies in addition to the Department of Education have offices in Capital Plaza Tower, so the system worked to inform Department employees of information and other governmental agency staff as well.) The closing date for applications ranged from April 26 to May 8. According to a newsletter sent to State Board members on May 8, the Department received over 6,000 applications. An April 16 newsletter published by the Department and sent to school personnel around the state announced, ''Boysen Beats Bushes for Brightest and Best.''

On May 10, the commissioner announced the makeup of the new Department (see Figure 9.6). The commissioner stressed that the new structure was focused more toward service than regulation. The organization chart identified deputy commissioner, associate commissioner, and division director positions. This organization chart called for four deputy positions, twelve associate commissioner positions, and forty-one division directors (seven of the division director positions would be in the newly formed regional centers). The old Department structure had three deputy positions, seven associate positions and thirty-seven division director positions (see Figure 9.7). While the new design did call for more top-level positions, the total number of positions in the Department did not increase.

Employees Notified of Status

Merit employees were notified of their employment status by certified mail. Two hundred nine of the two hundred twenty-seven, or 92 percent, of the support staff were retained by the Department. Of the 209 retained, some were demoted and a few were promoted. Of the professional staff, 166 out of 197, or 84 percent, were offered positions. Like support staff, there were demotions and a few promotions. According to a May 31 *Transition* newsletter, forty-nine ''employees did not match new requirements.'' Salary information was not included in the letters due to ''technical problems involving reclassification procedures.'' Employees were asked to accept positions without this information.

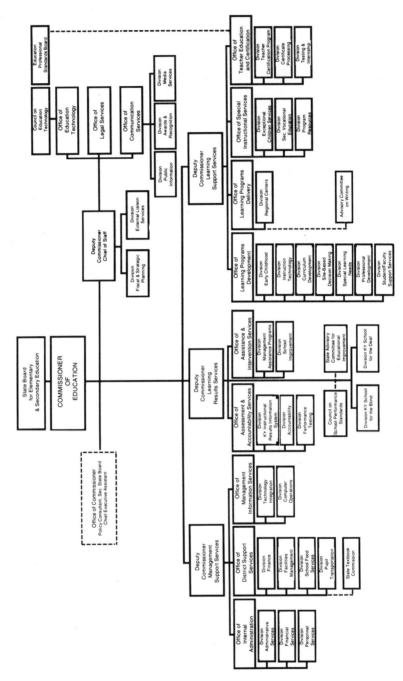

Figure 9.6. *Kentucky Department of Education Organizational Chart (after Restructuring). Source: Kentucky Department of Education.*

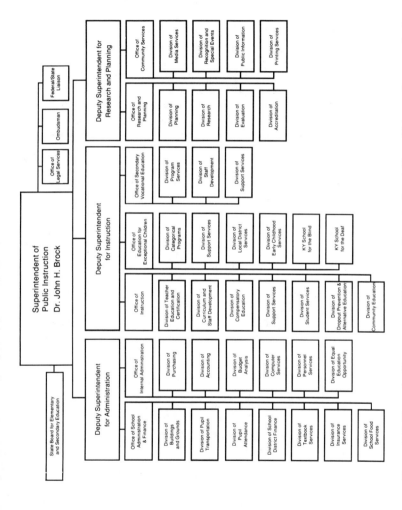

Figure 9.7. *Kentucky Department of Education Organizational Chart (Prior to Restructuring), July 1, 1990. Became Obsolete June 30, 1991.*

Most employees retained their salaries. The position notification letters did not offer employees specific positions, but did indicate the position classification they were being offered. The commissioner's May 31 *Transition* newsletter included the following statement, "During the past few months, the patience and professionalism demonstrated by department employees have been remarkable. Excellent performance under great pressure has been the rule, and that has been greatly appreciated." The statement is true!

Super Lines, Vol. 3, No. 18, contained the following KERA update.

> The national search for the best and brightest continues, and processing of more than 4,000 applications for 466 Frankfort-based positions has resulted in revised staffing timelines. Merit employees were notified by May 30 of their status within the organization: non-merit employees will be notified no later than June 15.
>
> The establishment of the Regional Service Centers will occur by January 1, 1992, pursuant to KRS 156.017. However, it is intended to proceed with staffing of regional centers this summer. There will be approximately fifty regional-based positions which will be re-advertised when the final design and location of the centers are known.
>
> ORGANIZATION—Meeting the timeline of June 30 for abolishing the current department of education is intense, due to the number of applicants, the number of interviews to be scheduled, the establishment of screening and interviewing panels, and the timely processing of that information. The intent of the process is to identify the best applicants for the positions which are available, and to focus the purpose of the department on service to the local districts as the implementation of KERA takes place.
>
> TIMELINES—The intent is that all positions, with the exception of Regional Service Centers, will be staffed by July 1. Support and professional level staff (consultants, branch managers) were notified of status by the end of May. Exempt employees will be notified of status by mid June. The statute has already put all department employees on notice that as of June 30, 1991, the current department and all positions are abolished.

Super Lines is the Department newsletter sent to all local district superintendents from the commissioner's office.

Deadlines Come and Go

On July 1, 1991, two of the four deputy commissioner positions, five of the twelve associate commissioner positions, and eleven of the forty-one director positions had been filled. Of the five associate commissioners named by July 1, two were associate superintendents in the old organization, and three were new to the state. On July 1, 1991, only two associate commissioners were working in the new Department, the associate commissioner for internal administration, and the associate commissioner for assistance and accountability. Of forty-one division director positions, twelve were filled with old Department staff and two were from out-of-state.

On July 1, 1991, in the newly reorganized Kentucky Department of Education, fourteen of the forty-seven deputies, associates, and division directors from the old Department remained in top-level management positions. Of the five newly named, out-of-state employees, one was present. A June 28 *Transition* newsletter announced twenty-four management vacancies that would be advertised again: two deputies, five associate commissioners, and seventeen division directors (seven additional division director positions for the regional centers would be advertised later).

The new organization took effect with over half of the management team not in place. The area with the most vacancies was Learning Support Services with one deputy, four associates, and twenty division director positions still to be filled. Two associates and five division directors had been hired. Many of the employees who were division directors in the old organization were demoted to merit positions as unit directors or consultants. Most had applied for director positions within the new organization, but they were not successful candidates. In order to keep the organization moving ahead, acting division directors and associates were named from existing staff. Present staff was told they could reapply for the director positions. If it was their intent to reapply, they would not be considered for the acting positions. Consequently, the acting roles were filled, for the most part, with consultants or with people who were told they would not be considered for appointment to the permanent positions.

THE OLD DEPARTMENT'S LEGACY: MATRIX MANAGEMENT

To put all of this into context, it is important to understand that the implementation of the reform initiatives was started under the old Department organization, continued during the January to June restructuring of the Department and will be carried forward within the new structure.

During the two years prior to the passage of KERA, Department staff had worked diligently to be more responsive to local district needs and enhance the technical assistance provided to districts. General feedback from the field seemed to reinforce the notion that these efforts were meeting with success.

When KERA was passed, Department staff worked quickly to organize staff into project matrix teams (Steffy, 1990) to carry forward the reform initiatives. Wilson (1989) contends that government agencies create their own organizational culture to meet their specific needs. The formation of matrix teams satisfied both a structural and cultural need. The organizational structure of the Department did not have staff assigned to areas such as school-based decision making, extended school services, performance assessment, preschool programs, or youth service centers. All of these areas were major program initiatives under the reform. Because staff was aware that the Department would be restructured under the guidance of the commissioner, it was decided to proceed with the matrix team structure rather than reorganize in April of 1990, and wait until the commissioner was chosen. There was also a strong cultural need within the Department to demonstrate that the current staff had the vision and competence necessary to carry forward the initiatives of the reform.

Matrix teams were operationally defined as voluntary groups of Department staff who had an interest in working on a particular reform initiative (Hansenfeld, 1983). Chairpersons or co-chairpersons were named for each of the initiatives and implementation efforts began. The work of the matrix teams was coordinated through the Administrative Council. As mentioned earlier, the superintendent of public instruction was actively involved in running for the U.S. Senate during this time. He continued to provide leadership and direction to the KERA implementation process, but turned the day-to-day implementation process over to the Administrative Council.

Using this structure, Department staff conducted KERA Awareness Sessions around the state to inform local district educators, university faculty, and interested community members about the specifics of the Act. House Bill 940 was a 900-plus page document that recreated and revised the new educational system mandated by the Supreme Court decision. Most everyone involved, including many of the legislators, were not completely aware of all of the provisions of the bill. There was a tremendous need for specific information about what the bill said. The old Department fulfilled that need, and from most accounts, quite well, earning editorial praise from leading newspapers.

The bill dramatically changed the funding formula for Kentucky schools. At the time the bill was signed into law, districts were attempting to develop their budgets for the 1990–91 school year, and they needed to know how much state funding they would receive. Management Support Services staff, working around the clock, were able to provide tentative budget information to districts by the end of May, 1990. Since many districts qualified for twenty-five percent increases in state funds, this was vital information. Research and Planning staff developed timelines for programmatic implementation and developed a comprehensive index for the bill. They also had responsibility for leading the site-based, decision-making initiative. Since every state regulation had to be modified, created, or reenacted, the State Board of Elementary and Secondary Education and the Department staff tackled the complicated task of regulation review and development. Instruction staff were responsible for the bulk of the programmatic initiatives. Within four months after passage of the bill, 130 school districts had approved proposals to begin the four-year-old preschool program. Because of the volume of work to be done, few members of the staff had time to think about the restructuring of the Department or what it might mean to them personally.

In January, the commissioner requested that the initiatives continue with the matrix team structure while the restructuring was taking place. Each matrix team filed a final report on June 30, 1991, describing the status of the program. These reports, combined with the reports completed in June, 1990, and December, 1990, provided clear documentation of the design, development, and implementation of each program.

STILL SEARCHING FOR THE BEST AND BRIGHTEST

Many of the programmatic initiatives embodied in KERA are reflected in the organizational structure of the new Department. There are divisions for accountability, site-based decision making, performance testing, and regional centers in the new design. Staff with specific expertise in these areas were sought to fill these critical positions.

While salary increases for Department staff retained in the new organization had to comply with personnel regulations, the commissioner was able to get approval from the Personnel Board to negotiate special contracts for newly hired, top-level, non-merit staff. By February, 1992, thirty-two of the agency's top administrators were being paid through a special contract (*State Journal*, Feb. 2, 1992). This included all four deputy commissioners. The average salary paid to division directors through the special contract was $61,900. The average salary for division directors on the Department payroll was $51,823 (*State Journal*, p. 46).

The new commissioner's salary, at $125,000, was about twice that of the superintendent of public instruction. Deputy positions in the new structure would pay in the upper eighties. Most deputies in the old Department made salaries in the sixties.

Administrative staff, who initially were optimistic about the potential benefits of restructuring, gradually began to voice concern about the delays, lack of specific knowledge about the design of the organization, and the procedures used to carry the process forward.

By late April and throughout May, current deputies and associates were consulted regarding the specifics of the structure at the division and unit level. There were individual meetings with the consulting firm or the chief of staff. How suggestions made by one associate or deputy might relate to suggestions made by another associate or deputy was never clear. By early June when interviews for division director positions took place, the high levels of stress and anxiety produced a climate of cynicism and distrust.

Division director interviews took place at a nearby hotel. The interviewing teams included current Department administrators and field-based school administrators. The interviewing teams were advisory to the commissioner. Some of the same problems that plagued the process for support and professional staff persisted.

When the day arrived to notify non-merit staff of their status (about the middle of June), one by one they went to the State Board room where they met with the director of personnel. Most were told they would be demoted without a salary cut. Some were told they would be demoted with a salary cut. Some were fired. A few were promoted. In some instances, the deputies knew about the decisions, and in some cases they did not. In one situation, the principal assistant to a deputy was fired. The deputy had not been informed of the decision.

The merit staff who were fired filed a class action suit contending that Section 42 of House Bill 940 as enacted by the 1990 General Assembly was unconstitutional and null and void. They unsuccessfully sought an injunction prohibiting the Department from carrying out the termination. This suit was later withdrawn because the governor intervened and assured terminated staff that every effort would be made to assist them in finding jobs in other governmental agencies. One terminated employee continued to report to work the first few days of July after his official termination date.

Because of fears regarding the uncertain emotional stability of some employees, security in the Department was strengthened during the transition time. Staff members were directed to get new picture identification cards and told that the old ones would not be valid after July 1.

At the time this chapter was being prepared (July, 1991), twenty-four top-level administrative jobs had been reopened. It was expected that advertisement, selection, and relocation would take several months to complete. Seven additional director positions and approximately fifty support and professional positions to staff the regional system were scheduled to be advertised later.

A BUREAUCRACY BY ANY OTHER NAME IS STILL . . .

The new organization design holds some potential for improved services to districts. While still essentially bureaucratic in design, in some ways it has been vastly streamlined, in others it has been expanded to more closely adhere to the programmatic initiatives reflected in KERA. With the exception of the firing of forty-nine merit employees, the reorganization that has taken place could have been accomplished without statutory language. In the past, it was quite customary for a newly elected state superintendent to reorganize the Department through executive order. In that process, merit positions could be abolished or added. Non-merit employees in the Department have always worked at the discretion of the old state superintendent of public instruction.

At the deputy level, the new structure has four positions. One of the deputies serves as chief of staff and acts as the commissioner in his absence. Three important Department-wide functions are attached to this deputy position: legal services, educational technology, and communication services. This office also has responsibility for fiscal and strategic planning and liaison activities with legislators, the federal government, other education associations, and governmental agencies. The Office of Communication Services and the three divisions attached to that office—Media Services, Awards and Recognition, and Public Information—were located in the old Bureau of Research and Planning. The Department planning function and the external liaison function were also in that bureau. When the top-level administrative positions are filled, this design should facilitate better coordination of the functions attached to the chief of staff. On July 1, 1991, two of the three associate commissioner positions and all of the division director positions reporting to the chief of staff were vacant.

The area that underwent the least amount of change was Management Support Services. There was consolidation of divisions in Internal Administration and District Support Services, and a new office of Management Information Services was created. This function had been at the division level in the old structure. Because of the vastly expanded emphasis on developing a statewide technology network, this function was elevated to an office level. Many of the division directors who were retained work in this bureau.

The most dramatic changes took place in the bureaus of Learning Results Services and Learning Support Services. Here, there was an attempt to integrate special education, vocational education, and regular education services; to consolidate district technical assistance functions; to expand assessment and accountability services; to accommodate the new regional technical assistance function; and to elevate the teacher education and certification function in keeping with the statutory creation of the Professional Standards Board.

The deputies responsible for these functions in the old organizations took other positions. Of the thirty-one deputies, office heads, and division directors in the Bureau of Instruction and the Bureau of Research and Planning, one office head and five division directors remained. It appeared that the area that underwent the most dramatic organizational change was also the area where there were the most unfilled, top-level positions as of July 1, 1991.

In a June 28, 1991, transition memo, Dr. Boysen had this to say:

> It has been said that a thing well begun is half done. As we begin the implementation of the new Kentucky Department of Education, let me warmly welcome you to the team and express my enthusiasm for the contribution that you are going to make, for the fun we are going to have in this process, and for the role we are going to play in putting Kentucky children and youth on top of the world.

Kentucky's restructuring of the Department of Education was hampered by the lack of specificity in the language of the statute, by the lack of other state models to follow, by the short timeline under which they were working, and by the complicated intricacies of a state personnel system.

ASSESSING THE LEARNING CURVE: LOOKING BACK AT WHAT HAPPENED

As other state legislators contemplate State Department restructuring as a means of improving the education system, it is hoped that the lessons learned in the Kentucky experience will be noted.

Legislators and new State Education Agency heads contemplating this kind of action are offered the following suggestions.

(*1*) Make every effort to effectuate the restructuring within the parameters of the present personnel system within the state.

(*2*) If statutory changes are contemplated, be sure the language is constitutionally appropriate.

(*3*) Be sure the federal constitutional rights of all employees are protected.

(*4*) Provide adequate time for the restructuring.

(*5*) Staff from the top down, not from the bottom up.

(*6*) Design the process carefully, share this information with staff and adhere to the timelines.

(*7*) Identify key staff in the present organization and enlist their help in each step of the process.

(*8*) Write specific job descriptions and have these available to applicants.

(*9*) If outside personnel are going to be used in the interviewing process, be sure they have an appropriate orientation.

(*10*) Maintain confidentiality of all applicant information.

(*11*) Be sure there is adequate staff to handle the volume of applications, interviews, and reference checks.

(*12*) Involve current staff in each step of the redesign. Most current State Department staff understand the complexity of the organization. Reorganizing a state department of education is far different from reorganizing a local school district. The interplay of the state agency with the federal and local education agencies is complex.

(*13*) The restructuring of a state department of education is only a means to an end, not the end.

The Kentucky Education Reform Act and the financial support provided to implement this Act remains one of this country's best models for effecting change in its public schools. Many other states have similar reform legislation, but lack the financial support needed to implement the reforms. Still other states are in great financial difficulty and are looking for ways to cut back on state budgets. Sometimes, reform is just a euphemism for fiscal retrenchment.

The Kentucky experience amply demonstrates that the restructuring of a state bureaucracy is far more complicated than anyone had perceived. What was viewed by some legislators as a means to purge its state education agency of incompetent, non-productive staff, turned out to be a self-defeating exercise that left the "new" agency gutted of top-level administrators, demoralized, and drifting without strong, aggressive leadership at a time when local school districts were relying on the state agency to guide them. Instead of the so-called "incompetents" leaving the sinking ship, some of the most well-qualified and competent staff, familiar with Kentucky and its problems, left the Department.

Perhaps the most galling aspect of the "restructuring" of the Kentucky Department of Education was that an unprecedented opportunity to de-bureaucratize the state agency and create a new design that facilitated the empowerment of change (Belasco, 1990) was lost. A far different kind of organizational model, one that was more fluid, less top heavy, "flat," and democratic (Davis and Lawrence, 1977) could have been born. This unprecedented opportunity was never fully understood by those guiding the process.

Instead, where a bureaucracy had existed before, it was resurrected again; with somewhat different functions, more aligned with the legislative language, but a bureaucracy nonetheless. The "phoenix" expected from the ashes of the old Kentucky Department of Education is exactly the same kind of bird as before, albeit with somewhat different colored feathers. The true enemy of an efficient, state education agency was not the popular media myth of "droves" of incompetents and drones on the Department payroll, but the structure of the agency itself.

The commissioner, his consultants, and key advisers, who were handed a once in a lifetime "window" to envision a new, different, and better structure for a state education agency, had no different vision. Anyone looking through the smoke and mirrors will see the "new" old Kentucky Department of Education in Frankfort today. "Restructuring" turned out to be the same old process of bureaucratic adjustments practiced by every new administration. The more correct title for what happened from January, 1991, to July, 1991, in the Kentucky Department of Education was simply *reorganization*.

Reorganization Continues

That reorganization continues to this day. By the late fall of 1991, the Department had been successful in filling most of the top-level management positions. Staff and furniture had been reconfigured and telephone numbers were published. New staff, coming to the state from other parts of the country, began the slow process of getting settled, learning about how state government works, and becoming acquainted with the people in the Department they would work with and supervise. Since most of the staff below the division director level were those who had made the transition from the old Department structure to the new Department structure, there was a general morale problem within the Department that is just beginning to dissipate.

By spring, 1992, there were definite signs of improved morale in selected divisions, although the overall tenor of the Department could be described as somber. The workload was proceeding at a frenzied pace due to the statutory timelines and the program approval process established by the commissioner. Program guidelines were often distributed to districts in draft form in order to provide districts with as much lead time as possible in completing required applications. A few of the programs requiring district application and approval included the Primary program, Preschool program, Professional Development Plan, and Family Resource and Youth Services Center proposals. These were in addition to the yearly 94-142 Part B proposal, Chapter I, Chapter II, Migrant, Drug and Alcohol proposals, and Vocational Education proposals. To add to the frenzy at the state and local levels, districts completed the first round of performance assessment during the spring of 1992 and the draft curriculum framework was released. Department of Education staff were crisscrossing the state conducting orientation sessions on various programmatic initiatives.

In the midst of all this activity, the reorganization of the Department continues. The deputy commissioner for management support services resigned and was replaced by a Kentucky superintendent. The deputy for learning support services became the deputy chief of staff and the deputy chief of staff became the deputy for learning support services. The Division for Professional Development was moved from Learning Support Services to Learning Results Services and a new division director was hired. It is expected that the reorganization will continue into the future as the focus for KERA implementation evolves.

WHAT IS NEXT

Most of the design work on the programmatic initiatives in KERA is underway or implemented. The next big initiative for the Department will be to build a school district support mechanism to deal with the school and district accountability features of KERA. Sanctions and rewards, schools in crisis, and distinguished educators will all materialize within the next two years. The focus of the Department will move away from program development to providing districts with the assistance they need to solve "schooling problems," which have traditionally kept almost a third of Kentucky's youth from graduating high school with high levels of demonstrated competence.

The statutory requirement for the restructuring of the Kentucky Department of Education was perhaps more of a symbolic gesture than a substantive measure. It still walks like a bureaucracy, talks like a bureaucracy, and looks like a bureaucracy.

REFERENCES

Belasco, J. 1990. *Teaching the Elephant to Dance; Empowering Change in Your Organization*. New York: Crown Publishers, Inc.

Boysen, T. 1991, *Transition Plan for the Kentucky Department of Education*. Unpublished raw data, pp. 1−4.

Coldiron, Madelynn. 1992. "State's Education Department Plagued with Morale Problem," *State Journal*, Feb. 3, l992.

Davis, S. and P. Lawrence. 1977. *Matrix*. Reading, Massachusetts: Addison-Wesley Publishing Company.

Elmore, R. l991. *Restructuring Schools: The Next Generation of Education Reform*. San Francisco: Jossey-Bass Publishers.

Goens, G. and S. Clover. l991. *Mastering School Reform*. Boston: Allyn and Bacon.

Hansenfeld, Y. 1983. *Human Service Organizations*. Englewood Cliffs: Prentice-Hall, Inc.

Jennings, M. 1991. "New School Chief Aiming for Speed, Fairness as He Makes Changes," *Courier Journal* (January 4):B1.

Jennings, M. 1991. "Boysen Outlines Quick Transition Department Faces," *Courier Journal* (January 5):A5 and A8.

Kentucky Department of Education. *Superlines*, 3(18).

Kentucky Department of Education. 1990. *Kentucky School Laws*. Frankfort, Kentucky: Banks-Baldwin Law Publishing.

Kentucky Department of Education. 1991. *The Kentucky Education Reform Act: 1990 Implementation Report*. Frankfort, Kentucky.

Kentucky Department of Education. 1991. *Transition Newsletter* (May 31).

Lewis, A. 1989. *Restructuring American Schools*. American Association of School Administrators.

Murphy, J. 1983. "Progress and Problems: The Paradox of State Reform," in *Policy Making in Education*, A. Lieberman and M. McLaughlin, eds., Chicago: The University of Chicago Press.

Steffy, B. 1990. "Matrix Management for a State Department of Education," *National Forum of Applied Educational Research*, 4(1):12.

Steffy, B. 1992. "Assault on the Bureaucracy: Restructuring the Kentucky Department of Education," *International Journal of Educational Reform*, 1(1).

Wilson, J. 1989. *Bureaucracy*. New York: Basic Books, Inc.

CHAPTER 10

Professional Development

THE professional development initiatives incorporated in KERA are designed to impact all components of preservice and inservice activities for educators. They are designed to impact the way teachers and administrators are trained and certified, the way university training programs are designed and accredited, the way teachers teach and the way administrators administer. These initiatives require the State Department of Education to design and implement a network of regional service centers and require school districts to work together to coordinate district professional development activities. In addition, through a joint resolution passed by the House and the Senate in 1990, all state universities are required to develop plans to demonstrate how the university system is assisting in the successful implementation of KERA.

GETTING STARTED

Prior to the passage of KERA, Kentucky law designed four days of the mandated 185-day school calendar for professional development. While districts were required to submit professional development plans to the state for approval, they were free to design the program based on a local district needs assessment. KERA, as enacted in 1990, mandated that districts address the following topics: "the Kentucky Education Reform Act; school-based decision making; performance-based student assessment; non-graded primary programs; research-based instructional practices; instructional uses of technology; and effective awareness and sensitivity training so teachers can motivate and nurture students of diverse cultures" (KDE, 1990, KRS 156.095).

Typically, district professional development plans are completed in the spring and submitted to the State Department for approval in May. Because of the new law-mandated inservice topics, districts were given additional time to revise plans and submit them for approval. The vast majority of the professional development activities conducted during the first year of KERA dealt with awareness-level training. The State Department delivered two series of awareness sessions in various locations around the state to inform district administrators about the contents of the statute and explain initial program implementation activities. Literally, programs were being designed, information was being disseminated, and districts were developing programs almost simultaneously. As explained in Chapter 7, implementation of the Preschool program by the beginning of the 1990−91 school year was mandatory unless a district applied for a waiver due to physical space limitations. In May, the Department of Education was providing awareness information about the program; in June, the funding formula was being explained; in July, district applications were being prepared; in August, districts were receiving program approval; and in early fall, 130 districts began the program.

At the same time, the state was being flooded with announcements of workshops dealing with all aspects of the mandated topics. Districts were bombarded by consultants claiming to have expertise. Since districts were free to choose whomever they wanted to deliver the required inservice, there was very little quality control. During this time, the State Department developed several awareness-level videotapes for districts to use at the beginning of the 1990−91 school year to provide training for teachers, parents, and community. As mentioned before, many of the professional organizations in the state also developed training materials to assist districts. In addition, the Kentucky Educational Television (KET) system was used to broadcast professional development programs. The KET satellite system enabled each school building to receive programming from the Lexington studio. During the first year of KERA, the Department of Education planned two day-long inservice programs. The first program dealt with site-based decision making and the second dealt with performance assessment. While the KET system has proved to be an invaluable mechanism for getting current, accurate information to districts in a timely fashion, the early experiment with day-long inservice programs was not continued. Most districts tape the KET programs and utilize them for professional development within their own districts.

In addition to the videotapes, the KET programs, and the general awareness sessions, the Department began to initiate institutes, conferences, and training sessions in all the mandated areas. Also, during this time, districts joined together to form ''consortia'' for the purpose of planning cooperative professional development activities.

KRS 1566.0951

(1) During the 1990−91 school year, the school district shall receive a planning grant to be used in conjunction with other districts to plan for professional development activities through the 1994−95 school year. By June 30, 1991, each district, except those districts with an enrollment of twenty thousand (20,000) or more students, shall have joined a consortium involving two (2) or more districts and shall have submitted a preliminary professional development plan to the Department of Education . . . When a consortium is operational, a consortium plan may replace plans for individual districts which are members of the consortium.

(2) During the school years 1991−92, through 1994−95, the consortia shall receive the districts' professional development funds to provide a high quality, coordinated professional development program to the staff of the member districts.

(3) After July 1, 1995, a school district shall be allowed to withdraw from the consortium and expend its professional development funds on any professional development activities it chooses. (KDE, 1990)

During the 1990−91 school year each district received $1 per student to support professional development planning activities. During the 1991−92 school year it was increased to $5 per student. For both the 1992−93 and the 1993−94 school years, $15 per pupil in average daily membership has been designated for professional development each year.

Among the state's 176 school districts, only two were not required to form a consortium. These were Jefferson County, serving Louisville with a student population in excess of 80,000, and Fayette County, serving Lexington with a student population in excess of 28,000.

The statute suggests that whatever inservice is required to enable educators to successfully implement KERA should be able to be delivered over the five-year period from April, 1990, to July, 1995. With the draft curriculum framework provided to districts in June, 1992, the statutory mandate that all districts implement the Primary School program by the beginning of the 1993−94 school year, and the implementation of the interim state performance assessment system during the spring of 1992 with its link to individual school sanctions and rewards, educators all over the state are becoming increasingly aware of the magnitude of the changes that are being required. Probably the most significant variable in this realization was the fact that the 1992 General Assembly did not significantly alter KERA. Prior to that session, there were still many non-believers who expected the reform to be short-lived. Now, they are beginning to understand the strength of the legislative commitment. Fortunately, the comprehensive professional development support system required to deliver the needed training is beginning to materialize under the direction of the Department of Education.

REGIONAL SERVICE CENTERS

One of the key components of this professional development support system is the Regional Service Center network. In the past, Kentucky had established a regional education network, but this system was abolished several years ago. KERA called for the design of a new Regional Service Center system to support professional development activities.

KRS 156.017 Regional service centers

Effective January 1, 1992, the commissioner of education shall establish regional service centers in the Commonwealth that primarily focus on the professional development of employees of school districts. The regional service centers shall be staffed by employees of the Department of Education . . . The regional service centers may include, but are not limited to, specially trained technical assistance teams and may facilitate the work of school district cooperatives or consortia. (KDE, 1990, p. 152)

During the time when the state had no formalized regional service system, districts formed informal networks called cooperatives. There are seven major cooperatives in the state. However, not all districts belong to a cooperative and some districts belong to more than one. In addition, each of the cooperatives is unique. Some offer extensive technology services; others focus on professional development and cooperative bidding; still others offer a combination of services. One cooperative serves more than forty districts. Another serves less than fifteen. Generally, the cooperative employs an executive director who works for the districts contributing to the cooperative. Cooperative employees are not State Department employees.

When districts were mandated by KERA to form a consortium to plan professional development activities, the consortia arrangement did not necessarily match the cooperative arrangement. In addition, each of the state universities operates a professional development center serving a designated number of districts. There are eight state universities. Now the state has a Regional Service Center system that is beginning to become operational and that is different from the cooperative system, the consortia system, and the university professional development system. For example, the Lexington campus of the University of Kentucky is the site for the University Professional Development Center, the Central Kentucky Cooperative, and a new state Regional Service Center. Currently, the staff of each one of these offices is working hard to develop a harmonious relationship to ensure that the work of each office compliments the implementation of KERA.

The State Department has established eight Regional Service Centers (RSC). Some of the Centers are located on university campuses and some are not. A director for each Center has been employed by the State Department. Staffing for each Center was completed by the beginning of the 1992−93 school year. The conceptual framework (KDE, 1991, *Regional Service Centers*) for the Regional Service Center system identified the purpose of the Centers.

> The purpose of each RSC is to enable school districts and schools, with the help of regional cooperative, consortia, and higher education, to implement KERA programs. More than providing assistance and brokering of services, however, each RSC is charged with helping client districts to assess professional development needs, diagnose appropriate implementation strategies and develop an internal capacity for change.

> Serving as a vehicle of communication and interaction between the field and the Kentucky Department of Education, each RSC will be involved both in the review of KERA Program designs as well as in their delivery at the school district level. Each RSC, with support from KDE Research and Evaluation staff, will also review and analyze both the appropriateness and effectiveness of all KERA related support services provided by affiliate partners.

The basic functions of the centers will include professional development, assistance in designing KERA implementation plans, technical assistance in program implementation, gathering feedback regarding the effectiveness of KERA programs, and leadership development. The Department solicited competitive proposals for the placement of the centers. The criteria for the selection of sites included facilities, accessibility, and numbers of districts and staff to be served by the Center. When completely operational, it is expected that these Centers will provide an important communication link between the State Department and local districts.

PROFESSIONAL DEVELOPMENT PLANNING PROCESS

In April, 1992, the Department of Education held a conference for district professional development coordinators. Each district in the state is required to have a person designated as the district's professional development coordinator. Since 124 of the 176 school districts in the state have a student population of less than 3,000 students (KDE, 1991, *School Financial Analysis*), this responsibility is usually one of the many functions assigned to the position of district supervisor. A supervisor in Kentucky's schools is generally a K – 12 staff position with duties similar to an assistant superintendent in many other states.

At the April conference, the Department formally introduced the newly hired Regional Service Center directors and reviewed the professional development planning process for the 1992 – 93 year. Since the Regional Service Centers were not fully functioning at that time, planning for professional development activities was coordinated through the district and consortia network.

While inservice topics were no longer mandated by statute, the Department encouraged districts to focus on nine areas (KDE, 1992).

(*1*) Preschool program

(*2*) Primary program

(*3*) Kentucky's learning goals, valued outcomes, and performance assessment of valued outcomes

(*4*) Research-based instructional strategies

(*5*) Development of school curricula aligned with KERA learning goals, the valued outcomes, and the non-cognitive school goals

(*6*) Educational technology

(*7*) Learning and assessment for diverse populations

(*8*) School-based decision making

(*9*) Leadership development

Figure 10.1 provides an overview of the roles and responsibilities of local schools, school districts, consortia, Regional Service Centers, a newly formed Standards Advisory Council, and the Division of Professional Development. Because of the short timeline for planning for the 1992 – 93 school year (plans were due to the Department by May 15) the planning process was recommended, but not required, to begin at the school level. In future years, the development of the plan will begin at the school site. Figure 10.2 outlines the process for developing, review-

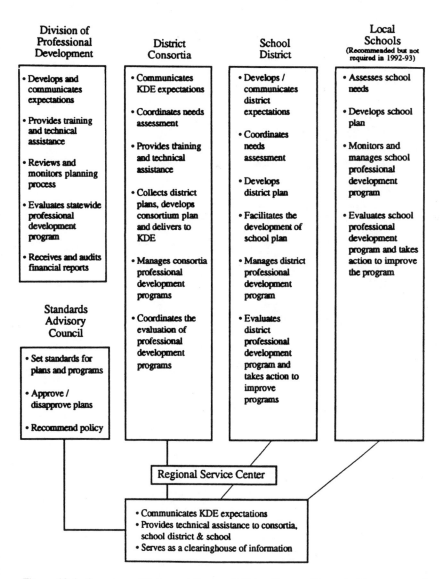

Division of Professional Development

- Develops and communicates expectations
- Provides training and technical assistance
- Reviews and monitors planning process
- Evaluates statewide professional development program
- Receives and audits financial reports

Standards Advisory Council

- Set standards for plans and programs
- Approve / disapprove plans
- Recommend policy

District Consortia

- Communicates KDE expectations
- Coordinates needs assessment
- Provides training and technical assistance
- Collects district plans, develops consortium plan and delivers to KDE
- Manages consortia professional development programs
- Coordinates the evaluation of professional development programs

School District

- Develops / communicates district expectations
- Coordinates needs assessment
- Develops district plan
- Facilitates the development of school plan
- Manages district professional development program
- Evaluates district professional development program and takes action to improve programs

Local Schools
(Recommended but not required in 1992-93)

- Assesses school needs
- Develops school plan
- Monitors and manages school professional development program
- Evaluates school professional development program and takes action to improve the program

Regional Service Center

- Communicates KDE expectations
- Provides technical assistance to consortia, school district & school
- Serves as a clearinghouse of information

Figure 10.1. Overview of Roles and Responsibilities. Source: Kentucky Department of Education, 1992.

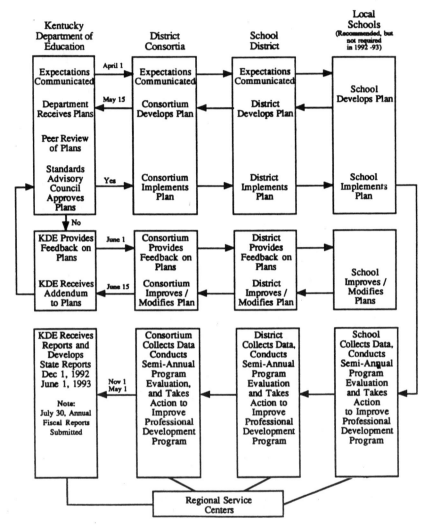

Figure 10.2. Overview of the Process. Source: Kentucky Department of Education, 1992.

ing, and approving plans. To assist districts and consortia with submitting their plans, the Department suggested a procedure to be followed (KDE, 1992, pp. 8—10).

The process for developing the plan for 1992—93:

(1) The Department of Education communicates expectations and standards to consortia and school districts:

— develops and communicates expectations for professional

development programs: roles, processes, and standards of performance
— meets with consortia directors to explain roles, processes, and standards
— provides training for professional development coordinators

(2) Consortium assists in communication of expectations and standards to local school districts:
— meets with superintendents and professional development coordinators to explain and interpret roles, processes, and standards
— provides training and/or technical assistance to districts and/or schools needed to facilitate the needs assessment and planning process
— interfaces with Department of Education staff on description of roles, processes, and standards that need clarification

(3) Each district develops structures and processes for planning based on state expectations:
— establishes goals and/or objectives for professional development (incorporates Kentucky Department of Education expectations; adds district focus)
— trains professional development committees and describes technical assistance resources available to local schools for planning and how to access these resources
— describes the content and planning process required for local school plans (school-level plans are recommended but not required for 1992–93)

(4) Each local school prepares professional development plans (recommended but not required for 1992–93):
— school goals and/or objectives for all school staff (incorporates district goals; adds school focus)
— identification of professional development needs relative to KERA components [who needs what kind of training (KERA component) at what level of development and when (timeline)]
— description of the professional development sessions/experiences and/or the type of programs and sessions/experiences required for professional growth of staff
— school's plan for supporting and encouraging the implementation of skills learned through professional development sessions/experiences

- school's plan for monitoring the selection and delivery of quality of professional development sessions/experiences
- school's plan for collecting data on professional growth and on the quality of professional development sessions/experiences, and taking action to improve professional development

(5) District aggregates school plans or develops a district plan.
- district goals and objectives for all school staff
- identification of professional development needs relative to KERA components
- description of professional development sessions/experiences to address district needs: format for activity, stage of activity (see Figure 10.3), sessions/experiences by KERA component, proposed providers of sessions/experiences, timeline for sessions/experiences
- district plan for ensuring the selection and delivery of quality professional development sessions/experiences
- district plan for evaluating and taking action to improve professional development programs

(6) Consortium collects district plans, aggregates needs assessment data, determines sessions/experiences to be provided by consortium, develops consortium professional development plan, and submits consortium plans and district plans to Kentucky Department of Education. The consortium plan includes the following:
- consortium goals and objectives for professional development
- description of professional development needs to be served by the consortium
- description of professional development sessions/experiences to be provided by the consortium, providers of sessions/experiences, and dates of sessions/experiences
- consortium's plan for ensuring the delivery of high-quality professional development programs and sessions/experiences provided by the consortium (e.g., reference check, review of training materials, etc.)
- consortium's plan for collecting data on professional growth and the quality of professional development sessions/experiences, analyzing data, evaluating programs, and taking actions to improve professional development programs provided by the consortium

(7) Department of Education with the assistance of district professional development coordinators from across the state conducts a

Stage of Professional Development	Desired Practitioner Outcomes for Training	Appropriate Training Strategies and Staff Development Processes for Maximum Growth
1. Orientation / Awareness Stage at which practitioners develop knowledge and understanding of key concepts, processes, and organizational structures of the program	• Be able to describe the general characteristics of the program and the requirements for use. • Analyze his/her role in the program based upon program characteristics and requirements and the program's demands on the user and the school. • Be able to identify the knowledge / skills needed for program implementation	• Provide information on key concepts • Address personal concerns • Present exemplars and non exemplars • Define competencies and requirements to implement program • Provide opportunities for exploration
2. Preparation / Application Stage at which practitioners develop the skills and processes to begin program implementation	• Develop the knowledge and skills needed for initial implementation of the program. • Identify the logistical requirements, necessary resources, and training for initial use of the programs. • Analyze existing resources to determine resources which need to be ordered. • Organize activities, events, and resources for initial use of the program.	• Model skills and processes • Simulate tasks and processes • Provide coaching and feedback • Observation of exemplary programs
3. Implementation / Management Stage at which practitioners learn to master the required tasks for implementation of the program in their workplace	• Develop the knowledge and skills needed to organize and manage resources, activities, and events related to day-to-day use of the program. • Analyze his / her use of the program with regard to problems of logistics, management, time, schedules, resources, and reactions of the student. • Make appropriate adaptations / modifications in program needed to address local managerial and / or logistical issues. • Develop a knowledge of long term requirements for the use of the program.	• Mentoring • Technical Assistance • Coaching • Networking of Resources • Visitation of successful programs in operation
4. Refinement / Impact Stage at which practitioners vary the use of practices to achieve maximum impact on student achievement	• Analyze cognitive and affective effects of program on students. • Develops immediate and long range plans which address possible / needed changes in the program to enhance student outcomes	• Networking with consultants and other practitioners operating at impact stage • Regional and national sharing conferences • Serving as training facilitators to other programs

Figure 10.3. *Stages of Development Related to Outcomes and Professional Development Strategies. Source: Kentucky Department of Education, 1992.*

    peer review of consortia plans. Peer review will be based upon standards and criteria for professional development plans.

(8) Standards Advisory Council approves plans or returns to consortia for additional work.

(9) Districts with approved plans are provided funding. Districts with plans that need additional work are provided assistance through consortia and Regional Service Centers.

(*10*) Consortia and districts modify plans with technical assistance provided by Regional Service Centers.

(*11*) Standards Advisory Council reconsiders revised plans.

(*12*) Department of Education collects statewide data on professional growth and on the quality of professional development sessions/experiences and provides periodic reports to consortia and school districts.

The process, as outlined above, is comprehensive and is designed to focus professional development activities on building high levels of competence. As Figure 10.3 shows, the professional development activities designed by schools, districts, and consortia are expected to provide a sequence of experiences which enables participants to begin at a level of orientation and awareness where they are gaining an understanding and beginning to build their knowledge base; enable the participants to begin program implementation; provide additional experiences so that participants gain mastery, and finally result in acquiring a level of expertise that enables the educator to improve student achievement.

FIVE ADDITIONAL PROFESSIONAL DEVELOPMENT DAYS

Because of the expectation that all educators acquire mastery-level expertise of the skills necessary to assure effective program implementation of all the components of KERA, it has become increasingly clear that four professional development days is not sufficient to provide all of the inservice necessary to achieve this objective. Consequently, the commissioner of education requested that the General Assembly approve a provision to enable local school districts to request five additional inservice days for each of the next two years. These additional days are subtracted from the number of required student attendance days. The provision was approved by the 1992 General Assembly. Local school boards may approve up to five additional professional days for all schools in the district or selected schools. Some districts have chosen to approve five additional days for the elementary schools in the district to enable them to prepare for the implementation of primary school. Some districts have requested one additional day. Still others have requested ten half-days. Districts are not required to request any additional professional development time if they feel it is not needed.

To assure the General Assembly that the additional professional development time would be used to deliver quality professional development, the state developed an approved series of training materials. If a district requests any of the five additional days, they must provide state-approved professional development. The state-approved professional development may be a component of the Integrated Professional Development series or a program provided by a consultant who has been approved by the state. The Integrated Professional Development series is designed as a train-the-trainer model. The series has been designed for five levels of inservice: preschool, primary, intermediate, middle, and high school. The topics addressed by each of the levels include valued outcomes, curriculum frameworks, educational technology, diverse learning needs, performance assessment, instructional strategies, effective instruction, and change strategies. During June, 1992, the Department trained a large contingent of university faculty, consultants, and other educators to deliver the series. Participants who successfully completed the training were certified by the state to deliver the training to districts requesting the five additional days.

During the 1991−92 school year, the Department worked with Susan Loucks-Horsley to develop a list of attributes of effective professional development (KDE, 1992, *Planning Professional Development*, p. 2). These attributes were used by the Department to assist in the design of the professional development planning and monitoring process. These attributes include:

(*1*) Focusing on instruction and student outcomes

(*2*) Promoting peer review, collegiality, and collaboration

(*3*) Encouraging flexibility, experimentation, and risk taking, rather than prescribing lockstep behaviors or punishing failures

(*4*) Involving participants in making decisions about content, format, timing, implementation specifics, evaluation, and other dimensions of the professional development sessions/experiences

(*5*) Including realistic time estimates for changes in practice, allowing participants sufficient time to be able to learn, plan for, and try out new skills, reflect on their success with helpful coaches, revise and retry, learn more, and get support for their efforts

(*6*) Increasing the integration and linkages among schools, districts, and consortia

(*7*) Gaining and maintaining the support of official leaders (e.g., superintendents and principals who know what to expect and how to be of assistance

(*8*) Providing participants with time to work on professional development and to assimilate new learning

(*9*) Encouraging participants to share and build upon their own experiences and perspectives, and acknowledge the personal concerns involved in making significant changes

(*10*) Including incentives and rewards for participation that are geared to individual participant needs, motivations, and the realities of the situation

(*11*) Addressing individual, school, district, and state goals, and doing so in a way that uses staff development to build capabilities to implement all KERA components

The skills necessary to provide leadership for the type of long-range planning required to effectuate these attributes are not commonly found. Professional development activities typically fall far short of the sustained, individualized coaching required to achieve teacher mastery of a new skill. The projected professional development system envisioned by the state requires districts to not only consider the educator's level of mastery, but also to consider the career stage of the educator (Steffy, 1989).

TEACHER CAREER STAGES

In the book entitled *Career Stages of Classroom Teachers* (Steffy, 1989), five teacher career stages are identified. These career stages are anticipatory, expert/master, renewal, withdrawal, and exit. A teacher's career stage is not linked directly to his/her chronological age or years of service. Instead, a teacher's career stage is more dependent upon the teacher's learning and motivation level. Application of the model suggests that in order to plan effective professional development on an individual teacher basis, consideration must be given to the teacher's career stage. For example, the professional development activities required to enable an expert/master teacher to achieve high levels of competence in implementing the primary school would be far different from the professional development activities required to get the teacher in withdrawal to the same high level.

The expert/master teacher is one who has demonstrated consistently that he/she can produce high levels of student achievement. Teachers in this career stage quickly establish a no-nonsense work environment in the classroom. Students know that they are cared for and respected by the teacher and the teacher knows the students respect him/her. The teacher knows the subject matter and how to design instructional experiences so that the level of student mastery in the classroom is high. These teachers maintain a vast knowledge of different instructional strategies. Students in their classrooms are comfortable taking risks and experimenting with new ideas. For the expert/master teacher, the seven critical attributes of the Primary program are already part of their instructional routine. The professional development required for the expert/master teacher to formalize this program may include a few workshops to upgrade some skills and then the expert/master teacher may be in a position to serve as a district trainer for teachers in other career stages. Many of the teachers in Kentucky who volunteered to pilot the Primary program could be classified as being in this career stage. These special teachers seem to self-actualize through their positions as teachers.

On the other hand, a teacher who could be characterized as being in withdrawal is one who may have grown cynical and sarcastic toward the system. Teachers in this career stage tend to be negative toward the system and resist change. They tend to instruct in a traditional, teacher-directed manner and often blame the students, parents, or society if learning does not take place. Professional development for a teacher in this career stage must begin by engaging the teacher in activities designed to change the teacher's attitude. Getting a teacher in withdrawal to mastery level in a new skill area takes time, commitment, and determination on the part of the supervisor. Teachers in this career stage must understand that maintaining the status quo is not acceptable.

The newly certified anticipatory teacher might require yet another type of professional development. Once the professional development process has begun, the coaching and support, the supervisory practices, the monitoring of the instructional planning process, and the recognition for improvement should be tailored to match the teacher's career stage. The level of expertise in the areas of human growth and development, motivation, change theory, and organizational development needed to design successful professional development activities in the nine KERA areas suggested by the Department of Education will require a comprehensive training program for district professional development coordinators. At the present time, it is not clear who will deliver the training and coaching that is needed. It is assumed that this will be provided by the emerging Regional Service Center system.

DEVELOPING LOCAL DISTRICT CURRICULUM MANAGEMENT SYSTEMS

In order to effectively manage the implementation of all the programmatic initiatives designed to provide Kentucky students with a "world class" education, the administrators of each local district will need to design and implement a curriculum management system. Based on the concept of curriculum alignment (English, 1992), this management system should address the relationship among the district's written curriculum, what teachers teach in classrooms, and the tests used to assess what students have learned. In Kentucky and in many districts throughout the country, the connections between the written, taught, and tested curriculum are undefined, loose, and textbook driven. This will have to change with the implementation of state authentic assessment measures that are primarily content free; designed to assess integrated, high-level skills; and linked to a system of school site sanctions and rewards.

In Kentucky, a district's ability to manage the curriculum through textbook adoption, teacher evaluation, and grade level designations is quickly coming to an end. The implementation of the Primary program with its mandate for cross-grade grouping, the new state provision to allow schools to use state textbook funds to acquire instructional materials in formats other than a text, the ability of school councils to determine the selection of instructional materials, and the basic KERA principle that *all* children can learn will have dramatic impact on how control of the school system is maintained. In addition, since teacher evaluation practices have never been shown to relate directly to student achievement (Posten and Manatt, 1992) districts will have to develop new mechanisms to monitor and support the improvement of student learning.

PRINCIPAL AND SUPERINTENDENT PROFESSIONAL DEVELOPMENT

To provide principals and superintendents with the skills necessary to design and implement effective curriculum management systems, KERA required professional development activities for all present and future principals and superintendents.

156.105 Principals Assessment Center; assessment of principals required

(1) Prior to July 1, 1992, the Department of Education shall establish a Principals Assessment Center, which shall consist of the National As-

sociation of Secondary School Principals assessment process or a similar validated process. The department may operate assessment centers regionally and shall provide for assessor training.

(2) In addition to any applicable certification and experience requirement, to be qualified and eligible for initial or continued employment as a school principal, effective July 1, 1994, the principal or applicant shall have successfully completed the assessment center process. A newly hired principal who is relocating from outside the state to begin his duties after June 30, 1994, shall successfully complete the assessment center process within one (1) year of assuming his duties as principal.

(3) The State Board for Elementary and Secondary Education shall adopt administrative regulations to establish the criteria for successful completion of the assessment center process. (KDE, 1990, p. 161)

By December, 1990, staff in the Department of Education had identified a Principal Assessment Advisory Committee, developed the required regulation, developed the necessary budget documents including the required personal service contract with the National Association of Secondary School Principals (NASSP) to conduct the assessor training, conducted the first of ten assessor training sessions, and planned for the first round of assessments for principal applicants which were expected to begin in late spring, 1991. Since that time, this program has continued to progress as planned.

The superintendent assessment and training component required the development of a totally new system.

156.111 Superintendents Training Program and Assessment Center; assessment of superintendents required; examination

(1) Prior to July 1, 1992, the Department of Education shall establish a Superintendents Training Program and Assessment Center. The assessment center shall be modeled after the American Association of School Administrators assessment process or a similar validated process. The department may provide assessment centers regionally and shall provide for assessor training. The center shall include, but not be limited to, training for superintendents in the following subjects:

(a) Core concepts of management;
(b) School-based decision making;
(c) Kentucky school law;
(d) Kentucky school finance; and
(e) School curriculum and assessment.

(2) At the conclusion of the training, each participant shall complete a written comprehensive examination based on the content of the training.

(3) In addition to any applicable certification and experience requirements, to be qualified and eligible for continued employment as a school

superintendent, effective July 1, 1994, the school superintendent shall have successfully completed the assessment center process. A person hired for the first time as superintendent in Kentucky after July 1, 1992, shall successfully complete the assessment center process within one (1) year of assuming his duties as superintendent.

(4) The State Board for Elementary and Secondary Education shall adopt administrative regulations to govern the training content, number of hours, written examination, and criteria for successful completion of the training and assessment center process. The board shall also establish the continuing professional development requirements for school superintendents, to become effective July 1, 1994. (p. 161)

During the summer of 1990 Department staff met with representatives from the American Association of School Administrators (AASA) and the National Association of Secondary School Principals (NASSP) to discuss the status of a superintendents assessment center like the one described in the law. It was determined that a number of generic superintendent assessment centers did exist, but they did not address the specific topics included in the law. With the advice of an advisory committee made up of representatives from the Kentucky Association of School Superintendents, the State School Boards Association, professors of educational administration, and the Department of Education staff, it was decided to develop a request for proposal for the development of the required training modules and the required assessment center. Proposals were due to the Department by April 1, 1991. NASSP and AASA were awarded the contract to develop the superintendents' assessment center and the Kentucky Association of School Executives was awarded the contract for the development of the training modules for law, finance, management, school-based decision making, and curriculum and assessment.

Figure 10.4 outlines the process the Department envisioned for implementing this program. All superintendents would complete the assessment center. However, if the superintendent was employed prior to July 1, 1992, he/she could ''test out'' of training modules. The training modules would relate to KERA components. If a superintendent did not receive a passing score on one of the areas, he/she would be required to complete the training module. Superintendents who successfully passed the exam would satisfy the requirement of House Bill 940 (KERA) Section 46 (KRS 156.070).

Assessment of current and future principals and superintendents was designed to ensure that persons in these roles had the skills and

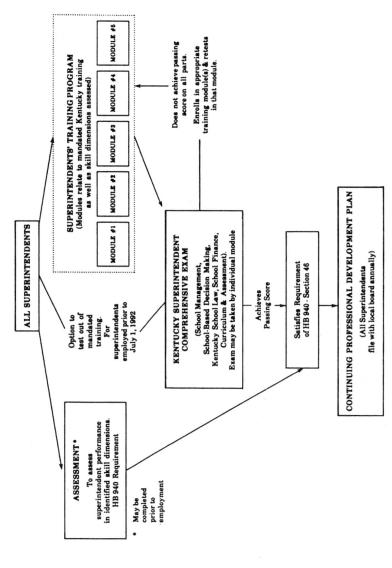

Figure 10.4. Planned Superintendent Training Program and Assessment Center *(to Be Implemented July 1, 1992). Source: KDE,* Request for Proposal, *1991.*

knowledge necessary to guide the development and implementation of all the components of KERA. It is still too soon to determine whether this assessment and training is sufficient to produce these results.

The programs and procedures for professional development discussed so far in this chapter have dealt with the inservice component. KERA addressed the preservice component as well through the formation of the Professional Standards Board.

EDUCATION PROFESSIONAL STANDARDS BOARD

The Education Professional Standards Board was established in KRS 161.028 of the Kentucky Education Reform Act (KDE, 1990, p. 312).

161.028 Education Professional Standards Board; authority to promulgate administrative regulations

(1) Beginning July 15, 1990, there shall be an Education Professional Standards Board, with the authority and responsibility to:

(a) Establish standards and requirements for obtaining and maintaining a teaching certificate;
(b) Set standards for, approve, and evaluate college, university, and school district programs for the preparation of teachers and other professional school personnel;
(c) Issue, renew, suspend, and revoke teaching certificates:
(d) Maintain data and submit reports to the Governor and the Legislative Research Commission concerning employment trends and performance of certificated personnel and the quality of professional preparation programs. The board shall study the problem of the declining pool of minority teachers in the Commonwealth and submit recommendations for increasing the number of minority teachers to the 1992 Regular Session of the General Assembly;
(e) Reduce and streamline the credential system to allow greater flexibility in staffing local schools while maintaining standards for teacher competence; and
(f) Develop a professional code of ethics.

As shown in Figure 10.5, the board is composed of eight classroom teachers, two school district administrators, two deans of colleges of education, a representative of a local board of education and two ex-officio voting members, the commissioner of education and the executive director of the Council on Higher Education. Members to this new board were not appointed by the governor until October of 1990, six months after the bill was passed. The board replaces a council that had

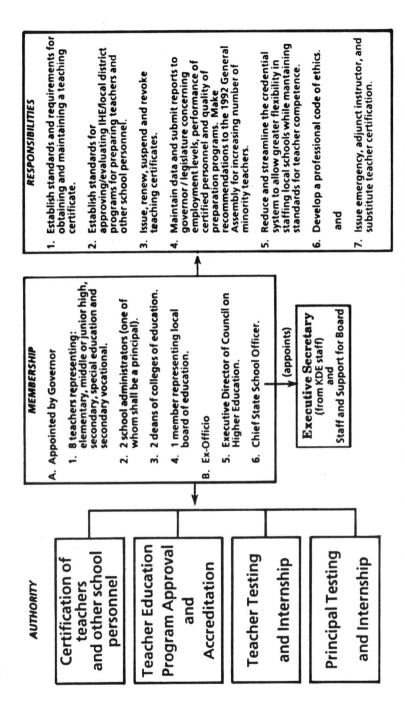

AUTHORITY

Certification of teachers and other school personnel

Teacher Education Program Approval and Accreditation

Teacher Testing and Internship

Principal Testing and Internship

MEMBERSHIP

A. Appointed by Governor

1. 8 teachers representing: elementary, middle or junior high, secondary, special education and secondary vocational.

2. 2 school administrators (one of whom shall be a principal).

3. 2 deans of colleges of education.

4. 1 member representing local board of education.

B. Ex-Officio

5. Executive Director of Council on Higher Education.

6. Chief State School Officer.

(appoints)

Executive Secretary
(from KDE staff)
and
Staff and Support for Board

RESPONSIBILITIES

1. Establish standards and requirements for obtaining and maintaining a teaching certificate.

2. Establish standards for approving/evaluating IHE/local district programs for preparing teachers and other school personnel.

3. Issue, renew, suspend and revoke teaching certificates.

4. Maintain data and submit reports to governor / legislature concerning employment levels, performance of certified personnel and quality of preparation programs. Make recommendations to the 1992 General Assembly for increasing number of minority teachers.

5. Reduce and streamline the credential system to allow greater flexibility in staffing local schools while maintaining standards for teacher competence.

6. Develop a professional code of ethics.

    and

7. Issue emergency, adjunct instructor, and substitute teacher certification.

Figure 10.5. Kentucky Education Professional Standards Board (to Be Established Beginning July 15, 1990). Source: Kentucky Department of Education, 1991.

a larger representation from the higher education community. The previous council recommended action to the State Board for Elementary and Secondary Education. The new board has regulatory authority.

Initially, the Education Professional Standards Board (EPSB) had no budget; consequently, the activities of the board were supported financially through the Department of Education. In addition, staff from the Kentucky Department of Education were assigned to the board. Since Department staff officially reports to the commissioner of education, and yet is assigned to work with the new board, there is a creative tension in the relationship between the two bodies. During the past eighteen months this relationship has matured and become more formalized.

The new board held its first meeting on November 26, 1990 (KDE, 1991, *Implementation Report*, p. 146).

> At the first meeting, the EPSB elected a chair, vice chair, and parliamentarian, approved the plan for expansion/integration of automation in the Division of Teacher Education and Certification, discussed legal and procedural issues related to certification revocation, and scheduled its December retreat. Three standing committees were formed at the second meeting: Issues and Policies, Teacher/Administrator Programs, and Licensing, Certification and Revocation. All committees began working in the areas of their assigned responsibilities. A three-member Executive Committee comprised of the chair, vice chair, and parliamentarian of the Board will oversee Board operations and planning . . .

From its first meeting to the present time, this board has worked diligently to carry out its legislative mandate. Initial meetings focused on orienting new board members to the operations of the state's certification, licensure, and program approval procedures; clarifying liability/insurance issues; and clarifying the board's role in establishing procedures for handling teacher certification revocation proceedings. Since that time the board has approved an alternate certification program for middle and high school teachers (see Figure 10.6), developed a code of ethics, implemented procedures to revoke teacher certificates, and began a major study that will lead to the development of a performance-based teacher and administrator preparation program.

The alternate route certification program is a three-phase process (KRS 161.049). Candidates must have a baccalaureate degree; a 2.5 GPA; a 30-hour major or five-year's experience in the subject field; achieved the state minimum passing score on the National Teacher Examinations, and have an offer of employment from a school district. The first phase of the program, lasting eight weeks, includes full-time

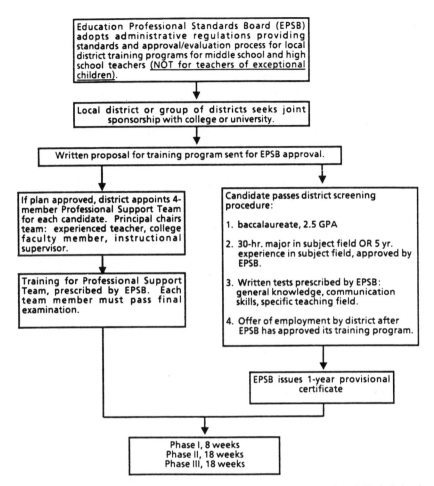

Figure 10.6. *Alternative Certification Program for Middle School and High School Teachers. Source: KDE,* Implementation Report, *1991.*

participation in seminars and practicum. The content of the eight-week experience must include, but is not limited to, introduction to basic teaching skills through supervised teaching experience with students; and orientation to policies, organization, and curriculum of the district that has offered employment to the candidate.

During the second phase, lasting eighteen weeks, the candidate is responsible for a classroom on a half-time basis. A professional support team composed of an experienced teacher, an administrator, an instructional supervisor, and a university faculty member is assigned to each candidate and one member of the professional support team visits and critiques the candidate each week. The team formally evaluates the candidate at the end of the fifth, tenth, and eighteenth week. Formal instruction continues during this eighteen-week period and emphasizes the following topics: student assessment; child development; learning; curriculum; instruction of exceptional children; and school and classroom organization.

During the last phase, also lasting eighteen weeks, the candidate may be assigned full-time classroom duties. The professional support team continues to supervise the candidate. Observations must occur at least every two months. During this time the candidate must be provided opportunities to observe other experienced teachers. At the end of phase three, the team chair prepares a comprehensive evaluation report on the candidate's performance. The team makes one of three recommendations: approved, recommend statement of eligibility; insufficient, candidate should be allowed to seek re-entry to a teacher preparation program; or disapproved, candidate should not be allowed to enter a teacher preparation program. The report is sent to EPSB with supporting documents and, if approved, the candidate is issued a statement of eligibility and may accept a teaching position. In order to receive a teaching certificate, the new teacher must complete the Kentucky Teacher Internship Program (KTIP). This first-year induction program is required for all first-year teachers completing university teacher preparation programs.

While the comprehensive nature of the alternate route certification program is outlined in statute, it characterizes the legislative intent to ensure that all teachers in Kentucky possess the skills necessary to implement KERA. This is further emphasized by the principles adopted by the Education Professional Standards Board and by the Code of Ethics the board established for all Kentucky educators.

Principles of the Education Professional Standards Board

In the spirit of KERA, the Education Professional Standards Board adheres to four basic principles about teachers and teaching. These principles serve as guideposts to Kentucky Department of Education staff who have been assigned to the Board, and are infused throughout Board policies and actions.

Without exception, only appropriately qualified and certified individuals should serve as teachers and administrators in public schools.

The profession of teaching encompasses a specific, well-defined body of knowledge, skills and ethics. All who desire to enter the profession of teaching must master and demonstrate competency in this body of knowledge, skills and ethics before being admitted into the ranks of the profession.

Teachers should pursue professional development activities to enhance their teaching and also to advance their careers.

Since a true profession monitors itself, members of the teaching profession should be actively engaged in determining and monitoring the standards and policies that direct and affect the profession.

Code of Ethics

Educators in the Commonwealth strive toward excellence, recognize the importance of the pursuit of truth, nurture democratic citizenship and safeguard the freedom to learn and to teach. Kentucky educators believe in the worth and dignity of each human being and in educational opportunities for all. Educators in the Commonwealth strive to uphold the responsibilities of the education profession according to the highest ethical standards. The commitment of all Kentucky educators is symbolized by this code of ethics of the education profession of the Commonwealth.

Education Profession

Shall exemplify behaviors which maintain the dignity and integrity of the profession.

Shall accord just and equitable treatment to all members of the profession in the exercise of their professional rights and responsibilities.

Shall keep in confidence information acquired about colleagues in the course of employment, unless disclosure serves professional purposes or is required by law.

Shall not use coercive means or give special treatment in order to influence professional decisions.

Shall apply for, accept, offer, or assign a position or responsibility only on the basis of professional preparation and legal qualifications.

Shall not knowingly falsify or misrepresent record of facts relating to his/her own qualifications or those of other professionals.

The Parents

Shall make reasonable effort to communicate to parents information which should be revealed in the interest of the student.

Shall endeavor to understand community cultures and diverse home environments of students.

Shall not knowingly distort or misrepresent facts concerning educational issues.

Shall distinguish between personal views and the views of the employing educational agency.

Shall not interfere in the exercise of political and citizenship rights and responsibilities of others.

Shall not use institutional privileges for private gain, for the promotion of political candidates, or for partisan political activities.

Shall not accept gratuities, gifts, or favors that might impair or appear to impair professional judgment, nor offer any such to obtain special advantage.

The Students

Shall provide students with professional education services in a non-discriminatory manner and in consonance with accepted best practice known to the educator.

Shall respect the constitutional rights of all students.

Shall not deliberately suppress or distort subject matter for which the educator bears responsibility.

Shall take reasonable measures to protect the health, safety, and emotional well-being of students.

Shall not use professional relationships or authority with students for personal advantage.

Shall keep in confidence information about students which has been obtained in the course of professional service, unless disclosure serves professional purposes or is required by law.

Shall not knowingly make false or malicious statements about students or colleagues.

Shall refrain from subjecting students to embarrassment or disparagement.

Shall maintain a professional approach to personal relationships with students. (KDE, *Code of Ethics*, 1991)

OUTCOMES FOR KENTUCKY'S PROFESSIONAL DEVELOPMENT SYSTEM

The professional development activities at the preservice and inservice level, embodied in KERA, are detailed, comprehensive, and integrated. Fully enacted, they have the capability of ensuring that *all* educators in the state are operating at the expert/master level. Three of the principles upon which KERA is built are these: *all* children can learn and most at high levels; we have the means to teach *all* children; and the quality of education that a child receives in this state is not dependent upon where the child lives. By applying these principles to the educators in the state, the principles might say this: *all* teachers can teach, and most can produce high levels of student achievement; the learning theory, pedagogy, and materials to enable *all* teachers to achieve high levels of student achievement is known or exists; and the achievement level of students should not be dependent upon which teacher the student is assigned. In other words, the quality of instruction delivered by the state's 35,000 educators should be consistently of the highest order and consistently produce high levels of student achievement for *all* the children of the commonwealth.

REFERENCES

English, Fenwick. 1992. *Deciding What to Teach and Test*. California: Corwin Press.

Kentucky Department of Education. 1990. *Kentucky School Laws*. Frankfort, Kentucky: Banks-Baldwin Law Publishing.

Kentucky Department of Education. 1991. *Kentucky Education Professional Standards Board*.

Kentucky Department of Education. 1991. *Kentucky School Personnel Code of Ethics*.

Kentucky Department of Education. 1991. *Public School Financial Analysis*.

Kentucky Department of Education. 1991. *Regional Service Centers of the Kentucky Department of Education: A Conceptual Framework* (draft).

Kentucky Department of Education. 1991. *Request for Proposal for Developing the Superintendents Training and Testing Program*.

Kentucky Department of Education. 1991. *The Kentucky Education Reform Act: 1990 Implementation Report*.

Kentucky Department of Education. 1992. *Planning Professional Development with a Focus on KERA: The Development and Approval Process for School Districts and Consortia*.

Posten, William K., Jr. and Richard Manatt. 1992. "Principals as Evaluators: Delineating Effects on School Reform," *The International Journal of Education Reform*, 1:3.

Steffy, Betty. 1989. *Career Stages of Classroom Teachers*. Lancaster, Pennsylvania: Technomic Publishing Co., Inc.

CHAPTER 11

Lessons for America

We can, whenever we choose, successfully teach all children whose schooling is of interest to us. We already know more than we need to do that. Whether or not we do it must finally depend on how we feel about the fact that we haven't so far.

—Ron Edmonds

THE Kentucky Education Reform Act has been described as the most radical in the nation. As noted in Chapter 4, the only other recent, comprehensive, legislated reform effort prior to the enactment of KERA was the Chicago School Reform Act of 1988 (Hess, 1991). With the exception of the formation of local school councils and their legislated authority to deal with school-related issues such as the hiring and firing of principals (already curbed by a decision of the Illinois Supreme Court), there has been little actual "reform" in Chicago beyond rhetorical bombast and media hype since the bill was enacted. In an April, 1992, report by North Central Regional Educational Laboratory that analyzed the impact of a reform plan developed by the Chicago Board of Education and approved by the Chicago School Finance Authority, there was very little documented reform that substantially changed instruction and student achievement at the classroom level (NCREL, 1992).

In contrast, the Kentucky Reform Act is more comprehensive and focused legislatively than the Chicago reform legislation. As explained in this book, programmatic initiatives in KERA are designed to interrelate and support one another. Essentially, every previous statute related to governance, finance, and curriculum of the state education system was reviewed and reauthorized or rewritten. This has made an enormous difference in the implementation process. Inevitably, in matters of implementation, there are gray areas where intent is not clear. For instance, the statutory language that established the Primary School program and the Extended School Services program is very brief and does not establish the parameters of the programs. On the other hand,

257

the statutory language that authorized the Preschool program is detailed and prescriptive. However, the fact that KERA is more focused and internally consistent is due to the manner in which it was crafted at the outset. These, and other observations, have led me to establish a tentative and formative list of "lessons" about Kentucky educational reform. I do not regard them as definitive, but as promising postulates deserving further analysis and empirical verification.

BACKGROUND FOR THE PRESENT RESTRUCTURING EFFORT

The present structure for public schools can be traced to the early to mid-nineteenth century. Michael Katz (1987) refers to the model chosen for the design of the system as "incipient bureaucracy." According to Katz, the advocates for this model supported a strong regulatory role for organizations dealing with social welfare and morality (p. 8). At that time there was a widespread belief that "families were in trouble." Industrialization, which caused the separation of the home and the workplace, seemed to be the source of the problem. While industrialization, capitalism, and a working class emerged throughout the Western world, in America there was the added component of evangelical Protestantism with its linkage to the political system (p. 15). All of this had an impact on the design of schools. As cities grew, there was a perception that "an epidemic of lawlessness and pauperism threatened the foundations of morality and the maintenance of social order" (p. 17). Schooling, it was thought, would provide the lower-class child with better role models and a better environment in which to gain the work habits of punctuality and regular attendance. In addition, the public schools offered society an opportunity to indoctrinate immigrant children into the mainstream, homogeneous American culture.

Katz argues that the early public schools existed to "shape behavior and attitudes, alleviate social and family problems, and reinforce a social structure under stress" (p.23). (These same comments were included in the rationale for the restructuring of Kentucky's schools.) The development of cognitive skills and intellectual abilities was of less concern even though the schools were perceived to be one of the key mechanisms for achieving social mobility. In promoting the concept of public education, advocates succeeded in causing citizens to believe that education was not only the "cornerstone of democracy," it was also the public institution that would solve most of the social problems of the day. Public schools would alleviate five problems: crime and poverty, cultural heterogeneity, poor work habits, "idle youth," and the anxieties of middle-class parents about their children's future (p. 115).

During the past 150 years, the schools have had little impact on crime, poverty, or delinquency. They have provided a place for "idle youth" and a mechanism for the transmission of a culture. The fact that the public schools did not solve the problems of the lower class did not significantly alter support for public education. Middle-class parents continued to support public schools because they believed their children had a better chance of "succeeding" in adult life if they did well in school. Now, it appears, public education is losing the support of the middle class.

The current attack on the public education system began a decade ago. The now infamous 1983 report, *A Nation at Risk: Imperative for Educational Reform*, warned that public education was "being eroded by a rising tide of mediocrity." A series of other national reports followed. In the same time frame, three scholarly critiques of secondary schools were published by Boyer (1983), Goodlad (1984), and Sizer (1984). The solution to the "crisis" was, in part, to increase graduation requirements, expand state testing, increase teacher salaries, and require more math and science courses (Farrar, 1990, pp. 3 – 13). In the book *Educational Leadership in an Age of Reform*, Jacobson and Conway (1990), divided the current reform movement into three phases. The first phase, from 1980 to 1986, focused on K – 12 education. The second phase, beginning in 1986, expanded the "root of the problem" to include the quality of teacher preparation programs and the caliber of students entering teacher preparation programs. The third phase quickly followed and focused on the inability of present school administrators to manage school improvement efforts. The central issue dominating this era of education reform is, more than any other, an economic one. There is common perception among political leaders and particularly among the business community that in order for the United States to maintain economic "world superiority," the nation's schools have to do better.

Doing "better" has been translated into achieving higher expectations for *all* students. Following this logic, the public schools of the future must produce graduates who are internationally competitive on emerging national and international authentic assessment measures. These assessment measures will evaluate students' attainment of integrated, high-level competencies. The current focus on restructuring requires holding the outcomes constant and making whatever organizational changes are necessary to enable *all* students to meet the expectations. Restructuring the system involves K − 12, higher education, parents, politicians, business leaders, and the community. In many respects the current restructuring effort incorporates the perceived vision embodied in the nineteenth century formation of this country's public education system. However, this time there is a recognition that in order to produce the results currently advocated, the required changes in the system will impact the political, social, and economic structure and priorities of the country. Many supporters of the restructuring effort are not optimistic about the success of the current initiatives because of the fundamental shifts in power required to make them successful.

One of the power shifts required is economic. Jonathan Kozol, in his recent book entitled *Savage Inequalities* (1991), vividly describes the consequences of the inequities among school districts in funding public schools. Kozol states that in the state of Texas in 1991 ''per-pupil spending ranged from $2,000 in the poorest districts to $19,000 in the richest'' (p. 223). In a descriptive passage from the *Chicago Tribune*, written by James D. Squires, Kozol quotes, ''It took an extraordinary combination of greed, racism, political cowardice and public apathy to let the public schools in Chicago get so bad . . . (they are the costly result of) the political orphaning of the urban poor . . . daytime warehouses for inferior students . . . a bottomless pit'' (p. 72). His painful stories of economic inequities in funding schools were repeated for New York, Ohio, New Jersey, and so on. In the last paragraph of his book, he makes a poignant statement (p. 233).

> Standing here by the Ohio River, watching it drift west into the edge of the horizon, picturing it as it flows onward to the place three hundred miles from here where it will pour into the Mississippi, one is struck by the sheer beauty of this country, of its goodness and unrealized goodness, of the limitless potential that it holds to render life rewarding and the spirit clean. Surely there is enough for everyone within this country. It is a tragedy that these good things are not more widely shared. All our children ought to be allowed a stake in the enormous richness of America. Whether they were born to poor white Appalachians or to wealthy Texans, to poor black people in the Bronx or to rich people in Manhasset or Winnetka, they are all quite wonderful and innocent when they are small. We soil them needlessly.

Equitable funding for the nation's 15,000 school districts is both an economic and a political problem; and there are others.

Seymour B. Sarason, in *The Predictable Failure of Educational Reform* (1991), contends that "schools will remain intractable to desired reform as long as we avoid confronting (among other things) their existing power relationships" (p. 5). Sarason argues that most education reformers do not talk about changing the system; in fact, they accept the system as it is (pp. 13, 14). He attributes this to the fact that almost everyone outside the system does not have a true grasp of the interconnected, complicated, politically grounded nature of the system. Nor does being part of the system guarantee a holistic view. According to Sarason, in order for true reform to take place, there will have to be a shift in power from central administration to the classroom teacher and from the classroom teacher to the student. From his point of view, the likelihood of such a shift is small.

In *Restructuring Schools: The Next Generation of Educational Reform* (Elmore et al., 1991), the authors conclude that the success of the current reform movement will be dependent upon the degree to which political, community, and professional interests coalesce around a common agenda (p. xv). They speculate that support for the present movement is partially related to the fact that, at the present time, the common agenda does not exist. Once it is clearly defined, opposition will surface from the groups that are negatively affected. "As long as the theme of school restructuring is fluid and unspecified, it functions well as a rallying point for reformers. But once the theme is defined, it may begin to divide rather than unite diverse political interests" (p. 4).

The themes emerging in the political discourse about restructuring are empowerment, accountability, and academic learning (p. 5). All of these themes are incorporated into KERA. Empowerment in and of itself is not sufficient. The discourse here centers on who has decision-making power. The empowerment issue does not sufficiently address the problem of responsibility. In the past ten years state departments of education developed state testing programs and increased graduation requirements. However, local school districts have been responsible for student achievement. Now, in Kentucky and in other states, teachers at the building level are being empowered to make instructional decisions. The idea of teacher accountability has high political appeal as long as it remains a vague abstraction (p. 7). Once specific implementation occurs we can expect controversy and lawsuits. Finally, according to many of the critics (Goodlad, 1984; Sizer, 1984; and others) "classroom activity for the average student is dull, perfunctory, and disconnected from what goes on in other classrooms or in the larger community" (p. 8).

The restructuring theme for improved academic learning is the need for integrated instruction of higher-order thinking and problem-solving skills. Teaching for understanding requires vastly different instructional skills than the typical teacher-directed model currently in place, particularly at the secondary level. If the current restructuring effort produces the required classroom transformation to produce these critical thinkers, it raises the question about whether society really wants a workforce that will question the status quo. If the worker is a member of a design team charged with making a better mousetrap, the answer is "yes." However, if the worker is employed in an environment where he/she is responsible for fulfilling a specific predesigned task such as assembling an intricate electronic device, I'm not sure how much critical thinking the employer would encourage. Nevertheless, these three themes: empowerment, accountability, and academic learning dominate current restructuring efforts.

Now that the foundation for KERA is in place, and there are new expectations for empowerment, accountability, and academic learning that impact the basic structure of how schools function, we are beginning to see signs that could lead to overt opposition. For example, in the area of improved academic learning, the state has established new high-level standards and empowered school councils to make whatever curriculum-related decisions are necessary to ensure that all students meet these standards (Chapter 2). However, the standards are general statements related to high school graduates. The mechanism for translating these standards into a district and school curriculum management system is unclear.

Some school councils are demanding full authority to define and deliver the curriculum without the assistance of central administration. Other school faculty are looking to the state and central administration for help in defining exactly what the state standards (valued outcomes) mean for the seventh-grade social studies teachers. Some local district board members and central office administrators are taking a "hands off" approach to the councils and is in essence letting them "do their own thing" without support or interference. In other districts, both board and central administration are taking a proactive approach toward the councils and attempting to assist them in any way they can. The issues involved in the formation of councils and the relationship of these councils to central administration and the local board involve issues of power, accountability, and academic learning. Everyone is becoming concerned about how to design a district system to support the autonomy of local school councils and their ability to make curriculum implementation decisions, and at the same time preserve the concept of a district where ultimate accountability resides with the local board of education.

The law suggests that local schools must meet student output expectations (baseline and threshold scores, see Chapter 3) or they will become ''schools in crisis.'' However, if a district fails to meet minimum student, program, service, or operational performance standards [KDE, 1990, KRS 158.685 (2)] the State Board shall declare the district ''deficient.'' Deficient districts are required to develop improvement plans. Failure to meet the interim performance goals in the improvement plan can result in state action to remove the superintendent and the members of the local school board from office. In addition, the Department of Education is currently piloting budgetary procedures that will enable local school councils to manage large portions of the instructional budget (Chapter 4). During the next two years, the shift in the power base through KERA provisions for empowerment, accountability and academic learning could determine the ultimate success of this important restructuring effort.

Now, after more than two years of implementation, some formative ''lessons'' are emerging. These lessons deal with the role of legislation; children and families; curriculum, testing, and teaching; and the role of administration in promoting educational reform. In framing the lessons, the reader needs to understand that from my point of view, the Kentucky Education Reform Act is, more than anything else, an attempt to force the state's most deficient districts to change long-standing practices that appear to subjugate the educational needs of children to the needs of adults to maintain power and protect the status quo. It is true that the programmatic initiatives in KERA are based on the premise that Kentucky can create a success-oriented school environment in which *all* children can learn. But, in my opinion, there would never have been a Supreme Court decision declaring the entire educational system unconstitutional if it hadn't been for the perception that it was the only way to address the educational neglect of children in the state's most deficient districts.

In the process of designing a mechanism to deal with those districts who flagrantly miseducate the children in this state, the legislature enacted a bill that could ultimately improve the educational opportunity for all of our children. But make no mistake, the true test of KERA is yet to come. This test will involve the State Board for Elementary and Secondary Education and its agent the Kentucky Department of Education; the Office of Education Accountability, created by the legislature to monitor the implementation of KERA and investigate wrongdoing; and the political power base supporting the administration and boards of the state's worst school districts. This is the arena for the true test of KERA. The vast majority of educators in this state are attempting to implement the provisions of the Act to the best of their ability. The chapters of this book speak to the comprehensive nature of the changes that are being required. Most believe in the vision. Most understand the significance of the legislation not only for this state, but for the future of public education in America. There are many lessons to come. This is a beginning.

LESSONS ABOUT THE CHANGE PROCESS AND LEGISLATION AS THE FULCRUM TO PROMOTE EDUCATION REFORM

Lesson 1: Comprehensive Change Will Not Sprout from the Ground Up (Like Some Form of Spontaneous Combustion)

The people, meaning the public, are inherently conservative about schooling. Nearly all have been to some sort of school. They remember what it was like when they attended a school. These experiences have been powerful shaping forces in defining schooling for them. Even if they were not successful in school, few parents have any comprehensive educational view of how to achieve educational change. The initial data from local school councils in Kentucky and Chicago support this observation. Parents and teachers serving on school councils may change school rules and implement new discipline codes; however, they generally will not, nor do they feel comfortable altering fundamental classroom curriculum management and instructional methodologies. While the people may favor "progress," parents' views of change do not include "experimenting" with *their* children. Parental, and all too often educator's, views of "experimenting" are largely ahistorical, i.e., they lack any real concept of what has been tried in schools before, as well as what constitutes an "experiment." For example, non-graded schools, an idea that has been around for over twenty years, and was the model of schooling for America for over one hundred years in the famed little red schoolhouse on the prairie or in the valley, is considered by most parents as "radical."

It is a fallacy that comprehensive educational reform can ever be crafted by people unschooled about schooling, ignorant of educational history and methodology, unable or unwilling to deal with how the future can be shaped into schools instead of using the past as the key to reshape schools. The past is dead. The future is not clear. The people cannot be expected to know how to translate uncertainty into an institution, craft its ethos, formulate methodologies that run true to that ethos, evaluate successes and failures, and engage in constructive alterations when things don't exactly work as planned. Providing the education required to produce bottom-up school restructuring will require more time and training than is currently available to most parents and teachers.

Lesson 2: There Are Powerful Vested Interests in Preserving Mediocrity in Education

Kentucky's poor schools didn't get that way by chance, nor were they preserved by some supernatural force beyond human imagination. Mediocre schools got that way and stayed that way because of very comprehensible reasons. Certainly, many were underfunded before KERA. They appeared to be administered by people who were more concerned about rule following and employing politically acceptable candidates than finding, hiring, and paying top dollar for quality classroom teachers and administrators. In far too many cases, school boards appeared more interested in supporting the existing political machine, maintaining their share of the power base, and deliberately ensuring the system was unresponsive to mandates for improvement from any other source.

In mediocre school districts, local taxpayers and corporations seemed more concerned about keeping taxes low than they were about doing whatever had to be done to ensure that the quality of education improved. This meant that new businesses and corporations that required educated people would not select such areas for development. This, in turn, reinforced the prevailing socioeconomics in place. Poor parents saw schools that had not served them well, and in which they did not do well; schools that had not changed since they were students. Lacking any incentives to support the school, and finding reasons to work against the school by fortifying family structures against losing children to the cities, many rural families opted out for generations from seeking better educational opportunities locally. In many of these communities it was more important to win the favor of a school board member by assuring a block of family votes and ensuring that a relative would be employed by the school district as a bus driver or a custodian than it was to insist that the schools improve. This was particularly true where there were high levels of unemployment with large percentages of families on welfare.

Children in these mediocre schools were used to raise funds, often in the thousands of dollars, to keep schools going and pay for the most fundamental services beyond minimal teacher salaries. Administrators became the "ward bosses" of these failing districts. Often lacking even rudimentary technical skills in planning, curriculum development, budgeting, and instructional evaluation, they were picked because of their loyalty to the status quo, and not on the basis of competence.

Years of low expectations, low financial support, incompetence, graft, and corruption breeds a contempt against competence, cynicism about progress instead of a faith in the promise of a better future, and legions of faithful defenders in mediocrity who *blame the evils of the system on the children*, who are, in reality, the victims of the system. You can't expect much from them, many say, so why bother? This stigmatization produces a self-perpetuating system of mediocrity.

Lesson 3: Outside Intervention Is Required to Initiate Fundamental Educational Reform in Corrupt School Systems

To keep hoping that change can be wrought by locals without outside intervention is to engage in wishful and unproductive thinking. Years of neglect and the pillage of strong local political traditions rooted in a fundamental respect for quality education and the tax base to support it have completely destroyed the local infrastructure by which reform can be conceptualized, take root, and grow to fruition. Outside intervention is a political necessity in totally corrupt systems.

The Harlan County School District received a $4.5 million increase in funds during the first year of KERA (Lucke and Mueller, 1991, p. 1), an increase of about 30 percent over the 1989–90 budget. By August, 1991, staff from the Office of Education Accountability were investigating reports of alleged wrongdoing in the district. In November, 1991, facing possible removal by the State Board for Elementary and Secondary Education, the superintendent, Robert Sheperd, resigned. He had lived his entire life in Harlan County and worked in the schools for twenty-three years. The resignation preempted the State Board's authority to name the new superintendent.

After accepting the superintendent's resignation, the Board named a twenty-year Harlan school veteran, Grace Ann Tolliver, as acting superintendent. The new acting superintendent proceeded to hire Shepherd as the district's technology coordinator. In January, 1992, three Harlan County board members were removed from office by the State Board. By the summer of 1992, after several legal judgements by the Harlan County judicial system to reinstate the board members, the case was before the Kentucky Supreme Court. By the spring of 1992, state officials were running the district. The State Board had removed Ms. Tolliver from office after she was indicted on theft and forgery charges involving school purchases in 1990. She has denied the charges. In May, at a meeting to review the 1992−93 school budget, $1.3 million in "lost" funds were found in a bank account in Louisville. The funds had previously been reported as part of a construction account when they were actually part of the general fund.

In the spring, 1992, opposition to the reelection of State Representative Roger Noe, Harlan, began to mount. Representative Noe was chairman of the Joint Education Committee when KERA was passed and was credited with helping to craft the legislation and get it enacted. Even the teachers joined the Noe opposition. After all, they reasoned, the board members who were ousted had given them a hefty raise and they felt that the ousted board was better than the one that replaced it. In May, Roger Noe lost the Democratic nomination for reelection. While all of these events were transpiring, there were 6,000 students attending classes in the Harlan County School System. Some did not have access to needed science materials. Some attended schools in total disrepair. The tough, state intervention provisions in KERA are there because of the Harlan Counties of this state. I am sure that there are good teachers and caring parents in Harlan County. But for many reasons, the negative political forces in the system, among the business leaders, and throughout the community have prevented this system from correcting the situation. KERA is about Harlan County. Outside intervention is required.

Lesson 4: Educational Reform Is Not a "Quick Fix" and Will Take a Lasting Presence, Perhaps a Decade or More

Mediocre schools can't be fixed by band-aids, fads, or other quick fixes. They won't be candidates for total quality management, or any other short run remedy. Mediocre schools, unless shut down, will take many years to bring to complete competence and educational quality.

The American people do not fully comprehend the enormity or the complexity of the task before them in "fixing" the schools. In many cases, schools are the mirrors of the communities they represent. They are not the bastions of embassies of some foreign country from the downtown bureaucracy. Mediocre schools are fueled by deteriorating expectations, declining moral and financial support, and attacks from those who have an agenda to destroy the institution. These antibodies have always been in the American system from the inception of its public schools.

Because the American people do not fully understand the task before them in overhauling their schools, they keep electing politicians who believe quick fixes or abandonment are the way the schools will be improved. Nobody is in it for the long haul. The change cycle far exceeds the elected term of local, state, or national officials.

Lesson 5: Reform Efforts Are Themselves Political Events

Educational reform is political reform. Those who believe that the schools can be changed "apolitically" are like Victorians who covered nude statues of antiquity with fig leaves. They won't or can't see what is before them.

The schools consume an enormous amount of public funds. Politicians and money are the handmaidens of government. Mediocre schools stay that way because these handmaidens have found it convenient to let them be mediocre. Among the advantages are patronage, profiteering, and power. Bad schools exist because "good" people prefer them to remain bad. To improve the schools would risk changing the people who control them and profit by them.

To find out which people prefer bad schools to stay bad, take this advice: Follow the money! The money leads to those who remain in power, and are the beneficiaries of the existing political arrangements in each community or state. If educational reform does not involve political reform, the effort is simply tinkering.

Lesson 6: Reform Legislation Must Be Sharply Focused, Comprehensive, and Internally Consistent to Have Any Lasting Impact

KERA, by comparison to Chicago and other reform mandates in other states, is simply more sharply definitive, comprehensive, and internally consistent than any other measure up to this time. It is not a perfect piece of legislation. There were some compromises made. However, as a whole, it remains the best piece of educational legislation yet adopted by any state legislature in the nation.

There are some things worth noting about how it was constructed. KERA was not a grass roots-designed piece of legislation. There was no ''People's Congress'' that formulated a grand design. Such a Congress is antithetical to the idea of radicality itself. The more the machine of compromise grinds on, the less radical a piece of legislation becomes in the process. Sharp edges are made round, and eventually the law looks like all the others before it.

Radical change must be protected in the process of definition, debate, and adoption. In Kentucky, a select committee of legislators and representatives from the governor's office identified a few key educational experts and crafted the legislation, largely outside the public eye and the ubiquitous lobbyists from educational and other watchdog groups.

Kentucky's educational reform is an example of ''expert reform.'' While there is no perfect way to formulate legislation, the encapsulation of comprehensiveness and continuity was one result of restricted access to the crafting of the law itself.

At first, this position appears undemocratic. Yet, it mirrors the way the U.S. Constitution was written, where a handful of authors actually crafted the bulk of the document, followed by debate of a restricted body of representatives.

Around the country we have some terrible examples of grass roots initiatives. Proposition 13 in California has systematically shredded public education in that state—similarly, Proposition 2½ in Massachusetts. There is no magic, nor quality in numbers. ''More'' is not better, especially in matters involving knowledge, technical competence, and experience.

Lesson 7: Top Down Change Does Work

The continued reliance on ''top down'' change has wrought a chorus of handwringers on the basis that it is ''undemocratic'' conceptually, and authoritarian philosophically. Professors who live in the sheltered halls of academe are often the first to condemn legisled change that is ''top down.''

Yet, the fact remains that in some cases and Kentucky was one of those, the ''top'' was all that was left to serve as the fulcrum of change for its public schools. There is also the legitimate expectation of the public that those in government are responsible "to do something" about conditions in their sphere of responsibility.

The key in Kentucky is to enlist the support of those not at the top once the legislation has been passed. That has occurred. Across the commonwealth, teachers, administrators, and parents are supporting KERA. Whether the reservoir of good will and support will continue remains to be seen. That will be influenced by the continuation of funds from Frankfort, as well as the perception that things are, after all, getting better, though glitches have occurred and are to be expected.

There has been a backlash against KERA in precisely those school systems where the political reforms have been felt the most. These are in the so-called "chronically mismanaged" districts in the commonwealth. In these areas the antinepotism provisions of KERA, the work of the watchdog accountability agency in identifying corruption and abuse, have posed a serious threat to "business as usual" politics of the status quo. The unseating of pro-KERA legislators may be the harbinger of ultimate weakening of the strong provisions signalling the end to patronage, or to the election of an "anti-tax" governor that would be a smokescreen for loosening the grip of KERA to promote change via funding. Changes in financial support would also serve to weaken support for change in the bulk of the school systems who by and large have not been guilty of bad management practices.

Top down change signals a change in expectations. It marshals public support. It clarifies and focuses the issues. It also tends to polarize and dichotomize and to create enemies where perhaps none existed before, simply because people don't like the change that was initiated. But the fact is that *top down change does work*. The true problem is that top down change cannot remain top down, or it will ultimately fail for lack of continuing support. To that end, the true beneficiaries of the change must come to see that it is in their best interests to support that change effort. These efforts must be rewarded.

Lesson 8: There Is a Difference between Schooling Reform and Educational Reform

Because educational reform is ultimately political reform, there is naturally great controversy regarding changes in governance. Governance changes portend changing the gravity of power within and outside school systems and related governmental agencies. These tend to overshadow necessary changes in educational processes. Schooling relates to organizational issues. Education refers to the actual instructional processes at work in the core technology with schools and classrooms. Education change is philosophical, curricular, and instructional.

KERA contained both schooling and educational reforms. The political alterations crafted within the law have received most of the public and media attention. Much less reported and controversial, but exceedingly important, were the changes regarding curriculum, testing, and instruction. These latter areas are the ones most likely to impact the work of teachers. They are the ones that will change the content and methodology of teaching. Unless reform is both political and educational, very little is likely to be different in the long run.

LESSONS ABOUT CHILDREN AND FAMILIES

Lesson 9: Improving Education Involves the Family and the Home (or the Lack Thereof)

The first school for any child is the home, or the lack of one. The first teachers for any child are his/her parents, or the lack of parents. The stabilizing force for children is the "curriculum of the home," and how well it has prepared a child for formal schooling.

Kentucky has taken steps to include the family or the lack of family in its conception of educational change. In this respect it is decidedly more radical than most other conceptions of educational reform. There is no doubt the family is one of the keys to improved success in schools. However, the American family has fundamentally changed. Fewer than 5 percent of American families now have both a mother and a father where the mother is not working outside the home. To keep insisting that education cannot improve until families change is to wait for a day that will never come. The past cannot be recreated. Instead, newer and bolder initiatives must recognize the reality and create new connections with families and schools. Kentucky has begun to do that through the creation of Family Resource Centers, the Preschool program and the Primary School program.

As these programs take shape there is renewed recognition of the critical partnership that must be crafted between the home and the school – a partnership that softens the lines between the two and bonds them together into a unified force to protect, support, and nurture the growing child. These partnerships are being born out of social necessity and they serve all kinds of children and families in all sorts of circumstances. As the positive bonds between the school and the family are strengthened, the school begins to take on a mantle once held but since discarded: the mantle of the school as the community center, the focal point for bringing citizens together to talk and debate, to learn and grow, and to serve one another and the total community. With the growth in before-school and after-school programs, the expansion of adult education to include day school activities as well as evening and Saturday activities, the integration of human service activities with educational activities, new ground is being broken and a new sense of community is being established.

Lesson 10: Schooling Must Start Earlier, Especially for Those Most at Risk of Failing in School

The rapid acceptance by parents of the opportunity to provide ''at-risk'' children with a half-day preschool experience speaks to the fact that these parents recognize the importance of this socialization experience and the benefits the program provides for their children. The myth that parents from low socioeconomic circumstances do not want their children to do well in school is false, repeated by educators unwilling or unable to change their instructional strategies to meet the learning needs of these children. The opportunity to work and play with other children; to listen to stories while cuddled in the soft arms of an adult; to visit farms, firehouses, and museums makes a difference in the acquisition of school readiness skills. The assumption that children cannot learn anything of significance prior to the age of five or that the home, no matter what the circumstances, is the most appropriate place for the child, is ridiculous. An environment where children can experience visual stimulation, good food, love, and friendship is always preferred over an environment where there is tension, fear, hunger, and danger. If the school can provide the nurturing environment and the home cannot, the child, whatever his/her circumstances, should be able to benefit from the school.

LESSONS ABOUT CURRICULUM, TESTING, AND TEACHING (EDUCATIONAL REFORM)

Lesson 11: No Curriculum Can Ever Be Purely Local, Children Are Citizens of the World, Inextricably Linked to World Problems and Cultures

On a recent hike at Logan's Point in Glacier National Park, I was not only struck by the awesome beauty of the place that divides the waterways of our country, I was struck by the friendly camaraderie that evolved among the people I met. At one point in my hike I encountered an Amish man with a long beard and binoculars showing a small, curious, Japanese girl a hiker, high atop the mountain. A group of French-speaking students quickly came to watch. Since I now qualify for senior citizen status (by some definitions) I added another dimension to the group. Our languages were different, our clothing was different, our homes were undoubtedly different. However, we were all the same in experiencing the majesty of the scenery and the friendliness of the moment. We were part of a world culture. Rather than preserving the one American culture of the past, the restructured schools of the future will increasingly socialize children into a multi-cultural world. The evolution of national and international standards will not be reversed. The standards embraced by Kentucky's valued outcomes are world class. They are not tied to specific content, yet they can be taught using the content of many different subjects, in a variety of languages, at all levels of schools and in a variety of settings. They could represent high expectations for students in Russia, or India, or the United States. They are appropriate for the state of Kentucky, the United States, and perhaps the world. They may be the beginning of an international curriculum.

Lesson 12: The State Has a Responsibility to Set Expectations That Are World Class, Not Culturally Closed or Locally Controlled

Students educated in the schools of Kentucky will routinely work, play, and live in many different parts of the world in the twenty-first century. Since the graduates of the year 2000 are currently in the sixth grade, it is essential that the curriculum they encounter in school prepare them for their role in a world culture. By empowering local school councils with the ability to use instructional material and textbook money to acquire the most appropriate material for the student population being served, teachers will be freed from the dictates of current state-approved textbook publishers about what to teach, how to teach it, and how to assess student achievement. Given the freedom to select whatever content they wish to use to achieve the valued outcomes, teachers will become vastly more astute at materials selection and they will demand materials that reflect the changing complexion of the world.

Lesson 13: Testing That Assumes Failure Is Required Is Antithetical to Reform Itself

School reform is synonymous with eliminating a single standard of performance for every child based on chronological age, testing that child, and labeling that child a failure based on the results of the test. The labeling and sorting mechanism attached to standardized assessment is beginning to show signs of a long-awaited death. Indeed, the untold trauma and stigma inflicted upon the youth of this country in the name of testing may remain one of the horrors of the twentieth century. The bright-eyed five-year-old, running from the bus to the classroom on the first day of school, is ill prepared for the humiliation heaped upon him/her by the inhumane testing practices of the past. With reform, there appears to be emerging a new set of testing procedures that serve to provide a benchmark for teachers, parents, and students about the progress being made toward acquiring the valued outcomes. Students are actively involved in assessing their own progress, setting new goals and then engaging peers and teachers as coaches in assisting them in achieving the desired outcomes.

LESSONS ABOUT ADMINISTRATION OF SCHOOLS

Lesson 14: Everything Cannot Be Decentralized to Schools

There are 176 school districts in the state of Kentucky and approximately 1,350 schools. If district central administration is abolished and all centralized activities are decentralized to the school, the state will have expanded the number of districts to approximately 1,350. The push/pull of school empowerment and maintaining a district system is one that is presently still a tug of war. The balance that is needed to provide flexibility at the building level and coordination across levels and among buildings will have to be achieved for the system to work. Transportation, technology, curriculum alignment to state assessments, desegregation, contractual agreements with unions, and taxation and finance are a few of the activities that require district coordination.

Lesson 15: Accountability Assumes Somebody (Singular) Is in Charge of the School and the School System

Accountability is a legal, not an educational concept. Liability requires accountability. Group liability is difficult to define and operationalize. The "people" cannot be accountable for anything. Teachers, as a group, cannot be accountable. Only individuals can be accountable.

The Kentucky reform makes it clear that the people can become more involved in their schools. As elsewhere, the benefits usually prove to be salutary. But the Kentucky reform also makes it clear that there is no special competence or wisdom in the "grass roots." This is particularly the case where improved technology, classroom methodologies, curriculum concepts, and testing improvements are what is required to improve the schools. These are matters that require some competence and professional experience to handle appropriately. Each of the issues cannot be handled as a referendum of the people.

The Kentucky Reform indicates that professionals, school administrators and teachers, are still necessary to work in and run the schools on a day-to-day basis. These professional educators are still, and ultimately, accountable for what goes on in our schools.

Lesson 16: Privatization Will Not Reform Public Education

It seems abundantly clear that choice or privatization will not reform public education. It will simply create a system of private schools. Fundamental reforms in schools and classrooms portend changes in the way schools have done business over many generations of parents. Conservative parents are not likely to support such changes, preferring to enroll their children in private schools that operate on the most conservative of educational agendas, both in a curricular and pedagogical sense. Privatization will be a force to reduce bold changes in schools that run counter to "common sense" versions of schooling. Such schools will pander to the most conservative of denominators in education.

Schools that challenge social inequities and the existing socio-economic-political system will not be embraced by those who already profit from the system. Parents representing the "haves" in our society will not run the risk of losing their position to schools that may loosen their grip on the good life.

The Kentucky legislature early on in its deliberations clearly dismissed choice as part of its reform except in rare cases. Part of their rationale was that too many schools were poor to make choice a viable option to the majority of children in the commonwealth. If substantial numbers of schools are mediocre, it is unlikely that choice schemes will be able to uplift large masses of poor children in their lifetimes. Privatization is an elite scheme to keep good schools good and bad schools bad. It is a chimera. The wealthy have choice now. Their choices are always real. The poor only have choice on a promise that things will get better sometime in the future. That day may never come unless the state guarantees that it will. Kentucky chose to leave choice out of its reform because it was an illusion.

Lesson 17: Legislated Reform Must Include Higher Education

The Kentucky reform is primarily an initiative aimed at K − 12 school systems in the commonwealth. The legislature considered but did not involve higher education within the commonwealth in this phase of the legislation. Instead, they passed a joint resolution calling for the university system to design plans to support the implementation of KERA. This may have been a mistake.

For too long higher education has considered itself "above" such problems. Yet there is much evidence that the university system, too, is in need of change. Many colleges within our universities and even colleges of education can become isolated from the field. Entire departments in some colleges look upon working in schools as "beneath them," or they feel their responsibility to the field is limited to conducting research after a program has been implemented. Too many professors have limited skills to offer schools or school systems in the way of problem-solving expertise. Some appear to take the attitude that teachers and especially administrators are "buffoons" or robots. The snobbery in some arenas of higher education regarding public education is a major barrier to improving the schools that feed them.

In too many universities, colleges of education are viewed as "cash cows" without any real academic purpose or true "university" program. This attitude harkens back to the elitism and sexism that resulted in establishing "normal schools" outside of liberal arts institutions, since the majority of students were female and women were not permitted to enroll in such male bastions.

Many times college- or university-level administrators come from a liberal arts background and they become infatuated with the latest management fad as the solution for the ills that face educators. The current popularity of total quality management (TQM) is an example of a business fad that is being applied to education, sometimes with the blessing of university administration. When challenged to design programs to support the improvement of public education, these administrators often have no idea how to engage in substantive educational reform at their own institutions, let alone within the public schools of their states.

When the time came for Kentucky higher education institutions to play a role in the reform of its public elementary and secondary schools, on most campuses, it was the colleges of education that were the most responsive to calls for assistance from the field. Just as KERA called for an alliance between the education community and the social service community, future iterations of the reform should require higher education to join in these collaborative efforts.

Lesson 18: There Are More Lessons to Be Learned in Kentucky

There are more lessons to be learned from the implementation of the Kentucky Educational Reform Act. As KERA continues to unfold in the nation's heartland, educators, reformers, policy makers, parents, and legislators should once again examine this bold educational experiment to see if the programmatic initiatives described in this book are working. As newer or more significant trends begin to sprout and take shape over time, they need to be documented.

Americans are an impatient people. In many ways they are an ahistorical people, forgetting to take time to learn again what has been tried before. Whatever happens in Kentucky in this decade, it is very likely to influence American education in countless ways as the nation crosses into the twenty-first century. It is hoped that we will not forget the formative lessons taking shape now.

Finally, the "Lessons for America" are most likely going to be contradictory. Contradictions are part of life. They are perhaps best epitomized in Frankfort in the state's capitol, where two statues stand enclosed in the same foyer, reminding Kentuckians of who its famous personalities are. One is of Abraham Lincoln. The other is of Jefferson Davis. Both were born in Kentucky about 100 miles apart. I expect similar contrasts to become part of the legacies of KERA. It will take time and a patient tilling of the data to fully understand who was right and wrong in improving public education in the commonwealth, what is working and what isn't. It is hoped that this book represents the first of many efforts to document the work under way in an integrated, holistic manner. KERA is not a series of isolated programs, it is a tapestry of interconnected threads. It is important that we continue to study, revise, and strengthen these connections as we implement this important educational restructuring effort.

REFERENCES

Boyer, E. 1983. *High School: A Report on Secondary Education in America*. New York: Harper & Roe.

Elmore, Richard F. et al. 1991. *Restructuring Schools: The Next Generation of Educational Reform*. San Francisco: Jossey-Bass.

Farrar, Eleanor. 1990. "Reflections on the First Wave of Reform: Reordering America's Educational Priorities," in *Educational Leadership in an Age of Reform*, Stephen L. Jacobson and James A. Conway, eds., New York: Longman.

Goodlad, J. 1984. *A Place Called School*. New York: McGraw-Hill.

Hess, G. Alfred, Jr. 1991. *School Restructuring Chicago Style*. California: Corwin Press.

Jacobson, Stephen L. and Conway, James A., eds. 1990. *Educational Leadership in an Age of Reform*. New York: Longman.

Katz, Michael. 1987. *Reconstructing American Education*. Cambridge, Massachusetts: Harvard University Press.

Kentucky Department of Education. 1990. Kentucky School Laws. Frankfort, KY: Banks-Baldwin Law Publishing.

Kozol, Jonathan. 1991. *Savage Inequalities*. New York: Crown.

Lucke, Jamie and Lee Mueller. 1991. "Harlan County School Reform Means Money for Status Quo," *Lexington Herald Leader* (October 13):A1, 5.

Murphy, Joe. 1991. *The Education Reform Movement of the 1980's*. Berkeley, California: McCutchan.

North Central Regional Educational Laboratory. 1992. *NCREL/SFA Chicago School Reform Study Project*, Oak Brook, Illinois.

Sizer, T. 1984. *Horace's Compromise*. Boston: Houghton Mifflin.

School-Based Decision Making: A Sample Policy

THE Fulton County School District adopted school-based decision-making policies on February 25, 1991. These policies are in keeping with the recommended policies provided by the Kentucky School Boards Association and adopted by many school districts in the state. Selected sections of Fulton County School District's policy follow.

SCHOOL-BASED DECISION MAKING
Extensive research in education over the past fifteen years has now culminated in a much clearer understanding of what makes an effective school. An effective school, as defined by this research, is a school where learning is occurring above and beyond what would normally be anticipated based upon the social and/or economic background of the students. Further, this same research makes it clear that the largest unit of effective change or improvement is not the school district, but rather the individual school or site when the individual school or site has, at a minimum, the following characteristics:

- consensus on explicit instructional philosophy, mission statement, goals, objectives, and values/beliefs
- district-level support for school improvement with Board and Administrative commitment to the effective schools research
- ongoing, school-wide staff development training
- individual school flexibility
- collaborative, collegial instructional planning
- a focus on basic skills acquisition
- an emphasis upon higher order cognitive skills
- teacher responsibility for instructional and classroom management decisions and performances
- teacher/parent accountability and acceptance of responsibility for students
- a safe, orderly, and disciplined school climate
- strong instructional leadership
- frequent monitoring of student progress

In response to this clear research, the Fulton County Board of Education endorses and supports the establishment of a school-based decision making process model in the schools that will improve instruction/learning and create the mechanism whereby many of the characteristics of effective schools can become a reality. The Board approves the implementation of this type of school-based decision making process model and further extends to school-based councils the authority for implementation as provided and described in Board Policy and state laws/regulations. This is done in order to increase student achievement and better meet the unique learning needs of the children served at each school. The primary purpose is to improve student performance.

New curriculum/instructional/cultural designs or plans must be in keeping with District and Board Policy, philosophy, mission statement, goals, objectives and values/beliefs. Visions and implementation strategies must be arrived at through a process of consensus involving members of the school and community who would be most affected by the curriculum/instructional/cultural changes.

The policies adopted by the Board should be understood to be an evolution of change, not a revolution. Authority extended to individual schools does not supersede District policy or decision making; neither does it mean that many of the traditional district-level decisions will no longer be made.

The process of school-based decision making works best when participants have access to current research so that decisions made are based upon the best information available. There will be a conscious and ongoing effort on the part of the school district to provide school-based teams access to such current information. Further, it is the responsibility of those actually involved in school-based decision making to request, and then to become familiar with, this research-based information in order to insure continuous improvement.

A caution to school-based teams that bears noting in this policy: there is a tendency for site-based teams to lose their understanding and, in effect, to become a new local bureaucracy. Therefore, we must constantly be aware of and remind one another that the movement to shared decision-making at the building level is not for the purpose of creating new, smaller bureaucracies to replace a larger bureaucracy, but rather a movement to involve all constituencies in our effort to fulfill the philosophy, mission statement, goals, objectives and adopted beliefs of our school system developed on behalf of the children we all serve—to improve student learning, performance, and achievement.

School-based decision-making policies, decisions and actions should be based on visions of excellence. Implementation strategies must be designed to improve student performance and move toward fulfilling the District philosophy, goals, objectives, mission statement and adopted beliefs.

Finally, the Board adopts these school-based decision-making policies for implementation within the limitations, provisions, and parameters stated herein and contained in the law.

WRITTEN PETITION TO ENTER

Teachers of a school who wish to enter School-Based Decision Making (SBDM) shall present a written petition to the Principal or Head Teacher, signed by a minimum of twenty-five (25%) percent of the teachers, indicating their desire to vote on the matter.

For the purpose of policies relating to SBDM, "teacher" is defined as all certified staff assigned to the school, except the Principal, Assistant Principal, or Head Teacher. In this context, an Assistant Principal or Head Teacher is one who spends fifty (50) percent or more of his/her time in an administrative role. Itinerant teachers shall vote at their designated home school and may serve on the council of their home school.

Home school is defined as the school where the itinerant teacher undergoes primary evaluation.

VOTING

On receiving a petition signed by twenty-five (25%) percent of the faculty, the school principal shall set the date, time and place of a meeting for the purpose of voting on entering SBDM. This meeting shall be held not less than five (5) and not more than ten (10) school days from the Principal's or Head Teacher's receipt of the petition to enter.

Notice of the meeting shall be provided to all teachers assigned to the school at least (5) school days in advance of the meeting.

The Principal shall chair the meeting at which the vote is taken. Voting shall be by the secret ballot. Ballots shall offer teachers the opportunity to vote for or against entering into SBDM. The Principal and one teacher chosen by the faculty shall count the ballots and announce the results at the conclusion of the meeting. The Principal shall forward the results of the vote to the Superintendent, the Superintendent will present the results to the Board.

If two-thirds of the total teaching faculty vote for SBDM, the school will enter SBDM. The Principal shall organize the elections to select teacher and parent representatives for the school council as specified in Board Policy on Election of School Council Members.

A vote to enter into SBDM shall be upheld no more than once every sixty (60) calendar days. The SBDM would begin the following school year.

If none of the schools decide to enter into SBDM, then the Board shall make the decision as to which school will enter into SBDM.

ELECTION OF SCHOOL COUNCIL MEMBERS

From the date of two-thirds (2/3) of the teachers voting to enter SBDM, the following procedures will be implemented for electing teachers and parents to the council.

Election officials for teacher members shall be the Principal and one teacher elected by the teachers assigned to the school.

The election officials will jointly give notice to all eligible teachers of the intent to elect teacher members to the council. The notice shall contain nominating procedures, eligibility criteria, the date, time and location of the election.

The election will be conducted not less than thirty (30) nor more than sixty (60) days prior to the end of the school year.

Nomination for the ballot shall be made in writing to the election officials no later than five (5) school days prior to the election. Election officials shall prepare a ballot listing the names of the teachers who have been nominated. Voting will be by secret ballot. Only eligible certified staff assigned to the school and the Principal shall attend the election meeting. The Principal shall chair the election meeting.

Election shall be by majority vote of all teachers present and voting. Balloting will continue until three (3) teachers are elected. Election officials will jointly count and report the results.

A parent must be a member in good standing in the parent organization of the school to be eligible to both vote in the election of parent representatives and to be nominated for election as a parent member of the school council.

A parent council member may be neither an employee of the school district nor a relative of an employee at the school served and must be a high school graduate or have earned a G.E.D.

The officers of the parent organization will select one member who will serve as an election official with the Principal. The election official will jointly file notice to all eligible parents of the intent to elect parent members to the council. The notice shall contain nominating procedures, eligibility criteria, the date, time, and location of the election.

The election will be conducted not less than thirty (30) nor more than sixty (60) days prior to the end of the school year. Nomination for the ballot should be made in writing to the election official no later than five (5) days prior to the election. At the election meeting, nominations may be made from the floor. The president of the parent-teacher organization shall chair the election meeting.

If the school does not have a parent-teacher organization, the Principal shall set the date and time for a meeting of parents to elect parent council members. The Principal shall provide reasonable notice of the meeting through the news media and through notes taken home by the students. In this case, the principal shall chair the election meeting.

The meeting to elect council members shall be held after normal working hours at a time and place convenient for parents to attend. The Principal shall notify the news media of the date, time, and place of the vote in a manner that gives sufficient time to provide notification to the community. Election shall be by majority vote of all parents present and voting. Balloting will continue until two (2) parents are elected. Election officials will jointly count and report the results.

Terms of school council members shall begin on July 1 and end on June 30 of the following year. Annual elections for the following year's term shall be held between thirty (30) and sixty (60) days before the end of the current school year.

Teacher and parent council members are eligible for reelection. Council members are limited to (3) consecutive terms.

A vacancy is created when a parent no longer has a child enrolled in the school or a teacher is no longer assigned to the school. A vacancy may be declared by the council for any member who misses three (3) meetings per term without council approval. The council will fill its own vacancies through appointment of members who meet the same criteria as the member leaving the council.

SCHOOL COUNCIL AUTHORITY
The council is a body united or combined for the purpose of policymaking for the school it serves. Said council is not empowered to borrow money; file suit; purchase, receive, hold or sell real property; or issue bonds. The Council shall operate within the financial restraints of the annual allocation.

Outside of a legally called council meeting, no council member other than the Principal, has decision-making or administrative authority conferred by office on the council. The Principal is the school's primary administrator and instructional leader. In order for a legal meeting of the council to take place, a quorum consisting of the principal, one parent and one teacher and at least one additional parent or teacher shall be present.

SCHOOL COUNCIL MEETINGS
The first meeting of the council shall be called by the Principal; the council shall set its own meeting schedule.

All meetings of the council are open to the public and subject to the open meetings law.

Meetings shall be held at times convenient to working parents. No council meeting shall be held during the scheduled instructional day. Advance notice of meetings shall be given to parents, teachers, and the media.

A written agenda shall be prepared and copies made available to the public at all meetings of the council. The agenda of each council meeting shall provide the opportunity for interested persons to address the council.

A quorum of the council shall be four (4) members. Four (4) affirmative votes shall be required for the council to take action. Representative of each group: parents, teachers, and the principal, must be there for Council action.

The Principal may be excluded from the meeting of the council only when a recommendation for employment for that position is being considered.

In case the Principal is excluded from the meeting, the council shall appoint a temporary chair for that meeting only.

The Principal shall be the Chair of the Council and shall be responsible for securing minutes that record the Council's actions. Minutes shall be approved by the Council, kept in a permanent file, and open to public inspection. A copy of the minutes of each Council meeting shall be forwarded by the Principal to the Superintendent who shall keep the Board informed of Council actions.

SCHOOL COUNCIL RELATIONSHIPS

Councils shall encourage parent, citizen, and community participation in council meetings and school activities and shall cooperate with independent school groups such as booster and parent organizations to assist them in their service to the school.

SCHOOL COUNCIL POLICIES

No policy shall be adopted by a Council at the meeting in which the policy is introduced.

The Council shall adopt policies that provide an environment that enhances student achievement and helps the school meet the mission and goals established by law and Fulton County Board Policy.

In the development and application of school policies as permitted by statute, schools operating under SBDM shall comply with Board policies, including, but not limited to those prohibiting discrimination based on age, race, sex, color, religion, national origin, political affiliation, marital status, or handicap.

APPEAL OF DECISIONS

Appeal of decisions of the council may be made by any resident of the district, parent, student or employee of the school.

Prior to being appealed, the issue must first be presented in writing to the council for reconsideration. Issues for council consideration shall be delivered to the Principal who shall bring the matter before the Council at its next meeting. If the matter is not satisfactorily resolved within ten (10) school days from the date the issue is presented to the Council, an appeal may be submitted in writing to the Superintendent.

If, within ten (10) school days of receiving the appeal, the Superintendent has not been able to satisfactorily resolve it, a further appeal may be made in writing to the Board. The Board shall act on the appeal within forty (40) school days of the Board meeting when the appeal was made to the board. The decision of the Board is final.

Actions of the Council will be reviewed on appeal based on whether the Council action was arbitrary, violated district policy, exceeded the authority of the Council or was otherwise unlawful under state or federal law.

COUNCIL BUDGET

Based on a formula to be developed by the State Board of Education, councils will be allotted funds for the development of a budget for their schools. These budgets may include instructional materials, school-based student support services, discretionary funds, activity and other school funds. Budgets are to show the use of allocations not to exceed the current allocation plus any funds carried forward from a prior year.

No deficits shall be incurred by the Council.

It is suggested that councils budget for a carry over of from 3% to 5%.

In order to comply with state accounting and bidding requirements, all purchases of goods and services will be made in conformity with board policy, state and federal requirements.

School maintenance and operations, food service, pupil transportation, and student accounting will be centralized.

SCHOOL PURCHASING

Subject to available resources, the Board shall allocate to each school an appropriation that is adequate to meet the school's needs for instructional materials and school-based student support services as determined by the Council.

The Council shall determine, within available resources, the instructional materials and student support services to be provided in the school.

In order to comply with state accounting and bidding requirements, all purchases of goods and services shall be made in conformity with board policy.

State law at present, does not permit schools to bid their supplies separate from the total bid of the school system, therefore, all schools in SBDM shall refer their purchase requests of goods and services to the Board for inclusion in the bidding process.

SCHOOL HIRING

After receiving notification of the financial allocation for the school from the Board, the Council shall determine, within funds allocated, the number of persons to be employed in the school in each job classification. The Council shall not have the authority to recommend transfers or dismissals.

When a vacancy exists in the position of school Principal, the Council shall select a new Principal from a list of nominees provided by the Superintendent. The Principal may be excluded from meetings of the Council only when a recommendation for employment for that position is being considered. In case the Principal is excluded from the meeting, the Council shall appoint a temporary chair for that meeting only.

A vacancy is created in the position of Principal by the resignation, removal, transfer, retirement or death of the current Principal.

When the position to be filled in the school is other than that of Principal, the Principal, after conferring with the Council, shall fill the position from a list of nominees provided by the Superintendent.

TRAINING OF SCHOOL COUNCIL MEMBERS
The Board shall approve areas of training and training programs to be required for all School Council members. Council funds may be expended only for training programs approved by the Board.

WAIVER OF BOARD POLICIES
The Principal on behalf of the Council, may submit to the Superintendent a written request to waive Board policy.

The Superintendent shall present the request to the Board within forty (40) days along with a recommendation to approve or deny the request. The Council shall have the opportunity to address the Board directly to support the request.

The decision to approve or deny the request shall include, but not be limited to consideration of the following:

(1) The legality of waiving board policy.
(2) If district goals will be advanced by the waiver.
(3) If student outcomes will be promoted.
(4) If in the District Mission Statement and goals, uniformity is required in the circumstances under consideration; and/or
(5) If the larger interests of the public will be served.

Within forty (40) calendar days from the date on which the Superintendent presents the waiver request to the Board, the Board shall rule on the request.

ASSESSMENT OF STUDENT PROGRESS
Each School Council shall adhere to the philosophy, conditions, and procedures for student assessment developed by Kentucky Statute, Kentucky Board of Education, and the Fulton County Board of Education.

ACCOUNTABILITY
By the October Board meeting each year, each Council shall submit, in writing, for Board Approval, its measurable goals and objectives for the school year. The goals shall be related to the mission statement of the district and the goals listed in HB 940, Part I, Sections 2 and 3. (See Chapter 2 in this book.)

By the October Board meeting each year, each Council shall submit, in writing, for Board approval, its plan for achieving the district mission statement, its goals and objectives and the method for evaluating the achievement of the plan.

By June 30 of each year, each Council shall submit in writing, its annual evaluation report to the Board. The Council shall be required to publish in the newspaper with the largest circulation in the area the school serves, an annual financial statement listing annual expenditures and receipts of the Council. This financial statement shall be published within sixty (60) days after the close of the fiscal year.

A performance-based testing based on the capacities listed by the State Department of Education will be used to evaluate the educational program.

OTHER BOARD POLICY

All board policies shall be reviewed and amended as necessary, to conform to the legal requirements of SBDM.

Ten Issues and Recommendations for Improving Education in Kentucky

THESE issues and recommendations are reprinted from John Augenblick's "An Evaluation of the Impact of Changes in Kentucky's School Finance System: The SEEK Program, Its Structure and Effects," *Report to the Kentucky State Board of Elementary and Secondary Education* (August, 1991).

Issue (1): *How will the SEEK Base Level ($2,305 in 1990−91) be determined in the future?*

One of the purposes of the SEEK Program is to assure that an adequate amount of funding is available for all pupils in the state. A rational approach was used to determine the Base Level in 1990−91 and an inflation factor was used to modify the Base Level for 1991−92. Similarly, an inflation factor is being used to adjust the Base Level for budget purposes for 1992−93 and 1993−94. Given the movement away from an "input driven" system to an "outcomes-based" system, it will be important in the future to link funding with pupil performance.

Recommendation: The Base Level should be adjusted by an inflation factor for no more than four consecutive years. The inflation factor should be a standard indicator, such as the Consumer Price Index (CPI), the elementary and secondary education equivalent of the Higher Education Price Index (HEPI), or an index agreed upon by a committee designed by the General Assembly. Every fourth year the Base Level should be evaluated by the Office of Education Accountability to determine its adequacy in light of state requirements placed on school districts, changes in technology, and the relationship between levels and pupil performance.

Issue (2): *What should be the relationship between the SEEK Program and the Statewide Salary Schedule or Professional Compensation Plan?*

Under the old Foundation Program, state aid was allocated on the basis of a statewide salary schedule and the state determination of an eligible number of teachers. The SEEK Program does not allocate funds on the basis of either of these factors. However, the state continues to operate a statewide minimum salary schedule, which is required to be restructured to consider a variety of factors in addition to the training and experience of teachers.

Recommendation: Initially, the state should assure that the SEEK Program provides sufficient funds to cover the costs of implementing the Professional Compensation Plan using numbers of personnel employed in 1989–90 plus any other personnel added since 1989–90 and deemed essential. Following initial implementation, the state should assure that increases in base salary of the Professional Compensation Plan should match the inflationary increases associated with the SEEK Program.

Issue (3): *Will state programs currently operating outside the SEEK Program be moved into the SEEK Program at some time in the future?*

Currently, the state operates some programs outside of SEEK, including programs for gifted and talented pupils and pre-school programs. These programs are not required or operate on a "pilot" basis. State aid for these programs is not wealth equalized. In the future, the state will allocate some funds to reward schools based on improvement and such aid will not consider directly the wealth of school districts.

Recommendation: All programs that the state mandates should be funded through SEEK. In addition, programs that are not mandated but that have been run on a voluntary, pilot, or competitive grant basis for five years should be run through SEEK. In most cases, such programs should be merged into SEEK through the use of pupil weights. In cases where weights are not appropriate (for example, when the proportion of pupils involved in the program is constant across all districts), the cost of the program should be added to the Base Level. As long as the amount of state aid allocated to reward schools is a small proportion of all state education aid (less than 10 percent) it need not be equalized in my opinion.

Issue (4): *Should the $.30 local equivalent property tax required in the SEEK Program be used exclusively for current operating expenses?*

During the SEEK implementation period districts are allowed to count a portion of voted debt levies toward the $.30 obligation under SEEK. The purpose of the SEEK program is to assure adequate and equitable revenue for current operations. The Facilities Support Program of Kentucky is specially designed to assure equity in generating fund for debt service.

Recommendation: Once the implementation period is complete, no district should be able to count any debt service levy toward the $.30 requirement.

Issue (5): *Should Tier I remain flexible or should every district be required to participate in Tier I to the fullest extent (15 percent)?*

Tier I was designed to "float" above the base in order to give school districts, through school board approval, the option of generating up to 15 percent more revenue than is provided in the base. Districts with less than 150 percent of statewide average property wealth per pupil receive state aid when they opt to impose taxes above the $.30 equivalent required as part of the base. The assumption made in the design of Tier I is that the base provides an adequate level of support.

Recommendation: At this point, there is no justification for requiring all districts to participate fully in Tier I. Most districts have chosen to participate in Tier I in 1990−91 although there is a variation in the extent of participation. Of some concern in the future is the possibility that schools in some districts that do not participate in Tier I to the fullest extent may also not meet performance improvement objectives. It may be appropriate in the future to require such districts to participate fully in Tier I.

Issue (6): *Should the magnitude of Tier II (30 percent above the sum of the base) and Tier I be reduced?*

Tier II affords limited flexibility for districts to generate revenue above the base and Tier I provided they receive approval from voters to raise the necessary taxes. The state does not participate in funding Tier II. Tier II serves two other purposes: (1) it places an absolute limit on the revenue generating ability of the districts as a way to control indirect equity and (2) by imposing such a limit it increases the likelihood that wealthy districts will have an interest in the Base Level (since their revenue limit is determined by the Base Level). As shown previously, about a third of all districts participated in Tier II in 1990−91 and, in total, about 12 percent of its revenue generating capacity was used.

Recommendation: At this point, there is no reason to change the magnitude of Tier II. Only a couple of districts approached the limit in the use of Tier II. No district received approval from the voters for Tier II taxes (in 1990−91 existing taxes were allowed to be used). At this time, there is no reason to believe that Tier II causes inequalities that violate the *Rose* decision. However, Tier II should be monitored carefully by the Office of Education Accountability and should its use increase, primarily in wealthy districts, the magnitude of Tier II may need to be adjusted or the way that Tier II operates may need to change.

Issue (7): *Should districts be required to spend the funds they receive from the state for specific purposes; that is, for example, should funds received on the basis of at-risk pupils be used exclusively to provide program or services for such pupils?*

Under the SEEK Program, a rational system is used to allocate state aid based on the needs of school districts. Counts of pupils actually participating in special programs or proxy counts of pupils who may need special services (as in the use for at-risk pupils) and weights designed to reflect the relative cost of providing such programs or services are used in the formula. However, once received, all funds are fungible and may be used in any manner the district deems appropriate. This approach is consistent with the general philosophy of HB 940, which specifies performance objectives for schools but does not specify how districts should organize their resources to meet those objectives.

Recommendation: At this point, it is not necessary to change the way the system operates. However, this issue should be monitored by the Office of Education/Accountability. Should the performance of particular groups of pupils not meet expectations and evidence becomes available that funds allocated for special programs for such groups are not being used to provide programs and services for them, it may be necessary to restrict the use of state aid.

Issue (8): *Should the definition of wealth used in Tier I remain constant during both years of a biennium or be allowed to fluctuate in the second year?*

In calculating the state's obligation under Tier I, change in the wealth of districts is not considered. If all districts increase in wealth during a biennium and the statewide average does not change to reflect those increases, fewer districts would be eligible to receive any state aid and those eligible to receive any aid may receive less under Tier I. At the same time, if property wealth actually decreases but the statewide average does not change, more districts may become eligible for more state support. Projecting the cost of Tier I is difficult both because it is necessary to predict the wealth of districts three years ahead of time and because the fiscal behavior of district cannot be predicted.

Recommendation: Given the likelihood that the per pupil property wealth of districts will change from year to year (given both improvements in assessment practices and changes in enrollment levels), the state has two choices: (1) it can either keep all parameters (district wealth, statewide average wealth, and property tax rates) in the system constant during both years of a biennium or (2) it can use actual property values, recalculate the statewide average, and use actual tax rates for the purpose of distributing state aid under Tier I. I suggest using the first approach despite its inaccuracy because: (1) the data needed to implement the second approach are not available when they are needed; (2) the system would be more predictable for both the state and the school districts; and (3) the system corrects itself every other year.

Issue (9): *What should happen to the minimum (8 percent in 1990 – 91 and 5 percent in 1991 – 92) and the maximum (25 percent) limits on state aid in the next biennium?*

The General Assembly placed limits on state aid in the current biennium to assure that no district incurred a dramatic loss in state aid or received an increase so large as to be unmanageable. The long run use of such limits could interfere with the operation of the SEEK Program, constraining its ability to achieve fiscal equity.

Recommendation: Since the limit on increasing state aid is likely to run its course in a couple of years (since no district was expected to receive more than a 75 percent increase in state aid, which would be achieved after three years with the 25 percent limit), this issue does not have to be addressed. However, some districts may continue to receive state aid beyond that determined by the SEEK formula long into the future. This practice should cease after the next biennium and the full implementation of the SEEK Program. No district should be guaranteed an increase in state aid greater than the inflationary increase applied to the entire system and such calculation should be made on a per pupil basis rather than on a total dollar basis.

Issue (10): *What definition of equity should be used to evaluate the SEEK Program?*

The SEEK Program was enacted in order to overcome inequalities in the old school finance system as identified in the *Rose* decision. However, no formal definition of equity exists and numerous options are available. Defining school finance equity is not simple and, typically, there are multiple equity objectives. It is probably impossible to achieve perfect equity under most circumstances (no court has ever required absolutely perfect equity).

Recommendation: In order to evaluate the SEEK Program it is essential to develop a definition of equity. The definition should consider the varying needs and wealth of school districts. It should focus on disparities in per pupil revenue as well as the relationship between such disparity and the wealth of school districts. The definition of equity should also take into consideration the multiple objectives of the SEEK Program, particularly recognizing that tax effort is a legitimate contributor to revenue differences.

An Educational Environment Designed around the Seven Critical Attributes

THE following material is taken from *Program Advisory: Action Plan for KERA's Primary Program*, published by the Kentucky Department of Education, Frankfort, Kentucky (1992, pp. 4 – 12).

DEVELOPMENTALLY APPROPRIATE CURRICULUM/INSTRUCTION

Experiences Stimulate Learning in All Developmental Areas

The curriculum is designed to achieve long-range goals for children in all developmental areas; physical, social, emotional, and intellectual.

The curriculum addresses the development of knowledge and understanding, processes and skills, dispositions and attitudes.

Teachers and administrators view each child as a unique person with an individual pattern of growth.

Integrated Curriculum

The curriculum is fully integrated so that children's learning *in all traditional subject areas* occurs primarily through projects and learning centers that teachers plan and that reflect children's interests and suggestions.

Teachers *fully implement* a language and literacy program to expand children's ability to communicate orally and through reading and writing.

Sub-skills such as learning letters, phonics, and word recognition are taught as needed to individual children and small groups through enjoyable games and activities.

The teacher's edition of basal readers may be utilized as a guide to plan projects and hands-on activities and to structure learning activities.

Teachers *teach literacy* as the need arises when working on science, social studies, and other content areas.

Teachers *fully implement* math programs that enable children to use math through exploration, discovery, and solving meaningful problems.

All math activities are integrated with other relevant projects, such as science and social studies.

Sub-skills are taught as needed to individual children and small groups through enjoyable games and activities.

The teacher's edition of math textbooks may be utilized as a guide to structure ideas about interesting math projects.

An abundance of math manipulatives are available and used on a daily basis.

On a daily basis, children have exposure to interesting board, card, paper and pencil, and other kinds of games.

Non-competitive, impromptu oral "math stumpers" and number games are played for practice.

Teachers *identify* social studies themes as the focus of work for extended periods of time.

Teachers *provide* opportunities for children to learn social studies concepts through a variety of projects and playful activities involving independent research in library books; excursions and interviewing visitors; discussions, the relevant use of language, writing, spelling, (invented and teacher-taught), and reading skills; and opportunities to develop social skills such as planning, sharing, taking turns, and working on committees.

Teachers view the classroom as a laboratory of social relations where children explore values and learn rules, social living and respect for individual differences.

Building on children's natural interest in the world, teachers *provide numerous* discovery science experiences.

Through discovery science projects, teachers help children learn to plan and to apply thinking skills, including hypothesizing, observing, experimenting and verifying.

Teachers *provide a wide variety* of health and safety projects to help children learn personalized facts about health and safety.

Art, music, movement, woodworking, drama, and dance, *are integrated throughout each day* as relevant to the curriculum.

Multi-cultural and nonsexist activities and materials are provided to enhance individual children's self-esteem and to enrich the lives of all children.

Teachers provide outdoor experiences daily so children can develop large muscle skills, learn about outdoor environments, and express themselves freely.

Guidance of Social and Emotional Development
Children have many daily opportunities to develop social skills in dealing with interpersonal problems such as helping, cooperating, negotiating,

and talking. Teachers facilitate the development of social skills at all times as part of the curriculum.

Teachers promote the development of children's consciences and self-control through positive guidance techniques including: setting clear limits in a positive manner; involving children in establishing rules for social living and in problem solving of misbehavior; redirecting children to an acceptable activity; and meeting with an individual child who is having problems or with those children and their parents.

Learning Centers/Work Stations
The *classroom is filled with learning centers/work stations.*

Learning centers/work stations are changed frequently so children have new ideas to explore.

Manipulative and Multi-Sensory Activities
All learning materials and activities are concrete, real, and relevant to children's lives.

A variety of work places and space is provided.

Balance of Teacher-Directed and Child-Initiated Activities
Teachers and children select and develop projects.

Frequent outings and visits from resource people are planned by both teachers and children.

MULTI-AGE/MULTI-ABILITY CLASSROOMS

Classroom Organization
Schools provide for heterogenous grouping, flexible age range grouping and/or family grouping.

Age ranges vary from five (5) to ten (10) with most children in a five (5) to eight (8) range.

Children are organized differently in class groupings from school to school, even within the same school.

In keeping with the philosophy of KERA's Primary Program, schools use the term *Number of Years in School*, when discussing classroom organization.

Children are assigned a primary teacher and remain in relatively small groups because so much of their learning and development is integrated and cannot be divided into specialized subjects to be taught by special teachers.

Specialists assist the primary teacher with special projects, questions, and materials.

Children with special needs are integrated into the classroom socially as well as physically.

Care is taken to avoid isolating special needs children in a segregated classroom or pulling them out of a regular classroom so often as to disrupt continuity and undermine their feeling of belonging to the group.

Primary program organization may include the following groupings:

Multi-year groups: groups of children from three (3) or four (4) years of the Primary Program, e.g., children in 1st, 2nd, and 3rd years (formally K,1, 2); children in 2nd, 3rd, and 4th years (formally 1, 2, 3); children in 1st, 2nd, 3rd, and 4th years (formally K, 1, 2, 3).

Dual-year groups: groups of children in two years of the program in one class, e.g., children in 1st and 2nd years (formally K, 1); children in 2nd and 3rd years (formally 1, 2); children in 1st, 2nd, 3rd, and 4th years (formally K, 1, 2, 3). (Note: Single-year groups will not satisfy the multi-age/multi-ability requirement.)

To honor the critical attribute of multi-age/multi-ability classrooms and to provide opportunities for children to advance at their own pace, tutor others, and mix peers of various ages, schools should group for the following purposes:

(*1*) Interest grouping.
(*2*) Needs-requirement grouping, in which students are instructed in a concept, skill, or value.
(*3*) Problem-solving grouping, in which learners are grouped around a common unsolved topic or problem.
(*4*) Reinforcement grouping, for learners who need more work in a specific area or task.
(*5*) Learning-style grouping, for those with a common pattern of learning.

CONTINUOUS PROCESS
Children progress at their own rate as determined by authentic assessment.

AUTHENTIC ASSESSMENT
Curriculum and assessment are integrated throughout the program.

Assessment results in benefits to the child such as needed adjustments in the curriculum or more individualized instruction and improvements in the program.

Children's development and learning in all the domains (physical, social, emotional, and cognitive) and their dispositions and feelings are informally and routinely assessed by teachers through observing children's activities and interactions, listening to them as they talk, and using children's constructive errors to understand their learning.

Assessment relies primarily on procedures that reflect the ongoing life of the classroom and typical activities of the children.

Assessment relies on demonstrated performance during real, not contrived, activities.

Assessment recognizes individual diversity of learners and allows for differences in style of learning.

Assessment supports parents' relationships with their children and does not undermine parents' confidence in their children's or their own ability, nor does it devalue the language and culture of the family.

Assessment is a collaborative process involving children and teachers, teachers and parents, and school and community. Information from parents about each child's experiences at home is used in planning instruction and evaluating children's learning.

Assessment encourages children to participate in self-evaluation.

Assessment addresses what children can do independently and what they can demonstrate with assistance, since the latter shows the direction of their growth.

QUALITATIVE REPORTING METHODS
Reporting reflects a continuum of the student's progress.

A regular process exists for periodic information sharing between teachers and parents about children's growth and development and performance. The method of reporting to parents does not rely on letter or numerical grades, but rather provides more meaningful, descriptive information in narrative form.

PROFESSIONAL TEAMWORK
Teachers (primary, art, music, special needs, Chapter I, physical education), librarians, and administrators use common planning time to prepare the environment so children can learn through active exploration and interaction with adults, other children, and materials.

POSITIVE PARENT INVOLVEMENT
Teachers view parents as partners.

Teachers and administrators schedule periodic conferences with each child's parents.

Teachers listen to parents, seek to understand the goals for their children and respect cultural and family differences.

Members of each child's family are encouraged to help in the classroom; to help with tasks related to, but not occurring within, the classroom; and to assist with decision making where appropriate.

S

T

U